The National Football Lottery

Also by Larry Merchant

. . . And Every Day You Take Another Bite

Larry Merchant

The National Football Lottery

HOLT, RINEHART AND WINSTON
New York Chicago San Francisco

Published simultaneously in Canada by Holt, Rinehart
and Winston of Canada, Limited

Library of Congress Cataloging in Publication Data

Merchant, Larry.
The national football lottery.
"Portions of this book have appeared
in Sports illustrated."
1. Gambling—United States. 2. Football.
I. Title.
HV6715.M47 301.5'7 73–4199

ISBN 0–03–010736–9

Endpaper photo: Bill Powers

First Edition

Printed in the United States of America: 065

for gail, always a two-touchdown favorite

Part I
Overture

Life loses in interest when the highest stake in the game of living, life itself, may not be risked.
—SIGMUND FREUD

Suddenly Respectable

A bank president became aware of a man with a savings account who deposited $500 a day every day for two years. Astonished, the banker left word for the man that he would like to meet him.

Shortly thereafter the man appeared in the banker's office. "I've been with this bank for 30 years," the banker said, "and I've never come across anything quite like this. If you don't mind my asking, what business are you in?"

"I'm a gambler," the man said.

"That's very interesting," the banker said. "But don't gamblers lose sometime?"

"Not if you know what you're doing," the gambler said.

"Why, that's extraordinary," the banker said. "Even the smartest businessmen don't win all the time."

"I'll prove it to you," the gambler said. "I'll bet you $500 that at noon tomorrow I'll show up here and you'll have square balls."

The banker stammered, fingered a letter opener nervously, and was surprised to hear himself say, "It's a bet."

Next day the gambler arrived on schedule, trailed by a horny dwarf.

"I see you made it," the banker said, appearing a bit flushed.

The gambler nodded.

Without a word the banker stepped around his desk and dropped his pants.

The horny dwarf's jaw dropped to his waist.

The gambler reached between the banker's thighs and felt his balls.

The horny dwarf fainted.

"What happened?" the banker asked.

"I bet him," the gambler said, "$1,000 that at noon today I'd have a bank president's balls in my hands."

You may search for your own moral in this story. For me it raises some intriguing questions.

Like: Do professional gamblers win all the time or just most of the time, and why? Do amateur gamblers lose all the time or just some of the time, and why? Are bookmakers really illegal bankers, merely skimming the interest off bets?

And, crucially, am I the horny dwarf?

There are other questions that intrigue me as well, because the gambling rage of our times is pro football. Betting and pro football is a marriage made in heaven. The ceremony was performed without benefit of clergy, but it is one of the few fads of the tumultuous sixties to endure and flourish.

How widespread is the phenomenon of pro football betting? What are its implications? Why and how do people bet? Who makes the betting line? Can it be beaten? How does betting affect one's head, one's life—socially, sexually, spiritually, financially? Should betting on football be legalized? How do bookies operate? Are there fixes? What is a Jimmy the Greek?

Also, can I, Larry Merchant, sportswriter, bet on National Football League games, win money, have fun, and find God and true love? And other fantasies.

There are several reasons why I chose to investigate

gambling, NFL style. Not the least of them was the fact that I have been betting on the pros for ten years and—gamblers are congenital liars but this is petrified truth—have never had what I consider a losing season. A losing season being a season in which I lost enough (as I once did in baseball) to cut down on taxi rides; I may have lost a few dollars in a season when the winnings and losings were so minimal that I didn't even keep casual track of them. One season I won $1,500. Another season I won $7,000. I've never started a season betting more than $100 a game, which is in my league, which means I can afford to blow a few hundred and shrug it off as an entertainment expense. Arnold Rothstein the legendary plunger I'm not, but look what all his betting coups got him. Rich, famous and murdered.

It occurred to me along the way that my involvement paralleled a lot of people's, that not many people who were involved understood the first thing about football or betting, and that, zounds, a book structured around my betting experiences might outsell the Bible. It would, too, confirm my prowess as a handicapper, for me if no one else, or expose me under pressure as a fraud, likewise. Either possibility had its charm. I envisioned myself betting $100,000 on the Super Bowl or winding up as a tragic Dostoevskian figure cleaning car windshields with greasy rags on the Bowery.

It also occurred to me that pro football bettors included vast numbers of the kind of upstanding citizens who used to think that a bookmaker was a fellow who made books. (I knew a fellow who got a job on an army newspaper because he listed his civilian occupation as bookmaker.) Before the pro football boom they bet only on the World

Series, the Kentucky Derby and a heavyweight championship fight. I have a theory about that. I have more theories than George Allen has game balls. Call this Theory No. 1.

The theory is that there is a symbiotic relationship between pro football and betting. Like lovers, they turn each other on.

The popularity of the game obviously is a turn-on for the degenerate with a compulsion to bet on everything that moves. It's always there on the telly, an overexposed goddess, beckoning and daring.

But there's something about the game that twitches the betting instinct in the ordinary fan too. That makes it fashionable to bet a dollar or two socially. That has transformed the NFL into a National Football Lottery.

A Louis Harris poll last year found that nearly one out of every four fans bets regularly; the percentage must be much higher in the population centers that have teams. This means that twelve to fifteen million fans break the law on any given Sunday or Monday.

These fans are the NFL's best friends, because pro football basically is a television sport—a small fraction of the fans who support the game actually go to games—and nothing short of the Second Coming or the Flood will uproot them from the 50-yard-line seats in their homes. A fan who has bet will sit there to the bitter or boring end, cheering and squirming for his money while getting his brain plugged into the sponsors' products. Small wonder that Merrill Lynch, Pierce, Fenner, and Whatshisface are so "Bullish on America."

It is implicit then that betting—social or serious—is a factor in the high TV ratings that yield an ever-expanding cornucopia of riches for the NFL.

Bookies furnish further proof. They report that an average televised game that doesn't feature the home team attracts as much or more betting than a nontelevised game of the home team, and two or three times as much as a game of above-average interest that isn't televised. Monday night games, with no competition, attract still-larger sums. One bookie I spoke to said that five of the top ten betting events of 1972, in all sports, were Monday night games.

All this feverish activity is good for pro football in another, important, way. It keeps the pot boiling for the six days of the week when nothing is going on.

Baseball, in contrast to football, is played every day. It thrives on vivid personalities whose exploits and antics can be closely identified with, strategy that a ten-year-old can fathom, and statistics that provide a meaningful reference. A world of fact and fantasy can be constructed from these elements—without necessarily seeing the games—shifting and portending with every home run, every final score. For those who care this world is fully contained, circular, like a baseball. Betting has no function in its mystique (although, because of the long schedule, there is a greater volume bet on baseball, with bookies, than on any other game).

Caring about a game or a team on a day-to-day basis, or even on a weekend-to-weekend basis, is difficult if not impossible for many adults. "Betting," says a priest in Boston who bets $10 a game on football, "adds to my enjoyment of the event." It stimulates the caring glands. That is why there is so much caring at a race track. Rooting for the home team is, for the bettor, kid stuff; he's rooting for a worthier entity—himself. Professional gamblers call themselves "players."

Football, in contrast to baseball, is an impersonal game

with few vivid personalities poking out from under all that armor, with strategy that frequently is unfathomable, and with statistics that as often as not are misleading. Football compels us primarily with its explosive choreography, its tense blend of skill pirouetting on a field mined with danger. It is a game of action that must be seen to be enjoyed. Once seen, the focus changes, sometimes within hours, usually within a day, to the next game. Enter, smiling seductively, bosom heaving, the point spread.

Like the weight handicap in horse racing, the point spread is designed, and divined, to neutralize the advantage of one team over another, in the mind of the betting public. Part of my purpose is to demonstrate that it often does no such thing, but for now the point is that the spread becomes the reference, the yardstick, for the center of football's between-games existence: the next game.

The point spread becomes the official common denominator on Tuesday when favorites and underdogs are established. Speculation in the media and conversation over drinks revolve around these roles. As Wednesday becomes Thursday and Thursday Friday, the buildup becomes a challenge to red-blooded aficionados. Fans have opinions, and opinions backed by cash are convictions. Or hunches. The weekend hysteria begins.

Allowing for a margin of error in the Harris poll, anywhere from one out of every fifteen to twenty people in this country answer the challenge weekly.

That's a heap of folks, folks.

A heap of money too.

The impact on the society of this massive involvement is enormous, clearly, but how can it be measured? One way is the infiltration of gambling attitudes and jargon into the consciousness and language, suggesting not that the work ethic is going to hell but that psychologically we are fessing up to homo sap's need to take chances.

In the process gambling, like aggression, has gained an air of respectability as one of those traits that makes homo sap such a wonderful lunatic, that adds zest to life when kept under control. Ambrose Bierce's observation that "The gambling known as business looks with disfavor on the business known as gambling" is losing relevancy as Damon Runyon's cynical "All life is 6–5 against" looms on the outside as a rallying cry of optimism.

Acknowledging the gambling imperative, businessmen-legislators are eager to raise tax revenues through pari-mutuel betting and lotteries; legal betting on football, baseball and basketball, as in Nevada, may not be far behind. Breathes there a governor with soul so dead that he hasn't bet a bushel of his state's fruit against another governor's alfalfa on the outcome of a game? And that was President Nixon himself commenting upon the appointment of George Allen as coach of the Redskins, "I'll bet they win a championship in a year or two."

One could hear, faintly, in the wind, the cooing response, "Er, how much, Prez?"

Consider this sampling of newspaper clippings: Advertising copy from a financial management service that propositions, "If you bet 8 cents on yourself, we'll bet $2 on you. Good odds?" An executive for an oil company noting of a big strike, "We're playing poker." Paul Simon regarding his first single recording after his breakup with Art Garfunkel, "It was time to take a gamble."

An artist is a cosmic gambler, and none gambled as outrageously as Fëdor Dostoevski. He gambled at the gaming tables, but his biggest gamble was a contract he signed with a publisher to produce a novel on a certain date or else forfeit the royalties on it and anything else he would write in the future. Three weeks before the deadline he hadn't written a word. On the due day he turned in his mini-classic, *The Gambler*.

This book represents a gamble for several upstanding citizens, myself among them.

My agent is gambling that I am not compelled by poor sales to put out a different, and deadlier, contract on him.

Early on in this project, when it was just a bright idea romancing investors, he broached it to business acquaintances. Said acquaintances flipped out and offered $100,000, take it or leave it, for all rights. Meaning that the book, as a property, would belong to them totally: Any monies generated beyond $100,000 (from, if any, a movie sale, paperback, reprint, book clubs, etc.) would be theirs, all theirs.

I thought they were stark raving mad.

But not as mad as my agent. He rejected it. I thought he should be committed.

His acquaintances were willing to gamble that this would be one out of, at a guess, every thousand books that earns $100,000 or more. They were not stupid men, or they wouldn't have that kind of money to bet. But I liked my chances a lot better than theirs.

Trouble was, my agent did not tell me about the offer until he had rejected it. Presumably he is not a stupid man either. It's just that he gambles too.

My initial reaction to the news of this wheeling-and-no-dealing was nausea. With $100,000 I could acquire some of the feeble amenities I deserved. I could start eating cherries again even though they cost $1.29 a pound. I could move out of my eleventh-floor garret overlooking Sheridan Square in Greenwich Village and overhearing the stereophonic clattering of garbage trucks every morning. I might even be able to make a down payment on a cottage in Sagaponack, Long Island, an enclave of potato fields and sand dunes where a city rat can get stoned on fresh air during the summer.

My second reaction was violent. I wanted to blind-side my agent. But he is eight inches taller and fifty pounds heavier than me, and a squash racquets champion.

Lastly it dawned on me that he was right, although not because I thought we could make a million, as he did.

If I am to conduct an unchartered odyssey through the cement jungles and crazed minds of pro football betting, I would lose all credibility if I had a sure thing going for me.

Besides that, Joseph Kennedy, father of the Kennedy clan, once said, "Journalists are the last of the talented poor." Three-hundred-dollar-a-week sportswriters aren't supposed to have $100,000. I accept that. It probably wouldn't be worth living on a planet where sportswriters had $100,000.

The bright idea then was submitted to four publishers. One bid, i.e., bet, $20,000. Three went to $25,000. One of the three raised to $27,500. Holt, Rinehart & Winston won me for $30,000. That's gambling.

The $30,000 was mine to do with as I saw fit. None of it was designated as a stake. I could bet moderately or immoderately. I could take the money and run. I had only to write a book on pro football and gambling. But no one was playing for as much as I was playing for.

I am playing for that worthiest of entities. I am putting myself on the line, as any author or self-styled expert does when he exposes himself.

Thirty big ones is not sliced eggplant either. I have

never had $30,000. I have never had half of it, which I will be lucky to have after expenses, a leave of absence from my job and various bloody cuts (by the government, my agent, and former first lady). If I lose $5,000 I will be sick. If I lose $10,000 I will be inconsolable. If I lose $15,000 I will be a heathen in my own eyes because I will have worked for nothing, and that's against my religion.

Yet I must bet meaningfully, bet enough to feel it in my gut. I may not be risking suicidal ruin, but I am not playing for toothpicks. As William Saroyan cried, leaping onto a dice table that was breaking him, "I don't care what Freud says, I want to win!"

I should note, before embarking on this odyssey, that being a sportswriter gives me no special advantage. Quite the opposite. As a breed we are, like players and coaches and others in the animal kingdom, notoriously bad handicappers.

Nor do I have access to so-called inside information. For which I am grateful. I don't believe in inside information. Show me a bettor who needs inside information and I'll show you a loser. My entire approach to betting on pro football is based on outside information, information available to anyone who wants it.

The trick is knowing what to do with it. If you know the trick you have a license to steal, tax free.

This approach may seem odd, but wait until you see where I take my preseason practice. In Monte Carlo.

Monte Carlo?

Gentlemen, I'll bet $500 you have square balls.

Ladies, I'll be with you in a moment.

The Red and the Black

Why not Monte Carlo?

Would truth, beauty and profit better be served in Tampa or Memphis or Birmingham or some such tropical furnace where NFL exhibitions are played?

I would just as soon spend the summer reading play books in the Gobi Desert. I would rather go to Transylvania, put on a low-cut gown and take a walk in the mist with Count Dracula.

I can do without exhibition games.

There are reasons. Esthetic reasons and grubby money-making reasons.

One: The summer is when I bury my head in sand and baseball and other summer things. I have a linear head. It rejects for as long as possible the next season until the current one is over. It absolutely banishes exhibitions of the next season while the current one is wending toward its climax. I go sockless and wear my seersucker jacket and drink gin and tonic until the leaves change color.

On Labor Day or thereabouts an alarm clock goes off in my uncluttered head, waking me to the new season and its possibilities. In midseason I'll be fresh and enthusiastic, and the guy who started in July will be confused, tired, poor, and into the next season. The seasons, betting or otherwise, should be savored as fully as a watermelon eaten to the rind. Mix at your own peril.

Two: Granted, exhibitions can be entertaining, in the

manner, say, that a band rehearsal can be entertaining. It's still a clothesline of jocks running and jumping, throwing and catching, rocking and socking. But essentially exhibitions are bloodless charades, lacking intensity and drama. Worse for the bettor, they are deceiving. They will, in the long run and pass of the season, be counterproductive.

A contradiction illuminates the deception. Professional gamblers are more successful betting on exhibitions than on regular games. Because they make it their business to know: which coaches experiment and which go all out to win, how much key veterans are going to play, whether a team is trying hard because management wants to sell season tickets. Anyone really tuned in can get the messages, but it is a tedious, professional chore to keep abreast of such developments on all games, and generally they will be reflected in the point spread anyway. Where the linemaker slips up, the professional pounces. The got-to-have-action amateur flounders. Fortunately for him, bookies limit bets on exhibitions.

The deception is twofold. When one wins and loses real money on fake games, one is likely to take them seriously and incorrectly evaluate the teams for games that count. This is like winning or losing in Monopoly and then buying or selling stock in the Reading Railroad. More fatal, when one wins with the kind of inside information that is valid for exhibitions, or loses because such information wasn't general knowledge, an attitude is encouraged that the road to everlasting happiness is paved with inside information. It isn't.

So I never bet on exhibitions. I like the summer, and I like football too much.

Three: Football isn't that mysterious. Picking winners

isn't that tough. Picking winners is the easy part. Managing your money—your emotions—is the hard part.

I went to Monte Carlo to test myself in management, in discipline. If you're going to suffer for your art you might as well suffer first class.

Additionally I hoped that through the prism of a concentrated period of gambling, a week or so, I would collect some clues to its fascination and some insights into my own motivations. So if I blew my advance and found myself contemplating a flying leap into Sheridan Square, I might be comforted by knowing why.

I was curious too about the relationship of sex and gambling. Partly because I am curious about the relationship of sex and anything and partly because I had a bad experience in gambling once. It was too painful, and I was too dense and preoccupied with the spastic frug of my daily rhythms, to ask myself or anyone else what it was about.

What happened of course was that I lost a bundle. Lost control, terrifyingly. And it shattered me. The sheer stupidity of it. A snake in the garden of self-esteem, exposing unsuspected vulnerability.

The bundle had $8,000 in it. I had to borrow from a bank, lying through the borrowing ritual, to pay it. The $7,000 I had won a year before was gone, invested in furniture and paintings before I could squander it. But the objects testified to my genius—in my mind's eye each was adorned by a bronze medallion with the legend of its origin, like "Green Bay minus 7 over Giants, November 18, 1965"—and convinced me of my omnipotence. I bet basketball and survived. I bet baseball and, on one long lost try-to-catch-up weekend, got knocked on my ass. I don't bet basketball or baseball anymore.

The monthly check to the bank irritated me mainly as

a reminder of my stupidity, which after a while I rationalized into a blessing-in-disguise-because-I-won't-ever-let-that-happen-again, as I once did after losing $20 in the shell game on a troop ship. Using subways instead of taxis seemed to be poetic penance; they actually got me to where I was going faster. It was the sixteen-pound shot that materialized in my chest that bothered me.

Sometimes it pulsed. Sometimes it burned. Sometimes it pressed against my sternum as though a heavy-handed masseur were working on me, air escaping from my lungs in gasps. Musing to myself about my next column, walking to the corner for a paper, drinking with the gang at the Lion's Head, eating dinner with Gail, pulling the covers over me, awaking, the sixteen-pound shot was my constant and closest companion.

It probably began to dissolve after I told Gail about it late one night in the darkness after months of holding it in, months when we communicated and touched even less than usual. The stupidity, the guilt, the shame trickled out like tears, with tears. It was a humiliating confession of weakness to me. A window into the dark secret heart I wanted to keep secret from myself. The confession was incomplete. I still couldn't be completely open. She asked me how much I lost, borrowed. "A lot. Too much." My lips would not form the numbers. I never told her.

Which brings us back to sex and gambling. The trauma, as traumas will, dehorned the horny dwarf.

I was prepared to cope with losing, to exorcise my demons, somehow. That was, in the end, fairly simple. But I was not prepared to cope with deeper man-woman complexities, complexities of myself. Games and other obsessions can be magnificent escapes.

The south of France is not bad in the escape department. Before Monte Carlo I sunned myself for three weeks at Saint-Tropez, a nipple on the bountiful breast of Provence, where the landscape is sensual, the food French, the women both. On my first afternoon in Monte Carlo I realized that I hadn't once thought of gambling in Saint-Tropez. I realized this when I saw a dowager, strangling in jewels, trussed in blue silk stockings and a brocade bathing suit. A relic of fading elegance, like Monte Carlo. I thought about gambling.

My plan of attack was as follows: I would play roulette exclusively. (One doesn't eat crepes in Yazoo City, Mississippi, and one doesn't shoot craps in Monte Carlo.) I would limit myself to 300 francs (about $60) nightly. I would use an international medley of systems. I would play 0 and 26, as recommended by a fashion photographer I met in Copenhagen who swore he never lost. I would play colors (black or red) as did Dostoevski's wealthy grandmamma in *The Gambler,* but only after one of them came up three times in a row, in which case I would let the money ride as long as I dared. (This was an adaptation of a baseball betting system I once read about: keep betting on a team that wins three games in a row, on the theory that you will catch some long winning streaks.)

A word about gambling systems: I don't believe in them. Systems substitute mathematical equations for human equations, a fatal flaw because humans must operate them. They would turn an essentially romantic pastime into a grind. On the other end of the scale they imply submission to a higher authority. Who? Why? The odds should be respected, but they don't have to be held in awe. What I did at Monte Carlo was pure whimsy. It would, I trusted, enable me to stretch out my investment of time and money. I did not expect to win.

I had had two previous experiences with roulette. Nineteen years before, as a sportswriter on leave from *Stars & Stripes* in Germany, I went to Monte Carlo with $30. I played 17 because it was the first two-digited number I picked up in French (*dix-sept*). On my last franc it hit. I put a few more francs on it and it hit again. I walked out with about $60. Two days after the 1969 Super Bowl, the Joe Namath Super Bowl, I put a $10 bill on 12 (Namath's number) in San Juan (at the standard 35–1 odds). The croupier handed the bill back to me because, he said, in a ruling that still mystifies me, I had to have a seat to play. Yes, 12 came up.

(One horse racing tale of woe. A day before the Super Bowl I went to Hialeah Race Track, determined to bet the 1–2 daily double, because of the zany week Namath was having. The driver of the borrowed limousine I was in got lost, incredibly, and we didn't arrive until the second race. The 1–2 won and paid $1,100.)

(Gamblers are selective in their memories. Few of us recall the incidents of games, horses or numbers that dropped dead after we almost bet them.)

Systems and numerology, whimsical or not, provide a hopeful framework, I suppose, for what we recognize as a streak of insanity. They resemble ethical or moral systems, religions, that try to hold things together, impose a discipline from without, make order out of chaos. If systems were any good the casinos wouldn't be so big and we wouldn't be so small.

On the first night, a Monday, I sallied forth from my hotel, the Metropole, a four-star Sidney Greenstreet of a hotel with its garden bar and birdcage elevator, and entered the big casino. I thought, "Bet nobody else is here for preseason practice." I thought, "George Allen, you don't go any first classer than me."

I expected Arabian princes with princely piles of chips in front of them. There were four wheels surrounded by peasants like myself. I sat down at a 10-franc-minimum table, exchanged 200 francs for chips, leaving 100 in reserve. I was ready to scrimmage, to do grass drills, to take laps.

I was not ready for the opportunity that came and went immediately, like a hole at tackle that opens and closes in a flash. I was not ready for what-might-have-been: a run to moonlight with a bag of gold crooked under my arm.

I won hundreds. I should have won thousands.

Zero came up on the third spin. Twenty-six came up on the eighth spin. I was ahead 14–0 in the first quarter. My eye began to roam, like a benchwarmer checking out the cheerleaders. I made mental notes of the pink marble columns and gaudy chandeliers and nineteenth-century palace decor. I sized up my playmates: a young couple out of a primitive painting of a French wedding party; an old couple playing clusters of numbers (at smaller odds than 35–1) with passionless prudence; an old man sitting next to me, charting every spin in quest of the wheel's glandular cycle; a Burgess Meredith type, directly across from me, playing with style and abandon, scattering 20-franc reds hither and yon.

My stack of 10-franc blues was depleting when I noticed the color red seemed to be repeating. There, another one. Another. I put a 100-franc greenie on red. Red. I hadn't been paying attention. I picked up one greenie, leaving one greenie on red. Red again. I picked up a greenie. Again.

I was stricken with a sense of panic. Not panic itself. The sense of being disoriented, missing the train in a crowded foreign depot, being at an uptown cocktail party and waiting for a girl to free herself and then, after scanning the etchings, watching another dude moving in.

I had blown it.

Black.

"Fourteen times," the old man next to me whispered, his pencil making jagged arthritic moves. "Red, fourteen times."

I felt warm, my insides percolating. Counted my money: 560 francs. Imagined that the people standing behind me could see my neck reddening. (When the sun rose and set on Joe DiMaggio I saw his neck redden, standing in the batter's box at Yankee Stadium, 0-for-7 in a doubleheader, getting booed. He tripled.) I played my numbers three more futile times. I was ahead 300 francs. The clock read 11:30; I had been there exactly an hour. I knew I would blow it all if I hung on. I felt hot. (DiMaggio was out trying to steal home.) I left.

Trying to compose myself at a café, I calculated that had I bet 20 francs on red after it had come up three times I could have won 20,240 francs. (There was a 10,000-franc limit.) It seemed like such a ridiculous figure—I mean I had never even won a bag of marbles at the Saturday matinee—that I cooled off.

Coolly, I had a meeting with myself.

"Fucked up again."

"Sure did. But what would I have done for an encore?"

"Don't rationalize."

"Rookies make mistakes."

"You didn't make a mistake. You lost the championship."

"Still walked out a winner."

"Three hundred francs. A three-yard gain. Some romantic you are."

"Paid for the day, plus. Let's be realistic: I'm trying to beat the house, not break the bank. I'm trying to have fun, not get rich."

"Twenty thousand francs would have been fun. Ten thousand would have been worth a few laughs. Three hundred is a bloody cop-out."

"Look, I'm in training. I had the control to get out while I was ahead. Inner discipline. It's a long season. I'll get them tomorrow."

"Bullshit."

"It's one o'clock. Curfew. Good night, George Allen, wherever you are."

Tuesday I got them.

Zero hit on the fifth spin. It is a thing of beauty and a joy, for a while at least, to score early when the odds are against you and you have bet on the underdog. Anxiety drains into relief as the prospect of instantly being wiped out is put to rest. What we all want if we can't have the money is a run for the money, evidence that we aren't ciphers.

My lead dwindled, without protest, to a handful of chips, and I have small hands. But I was into the game, concentrating, summoning, and when black came up for the third straight time I reached into my pocket for the last 100-franc note and placed it on black.

Black hit. I let the 200 ride. Black—400. Black—800. Heart, be still. Black.

I had found my price. I fetched 1,500 francs, leaving 100. Black hit again—200. Again—400. Red.

Zero came up in another few spins. I fondled a large rectangular 1,000-franc chip. I felt myself levitating, wanting to fly out. I threw 40 francs each on 0 and 26—nothing. It was 10:00 P.M., I had played for a half hour. I flew.

Fleeing through the great rooms of the casino after cashing in, I was lit up by an electric current. Was my nose blinking, my ears semaphoring? I had chills. My body was having an orgasm. It subsided, then returned as I hit the steps. Fantasmagoric. A multiple orgasm.

I once won $2,000 on a football game. I glowed inside for days. Winning this 1,500 francs, this measly $300, twanged an undiscovered chord in my ganglia. I was a Fourth of July sparkler, sizzling.

Over dinner I discussed it.

"Jesus, you're terrific."

"I know."

"I didn't think you had it in you to play black. Isn't it always red that has the streaks in novels and movies?"

"Black is beautiful. Have to keep an open mind."

"I have to admit that, in retrospect, you handled last night's situation the way you should have."

"I have to admit you're right."

"Remember that time in high school, playing against Jefferson, when the linemen said in the huddle they couldn't move that 320-pound guard, run thirty-six to the left? You ran right into the big bastard the first time, but the second time you veered left and found the hole."

"I'm a slow learner."

"Slow runner. There was a hole big enough for the First

Division to go through, and you made about seven. But I love you."

"Love you too. Night."

Wednesday I lost.

Zero and 26 performed nobly but indecisively. Up and down, down and up. Three reds came up once, and I played red and, because I had an odd chip and thought I might save 10 francs on one spin, I didn't play 0. It hit. My stomach flinched, as though steeling itself for a punch. The eyes of strangers condemned me. Discombobulated, I played colors indiscriminately, won some, lost some. I needed action. After two hours I was glad to come to any decision. The numbers seemed like random hieroglyphics. I was disappointed that I was not afflicted by vertigo instead of boredom.

"Now what was that all about?"

"I was about to ask you."

"Man, you have to hang in there."

"Gene Mauch once told me that young players lose their concentration quickly. Two hours is a long time to look at numbers, numbers, numbers. Nothing was happening. It was a grind. I didn't come here to grind."

"It's a long season. You came here to get ready for a long season."

"But there's no control, or illusion of control, as in football. No opinion to be right about. I feel no connection to roulette, even though I'm playing it, while in football I feel that I'm a part of it, even though I have nothing to do with the game."

"Crazy American, the bottom line is that you lost control of yourself, not the game."

"I'm still 1,500 francs to the good. I just got careless."

"They don't get careless when they have your money. They keep taking it. They're counting on you to get careless with their money. Don't."

"Just my humanity shining through. Let's mark it down as a good lesson."

"What are you drinking?"

"How do you say gin and tonic in French?"

"Gin and tonic."

"Perrier and Creme de Menthe. Sidney Greenstreet would drink Perrier and Creme de Menthe in Monte Carlo."

Thursday I won.

For variety and pizazz, and to broaden my vocabulary and horizons, I refined the system. I continued to play 0 and went to 25–26 and 26–27 instead of 26 alone, putting 10 francs on 26 and five each on 25 and 27, adding up to a 30-franc investment per spin, allotting me just 10 spins before the nightly stake could expire.

Twenty-six proceeded to mock my lapse of faith by scoring four times in a dozen or so spins. I was ahead 1,000 francs. Twenty-six, it dawned on me, was the number worn by Jack Mitchell, the original split-T quarterback at Oklahoma. As a sophomore last-string halfback I was given jersey 26 for the first game of the season after he graduated. Somebody thought better of it. For the second game I was 21.

Zero struck again and then, in succession, 26 and two 25s. It was a rout. I had an urge to punch the air triumphantly, to shout whoopee, something, but the stuffy decorum was intimidating. I searched for recognition or applause among my playmates. Unmindful, or resentful, of the great drama unfolding in their midst, they continued to root for their own money, the philistines.

Playing with the casino's money, 1,800 francs of it, I made my move. I doubled and tripled my bets, put 100 francs on 8, my daughter's age. In ten deliberately frenzied minutes I went through 1,200 francs. I took 600 in profit and fled.

"That was lovely. You took your shot and got out while you were ahead."

"I have 2,100 francs of their money. There's no way they'll get it all back."

"If you beat this silly game you ought to be able to murder football."

"I'm hip."

"You're fantastic."

"I'm horny. Got to share all these vibes."

At a discotheque a young German told me about The Sporting Club, an annex of the main casino where the high rollers roll. So that's what that Rolls-Royce motor pool was all about on Avenue Princess Grace.

Friday night I ambled into The Sporting Club with all the insouciance I could muster. The musky odor of power and the thick scent of sexcitement hit me the way Mike Curtis, the linebacker, forearmed a Baltimore fan who ran onto the field. I was stunned.

I have been around the very rich while they have their fun and games, and I have found them only more uptight than you and I. Here, playing out fantasies on an exotic Super Bowl grid, they seemed less uptight than you and I. There were men, princes of industry, most of them much past their prime, in the barely concealed frenzy of lions at feeding time. There were women, great beauties, diamonds cascading from every public part, lionesses in heat. There was a primal growl in the air.

My own fortunes interested me less than the real fortunes of others. Twenty francs was the minimum, so I raised my stake to 500. Zero and 25–26–27 rose to the occasion, steadily building a 700-franc lead. Then a bouncy little old man, animated as a chimpanzee, won 240,000 francs on four turns of the wheel. My 1,200 francs seemed puny. I decided I needed a bigger stake and went to the dice table. I pressed it to 2,300 and depressed it back to 600. Back at roulette I depressed it to minus 200, dug into my pockets for 500 more, and accepted a total loss of 700. I had gone 400 over my limit. The growl had jumped into my throat.

I had already caught a dizzying whiff of a card game called 30–40, where a man was playing for the limit, 40,000 francs (about $8,000) per hand. He was losing heavily; markers on the table counted up to 600,000 francs. His eyes were glassy with resignation, his mouth expressionless, waxy with death. As his losses mounted to 800,000 his body seemed to sag. I wondered what the autopsy would show.

Then, gradually, he reduced the row of markers. As he did his mask of tragedy transformed through stages of aliveness to hope to anticipation to victory, and finally to celebration. Marcel Marceau, the mime, couldn't have done it any better. When the last marker was wiped out the man toured the room jubilantly, hugging and kissing women.

I felt that I had seen a man dig his own grave and climb out.

I was sure that he had an electric current sizzling through him.

Psychiatrists tell us that tempting fate—engaging in a life-death struggle—is one of the subconscious forces egging on the compulsive or pathological gambler. It could also be, they say, a desire to expiate guilt or seek love or return to the infantile state of being at the center of the universe. I don't know how guilt-ridden, love-starved, or well-diapered this man was, or whether he was even a case for the couch, but he certainly managed to stir himself viscerally by dying and being reborn.

Which, thankfully, brings us back to sex. On another level, psychiatrists tell us, gambling is a surrogate sexual experience. Whether it is a substitute or a supplementary entry for the real thing is up to the individual. Whatever, the heart-pounding risk of gambling is an erotic quick release that simulates the intensity of sex.

Those of us who gamble only from time to time are not, by the psychiatric definition, gambling at all. A clinical gambler is a screeching-with-anxiety neurotic who can't relax until he loses. The rest of us are getting a cheap thrill by creating an easy gut involvement.

My involvement in betting on football, particularly in how I handicap games, is, I began to understand in Monte Carlo, an extension of misspent youth as a player and high school backfield coach. The competition. The planning. The tension. Winning and losing.

But gambling for fun has its risks too, no less than social drinking. I've suffered a lapse gambling. A time or two I've gotten smashed drinking. Getting smashed is cheaper.

"You got manic in there, stud."

"No use gambling if you can't lose your head once in a while."

"Forget the book?"

"When you get into it, there's no book. First you live it, then you write it."

"Is that what you got out of your preseason practice?"

"That, and 1,400 francs, and a dynamite suntan."

"Lots of luck."

"Rather be good."

"Better be good, or you'll be good and broke. What's that ringing?"

"The alarm clock in our head, shmuck. Football season."

Part II
The Season

The race is not always to the swift—nor the battle to the strong—but that's the way to bet.
—DAMON RUNYON

First Week

MONDAY, SEPTEMBER 11

So, as it says in the Old Testament, I begin. I begin to play God with the National Football League and the point-spread prophets by going back to last year's standings. It has to begin with last year because there are few dramatic changes from year to year. A few teams jump up, a few teams fall down, most teams slide along even as you and I.

AMERICAN FOOTBALL CONFERENCE

	w	l	t	pts.	op.
	Eastern Division				
Miami Dolphins	10	3	1	315	174
Baltimore Colts	10	4	0	313	140
New England Patriots	6	8	0	238	325
New York Jets	6	8	0	212	299
Buffalo Bills	1	13	0	184	394
	Central Division				
Cleveland Browns	9	5	0	285	273
Pittsburgh Steelers	6	8	0	246	292
Houston Oilers	4	9	1	251	330
Cincinnati Bengals	4	10	0	284	265
	Western Division				
Kansas City Chiefs	10	3	1	302	208
Oakland Raiders	8	4	2	344	271
San Diego Chargers	6	8	0	311	345
Denver Broncos	4	9	1	203	278

NATIONAL FOOTBALL CONFERENCE

	w	l	t	pts.	op.
	Eastern Division				
Dallas Cowboys	11	3	0	406	222
Washington Redskins	9	4	1	276	190
Philadelphia Eagles	6	7	1	221	302
St. Louis Cardinals	4	9	1	231	279
New York Giants	4	10	0	228	362
	Central Division				
Minnesota Vikings	11	3	0	245	139
Detroit Lions	7	6	1	341	286
Chicago Bears	6	8	0	185	276
Green Bay Packers	4	8	2	274	298
	Western Division				
San Francisco 49ers	9	5	0	300	216
Los Angeles Rams	8	5	1	313	260
Atlanta Falcons	7	6	1	274	277
New Orleans Saints	4	8	2	266	347

I begin with some simple observations and questions to myself:

The offense of the Colts wasn't that good, yet only four teams outscored them. Reason: Their defense overwhelms the opposition and makes it easy for their offense to operate. The offense is in trouble when the defense doesn't dominate the game.

The Jets won nearly half their games without Joe Namath. He's back.

Why did the Browns win nine and the Bengals win four, when they had almost identical point totals? The Browns could be less than meets the eye, the Bengals more.

The Packers, like the Bengals, had a better point ratio than their record indicates. Curious.

This is my way of getting oriented for the new season. The musings may or may not give me a useful clue, but they serve a useful purpose: the focus of season-to-season continuity. People who have been razzled and dazzled by the grim hokum of exhibitions usually need the hard results of the first two weeks to get jolted into that focus. If they are bettors they may have missed some good bets.

It can be argued that the converse is true too. That by giving too much weight to last season you may overlook the significant drift of the present one. I agree. But significant drifts are obscured by exhibitions, because there are so many meaningless and so few meaningful happenings. Which are which? You'd have to be closely tuned in to all twenty-six teams—hello there, 26—and not only wouldn't I wish that on my worst enemy, but I don't think it's possible. You are going to get sucked in by the false hopes and despair that even fake winning and losing inevitably yields.

There's a more reliable way to get tuned in. Theory No. 2 holds that teams that add good players generally do better than they did the year before and teams that subtract good players generally do worse. Rookies generally are unreliable: Those who contribute importantly (make the difference in winning games) are as rare as Academy Award-winning actresses discovered on drugstore stools.

To refresh myself about the measurable additions and subtractions (trades of known quantities and qualities, serious injuries to key players), and to pick up whatever vibrations I could, and to amuse myself, I spent the afternoon trying to make sense of all the nonsense in the exhibition issues of *Pro Football Weekly,* which furnishes a comprehensive picture of the week that was. It is possible, of course, that I was making nonsense of the sense. The bottom line on the betting season that was will be the final arbiter of that.

The impressions I came away with, team by team, as they finished in the playoffs and standings, were these:

Cowboys Subtracted quarterback Roger Staubach with injury, halfback Duane Thomas in trade; added receivers Billy Parks, Ron Sellers in trades. Staubach and Thomas got the Cowboys a championship with their ability to make exceptional plays. The Cowboys are strong but unlikely to win it all again without them. They are a bad bet with Craig Morton at quarterback.

Dolphins Added former league-leading receiver Marlin Briscoe and defensive tackle Jim Dunaway in trade. Halfback Mercury Morris pushing Jim Kiick for starting berth. Young team that can only improve.

49ers No significant changes. Can beat anyone, but erratic.

Chiefs No significant changes. They overpower weak teams, have problems scoring on strong teams.

Colts Subtracted Bubba Smith with injury. Smith is the kind of defensive lineman who makes teammates around him look better than they are. Who rushes the passer now? Puts a greater burden on the offense and who carries it?

Redskins Added receiver Charley Taylor, quarterback Sonny Jurgensen, who were injured last season. Redskins didn't lose until Taylor was injured. Will be hard to beat if all their key personnel stay healthy.

Browns Subtracted defensive end Jack Gregory from already soft defense in trade. I like Mike Phipps, who is replacing Bill Nelsen at quarterback, but he has to show he can do the job. Once-great halfback Leroy Kelly is a year older. Could be the start of a slide for this team.

Vikings Added quarterback Fran Tarkenton, receiver John Gilliam, subtracted receiver Bob Grim in trades. Tarkenton should manufacture enough offense to make them favorites in every game. Combined with great pass-rushing defense, this could mean lopsided wins over mediocre opposition.

Raiders Added Mike Siani, rookie receiver who may help right away. Strong team again, but inconsistent quarterbacking, lack of big-play threat and pass-rush make them a dangerous bet.

Rams Added defensive end Fred Dryer, offensive lineman John Williams, subtracted defensive end Deacon Jones in trades, but these positions are already well-manned. Quarterback Roman Gabriel missed most exhibitions with a punctured lung and may have trouble with his arm. Iffy team. I like the coach, Tommy Prothro.

Lions Subtracted tight end Charlie Sanders with injury, which minimizes the team's passing threat, and the team is offense-oriented. Look for the right spot to bet against the Lions until Sanders returns in midseason.

(Revealing note on the Lions: Joe Schmiesing, formerly of the Cardinals, a weak defensive team, has won a starting berth at defensive tackle. Players claimed on waivers as the regular season approaches may also be a more accurate commentary on a team than the coach's chronic optimism. The Rams picked up a cornerback, Al Clark, from the Lions, who themselves picked up a cornerback from the Falcons, suggesting that both teams are shaky at that position.)

Falcons Added Joe Profit, top halfback prospect who missed rookie season with injury. Expansion team coming off first winning season, should be on the upgrade. They play hardnosed Norm Van Brocklin football but lack a Norm Van Brocklin quarterback, and speed at flanks. I'm a Van Brocklin man.

Chargers Added defensive linemen Deacon Jones, Lionel Aldridge, Paul Costa, fullback Cid Edwards, Duane Thomas (if he is able to overcome mental-emotional problems to play); subtracted Billy Parks in trades. Possible sleeper team if the old defensive studs have anything left; if Thomas. Offense can score.

Eagles Subtracted linebacker Tim Rossovich in trade, running back Les Bougess with injury. No significant additions to a team that needs them. Some good horses on defense though.

Patriots Added tight end Bob Windsor in trade. Moved up last year with quarterback Jim Plunkett, a coming superstar. But five rookies are starting on defense.

Bears Subtracted entire front four: Ed O'Bradovich retired, George Seals playing out his option, Jerry Staley and Willie Holman injured. Top offensive player, receiver Dick Gordon, playing out his option. Quarterback Bobby Douglas said to be lacking in play-calling ability, but he can't pass either. Bet against these loves.

Jets Added Joe Namath, defensive tackle John Elliott, both injured last season. Dynamite offense, defense suspect.

Steelers Added fullback Franco Harris, highly regarded first-round draft pick, may be the answer to their big back need. Secondary suspect. George Allen says they will win their division. Watch.

Packers Added rookie cornerback Willie Buchanon, a highly regarded high first-round draft pick, rookie field goal-kicker Chester Marcol, running back MacArthur Lane in trade; subtracted running back Donny Anderson in trade. Much muscle here but lack of passing should hurt them against strong defenses.

Saints No significant changes. Lots of holes. They pulled some big upsets last season with rookie quarterback Archie Manning.

Broncos Subtracted Paul Costa in trade. Solid front four of last few years broken up. Who quarterbacks? New coach: John Ralston, Stanford.

Cardinals Added Donny Anderson and highly regarded first-round draftee Bobbie Moore, a receiver; subtracted MacArthur Lane. Team going nowhere.

Oilers No significant changes. Some good defensive horses, top quarterback prospect in Dan Pastorini. New coach: Bill Peterson, Rice.

Giants Added running back Ron Johnson, injured last year, and Jack Gregory, receiver Bob Grim, quarterback Norm Snead; subtracted Fran Tarkenton, Fred Dryer in trades. Snead has never had a winning season, Giants have had one in eight years. I don't think Alex Webster can coach.

Bengals Added highly regarded first-round rookie Sherman White, defensive end, second-round safety Paul Casanova, who must be respected because Paul Brown seldom makes mistakes. Team has makings of solid defense, but the passing game is erratic.

Bills Added top draft pick, defensive lineman Walt Patulski, subtracted receiver Marlin Briscoe in trade. O. J. Simpson might win some games himself. Lou Saban returns as coach.

These impressionistic team personality sketches are references for the first few weeks of the season. Since they represent my own opinions, they could be as counterproductive as betting on exhibitions, for opinions, once drawn, can be difficult to erase: There are coaches who would rather give an enema to a constipated rhinoceros than change the game plans they have painstakingly conceived, even in the face of evidence that they aren't working. Undoubtedly some of my opinions are bummers. They will have to be adjusted. He said.

The important thing to remember is that it isn't necessary to be right on everything. What is necessary is to be one jump ahead of the oddsmakers—who are human and make mistakes too—in evaluating just a few teams.

It took about four hours to piece together the puzzle of the new season to my satisfaction. When I think of all the time I saved this summer by ignoring exhibitions, I could kiss myself.

I have gotten an almost tactile pleasure out of playing

with the puzzle, manipulating the pieces, starting with the straight-edged certainties as a framework (the Dolphins, Redskins, Vikings, Bears), filling in the landscape with similar colors (Chiefs and 49ers, Lions and Falcons), confused by the clouds and skies of uncertainty (Colts, Rams, Jets, Steelers, Bengals, et al.).

Trying to apply logic to twenty-six teams is a fun doodling exercise, a way of expressing my retarded adolescence. But I wonder how much of the logic is illusion. Whatever experience and wisdom I think I can bring to bear on pro football, I wonder if there is any real difference between it and roulette. And whether, despite the trappings of rationality, I am trying to make order out of chaos with—a system.

Tuesday

Ordinarily I get the "line" today, but I missed the call from Doctor, my favorite bookie. Just as well. I have my own line to make.

The official line, or point spread, comes out of the West, I know not where, probably Las Vegas. I intend to chase it down to the linemaker himself this season. It is also my intention to match my line against the official line in an attempt to show that it's no big deal to figure out, and that the official line is grossly overrated for its accuracy. There are 189 games in a season, and the line is way off much more often than it is close to the final score. When it is close, bettors tend to swoon or curse the powers-that-be out there in the vast unknown. This has the unfortunate effect of intimidating bettors on those many occasions when the powers-that-be blow one. Or two. Or more.

In fact, what the fan may view in retrospect as a blunder in the line may be an accidental inspiration. A good line as far as a bookie is concerned is a line that stimulates action on both teams in a game. But a better line for him is one that stimulates more action on one team than the other and winds up with the other winning. He, in that case, is the other.

As an example, the Colts were made 17-point favorites over the Jets in their Super Bowl. The Jets won the game, so in terms of providing an accurate gauge of the matchup the line couldn't have been wronger. But the betting public actually was convinced that the Colts were a bigger favorite than that. They bet so much money on the Colts that the line went up to 19 and 20. Which left most bookies with more money on the Colts than the Jets. Which left them with a fat profit.

As a rule, though, bookies don't like to wind up with too much money on one team because that puts them in the position of gambling, and they prefer their customers to do the gambling. All bookies are former customers who decided they would rather pay the rent on time every month.

Whether the line itself influences betting is another question I intend to examine. If the Colts had been made, say, 6-point favorites, would it have slowed the surge of Colt money by convincing bettors that the Jets had a chance? Or would it have caused a bigger landslide for the Colts?

The public influences the line far more than the reverse, and that creates openings for sharp handicappers. The linemaker, for example, may have been convinced that the Jets–Colts was much closer than 17 points but foresaw heavy sentiment and money on the Colts (because the NFL representative in the previous two Super Bowls, the Packers, pulled overwhelming support).

Just as the linemaker may be influenced by the public in putting out the national line, local bookies will adjust the line to regional prejudices. The Jets were 17-point underdogs in New York. The Colts were 20-point favorites in Baltimore.

This is my line for the first week (first team is the favorite except for P for "pick," or even, games):

Falcons	6	Bears
Bengals	3	Patriots
Cowboys	13	Eagles
Lions	9	Giants
Rams	10	Saints
Colts	6	Cardinals
Packers	P	Browns
49ers	1	Chargers
Oilers	3	Broncos
Jets	4	Bills
Dolphins	1	Chiefs
Raiders	4	Steelers
Vikings	P	Redskins

How I arrive at a line illustrates my handicapping methods. As a first-week special I'll discuss all thirteen games on the schedule; hereafter I promise to limit this stuff to the games I bet on.

Falcons vs. Bears The Falcons will run against the patched-up defensive line of the Bears. I can't imagine what the Bears will do for points.

Bengals vs. Patriots Too early for a reading on either team. Bengals have superior defense. Paul Brown teams don't fumble much.

Cowboys vs. Eagles The Cowboys are stronger and more skilled than the Eagles at virtually every position. But Craig Morton may keep the Eagles in the game for a while.

Lions vs. Giants This would be a 14-point game with Charlie Sanders playing. Neither team has much defense. The Lions, with Greg Landry at quarterback, should move the ball more consistently.

Rams vs. Saints Rams should dominate this game with their offensive and defensive lines. Saints are more explosive.

Colts vs. Cardinals Colts' defense should contain the Cardinals even without Bubba Smith, but Colts' offense is drab enough not to push the Cardinals around.

Packers vs. Browns I have no opinion on this game.

49ers vs. Chargers Pass-rush of Deacon Jones was one of the main reasons why the Rams usually beat the 49ers. I give the Chargers a shot at an upset. 49ers figure to be favored by a touchdown.

Oilers vs. Broncos Broncos probably will be favored at home, but I like Pastorini and I think the Oilers' defense should be able to cope with a Charley Johnson at quarterback.

Jets vs. Bills I like the Jets, but I don't trust their defense.

Dolphins vs. Chiefs Chiefs the probable favorite at home, but they couldn't beat the Dolphins in six quarters of a playoff game last season, and the Dolphins have improved themselves since then.

Raiders vs. Steelers Raiders should be able to score on the Steelers' secondary. I'm not that crazy about Terry Bradshaw, Steeler quarterback.

Vikings vs. Redskins (Monday night) Vikings will be favored at home. Their great defense has had problems against teams with a balanced offense, which the Redskins have: If you run at the Vikings you neutralize their famous pass-rush. I'm anxious to see what Fran Tarkenton does for the Viking offense; but George Allen has always had success defensing him.

That's it, folks, and the subliminal message is that I view football as a game of strength vs. strength and strength vs. weakness—cause and effect.

Illustration on cause and effect: Put Joe Namath, Paul Warfield and a football on a patch of grass. Have Joe Namath throw every pass in his arsenal to Warfield. They will have a completion percentage of, say, 98 percent. Now put a defensive back between Namath and Warfield. Depending on his ability, the percentage will drop. Now put nineteen other players between Namath and Warfield and tell some of them to charge Namath and scream and wave their arms and bare their teeth. The percentage will drop again. Now tell Namath to mix in running plays with his passes. The percentage will rise. Now put a twenty-mile-an-hour wind into the picture and tell the defense to mix its coverages. The percentage will drop. Now tell the defense to look for a long pass and have Namath throw a short one. The percentage will rise.

There are an infinite number of factors that can be injected into this illustration to make the point that things don't just happen out there. Somebody makes them happen. Somebody controls the tempo of the game and makes the other guy play the way he doesn't want to. Somebody has the poise to play well in the face of adversity and the clock. Somebody doesn't.

These are factors that can be used in an equation to try to visualize how a game will be played, much the way a track handicapper tries to visualize the running of a horse race. Equally important, when the game is over they can be applied to determine what went right and what went wrong in the equation. I am not satisfied to rationalize a defeat on unlucky breaks. I know that I may lose because of a fumble or a blocked punt or a controversial call by an official; I can win that way too. I know I will win and lose some games because of factors I overlooked or miscalculated. But the more I know about the possible causes and effects the better chance I have to arrive at a winning equation.

This perspective was passed down to me from my great-grandfather, who, my mother tells me, used to say, "I'd rather lose with a smart man than win with a dumb man, because at least you know what you have with a smart man." My translation is: It's better to be good than lucky because if you're good you're more likely to have the team that makes its breaks and overcomes the other team's breaks.

I have omitted from the equations the intangible factors we are bombarded with so incessantly in football. The home field advantage. Emotion. Momentum. Hot games. Teams going flat. And other catchy abstractions favored by coaches and losers. I omit them because, to whatever degree they exist, which is problematical, I am certainly not smart enough to give them specific weight in an equation. Pros are supposed to perform to specified standards and I can't judge the variables in performance in advance. I choose to give credit or discredit to the other fellow when a pro of proven stature doesn't perform to his standard or performs way above it. I don't want to alibi for his poor performance or overvalue his great performance. If I do I will keep making the same mistakes.

Linemakers, handicappers and bettors usually do give a specific weight to the home field advantage, two or three points. I don't. Theory No. 3 is that the home field advantage of yesteryear has been largely neutralized by three developments:

1. The officiating is fair. (In the early stages of a pro sport, officials who are swayed by local sentiment may be suffered for commercial considerations: When the home team wins, it draws more spectators.)
2. Young people are more accustomed to travel today than they used to be. George Allen lectures the Redskins that a game on the road is "just a business trip."
3. Television. The notion that players play better at home suggests they fight harder to defend their turf in front of loved ones and community. But loved ones and a bigger part of the community see televised games, and they see games in more detail than they can in a stadium, exposing the players to closer scrutiny.

In basketball, with the crowd pressed around the edges of the court, officials are more likely to be swayed. And cheers reverberating like a lightning storm in a closed arena may have a measurable impact on a team. I am skeptical of such an impact in pro football.

I understand, now, having set all this down for the first time, that my approach to pro football as a bettor is an extension of my own semimarginal background in the game. As a player I enjoyed the hitting—it was easier to hit a man than a curve ball. Hitting is still the fundamental name of the game, which is why my evaluations always start with the matchups of the real or imagined strengths and weaknesses of the opposing lines. As a coach I dug doodling with X's and O's, matching wits with the other guy, working toward perfection with a group of young men, getting the instant win-lose gratification-judgment of seeing whether I had done the job.

My rewards as a pro football bettor are related. The high is investing myself—through my money—in a contest that will or won't unfold as I had foreseen. The money is a stimulus to an involvement that retreats securely into a part of my youth that seems relatively happy and uncomplicated. The biggest differences, I'd like to believe, are that I don't run quite as fast or get up quite as early as I used to. Also, I've gone from crewcut to rarely cut, Coke to Tab, Betty Grable to Liv Ullmann, and betting little nickels on softball games to big nickels ($500) on football games.

Wednesday

The line came. I placed my bets. I gave season's greetings to my bookies.

Doctor (a pseudonym for his pseudonym) called with the line:

Falcons	5½	Bears
Bengals	3	Patriots
Cowboys	14½	Eagles
Lions	10	Giants
Rams	11½	Saints
Colts	7½	Cardinals
Browns	2	Packers
49ers	5½	Chargers
Broncos	3	Oilers
Jets	7	Bills
Chiefs	3½	Dolphins
Raiders	3	Steelers
Vikings	3½	Redskins

The Jets were stronger favorites than I expected. I anticipated the rest of the games within a point and a half, with the exception of those I took a stand on. By taking a stand I mean making a primary judgment that the margin of victory or defeat will be greater than the anticipated official line. The difference between my line and the official line is a likely basis for a bet.

As soon as Doctor read off the line I blurted, "Give me the Falcons for a nickel. Give me the Dolphins for a nickel. Give me the Redskins for a nickel. Give me the Chargers for a nickel."

A nickel in bookie-bettor code language is $500. A dime is $1,000. A dollar is $100.

I have no idea why I decided to open the season at a $500 standard bet. It seemed properly risky. A bettor should calculate his potential losses before his potential winnings, and I had risked enough for the first week to put me well on the way to poverty.

I was slightly breathless, though, when I hung up the

phone. The first three bets were automatic. Zip, zip, zip, pay me the money. I liked the Chargers, but I was sorry I made the bet as soon as it fumbled off my tongue. It was a hunch, not a conviction.

Theory No. 4: Play convictions, not hunches. A conviction probably has some solid logic behind it.

Time for my first regular season meeting with myself.

"Why'd you do that?"

"I don't know."

"Some cause-and-effect that is."

". . . ."

"Slow down. It's a long season, remember? You can't win it all in one weekend."

"Check."

"Four is too many games. Cut it down."

"Check. Anything else?"

"If a nickel is $500 and a dime is $1,000, how come a dollar is $100?"

"Don't ask me."

I had made an appointment with Doctor for him to call me Saturday, when I would start checking fluctuations on the line until game time, should I decide to make additional or supplementary bets. I have to make appointments with Doctor because he cannot be reached by phone, directly, as most bookies can. He gave that up two years ago when his clerk was arrested trying to pull a swindle with some Harlem swifties. Doctor roams around the city with rolls of dimes in his pockets, calling his customers from bus terminals, office buildings, etc. He is a dapper little penguin of a man of about sixty, a veteran of forty years in the business, a loner. He knows as much about football as the Dalai Lama—he calls a field goal "that 3-point thing"

—but I'd rather do business with him than many of the shopkeepers in the legal marketplace. You practically have to submit a Dun & Bradstreet rating to him before he'll handle your action. I had an introduction to him from a newspaper executive. Doctor and I have never hassled about money, and we have a vague understanding that when either of us owes the other a couple thousand dollars we'll settle up (rather than meet every week as many bettors and bookies do). This hasn't happened in so long that I haven't seen him in two years. We don't speak from one football season to the next and when I spoke to him today he said he owed me $70 from last season that I had forgotten about. It is as though I've been making mind bets—bets in my imagination—and a great bookie in the sky has been entering them on a ledger.

One of Doctor's philosophical cornerstones is that "The 11–10 takes care of everyone," i.e., does them in. The 11–10 is the odds you must lay a bookie on a football game. The four $500 bets I have are really my $550 to his $500.

I look upon this 10 percent—known as the "vigorish" or "vig" or the "juice"—as a legitimate handling charge. I have to win eleven bets for every ten I lose, or about fifty-three bets out of one hundred, to break even, assuming that the bets are for the same amount (which is assuming a lot). Regardless, I feel that if I can't win that many bets I should find another passion. Raising purebred titwillows might be fun.

I have two other bookies. If you're serious about betting pro football, you should have at least three bookies so you can shop for points and half-points. One of them may have a game at 2½ while the others have it at 3. The half-point could be the difference between winning, losing or tying. Across a season four or five games like that make a difference in your wallet and your sanity.

I am using Billy and Mr. Rhodes as backup bookies to Doctor, and to get as much information as I can on how they function. Mr. Rhodes serves as my comic relief as well.

Billy, who is in his late thirties, is the only one of the three who knows I'm doing a book. He has promised to discuss his operation freely and let me observe him in action. His wife is his assistant. "The greatest woman bookie in the world," he says. "She's the expert in numbers."

Billy is a "runner" for a big bookmaking office. I know that he turns in bets to the office, but I'm not certain what the financial arrangements are. He has a phone number in the city I can call directly, and so has his office. I have a code name at his office: "Marine for No. 6." Marine as in Merchant Marine. No. 6 is Billy's code number. I like that. It is as lightly ominous as the skull and crossbones on a bottle of iodine. Both he and I will be credited for the bets I make. We reached a settlement figure of $1,500.

I haven't used Mr. Rhodes for several years, since we had a disagreement on who owed whom what. I made four bets with him one weekend and he told me later that I had made a "round-robin" of them. A round-robin is a four-way parlay. You link each team with every other team, giving you six two-team parlays. I regard one two-team parlay as terminal cancer, so why would I bet six of them? In a parlay both teams must win and you get paid off at 13–5. If you bet the games individually and won you would get paid off at 11–10 each. If you win one and lose one, which is most likely, you lose everything on the parlay but just the vigorish on one game in the individual bets. Parlays are get-rich bets that make you poor. I argued with Mr. Rhodes until he agreed to give me credit for individual bets (three of them losing). A couple of weeks later I bet a game taking 16½ points. The game came up 16, and Mr. Rhodes insisted there was no half-point. I closed my account with him.

This is not to imply that Mr. Rhodes is not an honorable man. In the hurly-burly of the pregame rush he takes dozens of bets and occasionally there is bound to be a slipup. Sometimes the bettor may unwittingly pick a team he didn't intend to, sometimes he will hear the response from the bookie (who always repeats the bet) incorrectly. I just thought that the proximity of our two slipups was curious. The Better Business Bureau refused to hear my complaint and I took my account elsewhere.

(Considering the number of transactions I've had with bookies, I've had remarkably few disputes. But my first transaction was made through a colleague at the Philadelphia *Daily News* and it cost me $400. I won $1,200 and got only $800. My colleague, it developed, had deducted his $400 in losses. The Newspaper Guild refused to hear that complaint.)

Further in Mr. Rhodes' behalf let it be noted that he buys Christmas presents for his clients. The year I lost the $8,000 he got some of it, and I got two silk Sulka ties from him. Fortunately I had recovered from the loss by that time, else I might have hung myself with them.

Doctor does not give Christmas presents, but he provides one formidable extracurricular service. He can get sixth row center theater seats for top shows on about an hour's notice, without paying a scalper's fee. I figure some high-powered show biz magnate owes him a couple hundred thou.

Anyway I am back with Mr. Rhodes, for the purposes of the book, because he amuses me. He is a Broadway character, forty-five or fifty, out of Nathan Detroit by Big Julie. His main source of income, it is said, is pornography shops. He dabbles in bookmaking to keep his hand in, like an old bank robber copping change off newsstands. It's in his blood.

I got through to Mr. Rhodes on his answering service. He informed me that his limit had deescalated from thousands to $200. He also informed me that the line wouldn't be made available to me until the weekend.

"There's an old man on my block who has a grocery store," Mr. Rhodes explained. "He gets up at dawn, and he works late. He has to work hard because there's a supermarket down the block. The old guy has a few regular customers he's been selling milk and potatoes and string beans, giving them an honest count. He don't sell that white powder, so much white powder that they don't care if they lose.

"I'm that old guy. I got a few customers who bet baseball every day. Them, I service with an early line. You, Saturday. This way you don't have to give me my money back out of the goodness of your heart because the game went from 6 to 8. Understand?"

What Mr. Rhodes is saying here is that he is small potatoes. Unlike the big Idahos who are connected to the underworld and who can afford to take a beating some weekends because of the profits from heroin, he has to eke out his percentage. He is concerned that sharpies might have inside information—on injuries, which I usually ignore unless the very top players are involved—and get an edge by betting early in the week. Thus, if a game went from 6 on Tuesday to 8 on Saturday, I could only bet at the adjusted line of 8. At 6 he might get swamped with money on one team. (Many small potatoes bookies operate this way, and not a few get 6–5 odds on bets under $100.)

Mr. Rhodes and I fixed $500 as our settlement figure, whereupon he made a proposition to me. I write a sports column for the New York *Post,* a liberal paper, and Mr. Rhodes enjoys agitating me about its editorial policies, which he disagrees with, conservatively, 105 percent of the time. He is especially incensed about the crime issue these days, an irony that is delicious coming from a man who lives outside the law, the parallel being General Motors blowing a gasket over air pollution.

"I'll make a deal with you," Mr. Rhodes said. "Your rag thinks it's so safe to walk the streets; if you walk six blocks up Seventh Avenue in Harlem at four o'clock in the morning, and come out alive, I'll give you the pro line on Tuesday."

I told him I'd think about it.

THURSDAY

Gail called, from Chicago, where she is acting in a play. Like nicotine addicts who quit smoking regularly, we have split three times in the last year. She insists on coming to town Monday and Tuesday for the start of the fourth quarter. I sublet the garret I live in from her. New York is teeming with great love stories like this.

It might be enlightening, or therapeutic, to examine the subtle and perhaps not-so-subtle lights and shadows that gambling casts on an ongoing relationship. I will have to improvise.

But I still regard Gail as the first-string quarterback, my once and future love, though at times we have played out our options and joined other teams temporarily. For all we know this may be the quintessential modern romance.

FRIDAY

Had my physical today. Brain waves, blood tests, cardiogram, pulmonary, the works. Object: Compare to similar physical late in the season to find out if my nerves are shattered, brain decomposed, heart diseased, stomach ulcerated, penis shriveled as a result of roller-coaster betting experiences.

Three terrific developments:

I stand 5′7¼″. All my adult life I have been living under the stifling impression of being only 5′6½″, of having lied on every driver's license application when I listed myself at 5′7″, of rationalizing that I would have captured Norma Tate, a campus beauty, if only I were a fraction of an inch taller.

I weighed 161½—my best betting weight.

I'm communicating with my glands, specifically my kidney, which I take as a positive sign, the way a race driver must feel when he is in touch with the carburetor. I have trusted my kidney ever since that time I tried to join the marines as a candidate for officer's training. Given a pint bottle to produce a specimen, my kidney stiffened in horror. After fifteen minutes I got the message, and eventually let the army come and get me. I have never regretted the decision of my kidney, which apparently had a better instinct for survival than I did at twenty-one. Today it instantly produced three golden ounces.

Played a parlay card at my office, putting $20 on the Falcons, Dolphins, Chargers, and Oilers. Parlay cards list all the games and offer terrible odds if you can pick at least four out of four correctly. Parlay cards are great because they provide the small bettor with as much action as he wants at negligible risk. The risk is negligible because the odds are so transparently terrible that nobody in his right mind risks much on them. To pick four games you get 9–1 odds on a 15–1 shot (calculated by doubling up the original bet four times).

It is, I find, a good way to make hunch bets—the Chargers and Oilers in this case—without jeopardizing my bankroll. I win one of them every two years and take bows all around the office. That's what it's all about. No office should be, and few are, without them.

The day was made complete when I bumped into Doctor in the subway. Told him I'd like to cancel the bet on the Chargers. "Done," he said with a grin. Most bookies would make you bet the other side to cancel the bet, so that you would have to pay a penalty of the vigorish (losing $550, winning $500, the penalty would be $50). The moral is that it pays to do business with an old established firm.

Saturday

I was hit with a new concept today—the "outlaw line." Lem Banker was the hitter.

Lem Banker is a professional gambler in Las Vegas. He bets football, basketball and baseball exclusively, and he says he has declared his earnings as income on his tax return for years. He also writes a twice-weekly column on betting for the Las Vegas *Review-Journal.* We are going to exchange views on the season from week to week. In November I will be going to Vegas to meet the shakers and movers on the pro football gambling scene, and Lem will be a sort of bettor of introduction for me.

The outlaw line, he said, is the early or test line put out on Sunday or Monday by assorted bookies, some of whom are licensed. A select few bettors are allowed to bet limited amounts into this line. Within a day or so a consensus is formed, and somehow an official line is derived from it. That somehow is what I'd like to pin down later. It may be easier to pin down the Loch Ness Monster.

The outlaw line was this:

Falcons	3	Bears
Bengals	1	Patriots
Cowboys	14	Eagles
Lions	10	Giants
Rams	9	Saints
Colts	7	Cardinals
Browns	3	Packers
49ers	5	Chargers
Broncos	3	Oilers
Jets	6	Bills
Chiefs	5	Dolphins
Raiders	3	Steelers
Vikings	5	Redskins

Comparing this line to the official line that emerged in New York, money had come in on the Falcons, Bengals, Cowboys, Saints, Colts, Packers, 49ers, Jets, Dolphins and Redskins.

Very obviously it is a tremendous advantage for a knowledgeable bettor to have access to this line. For two reasons:

If you know what you're doing you will give fewer points on a favorite and get more points on an underdog. I would have gotten 5 on the Dolphins and Redskins instead of 3½, and I would have given 3 on the Falcons instead of 5½. That is bound to be the difference in some bets during a season.

In addition it presents an opportunity to hit more "middles." A middle for the football bettor is the equivalent of pulling to an inside straight in poker, getting a double yolk in an egg, having a multiple orgasm. It is winning both sides of a bet.

For example, if I took the Dolphins with 5 points on Sunday or Monday, and then, if the money on the Dolphins drove the price down to 3 points by game time and I bet on the Chiefs, I would win everything if the Chiefs won by 4. I would win my bet on the Dolphins because I took 5; I would win my bet on the Chiefs because I gave 3.

Assuming I bet $500 on both sides, I would win $1,000. Assuming that one team won by a bigger margin, I would lose only $50. Hitting a middle then is a 20–1 shot. It is unwise to bet the same amount on both teams because of the odds, so the knowledgeable bettor will bet a fraction of his original bet on the other team because he still would rather win money than put it all on a long shot. If the middle comes in, drinks are on him.

I have hit one middle, when I gave 6½ and took 7½ on a game that wound up with a 7-point margin. I've had several "sides." A side is when, in the example given above, the Chiefs would have won by 3. In that case I would win on the Dolphins with 5 and get "sided" or get a "push" (tie) on the Chiefs giving 3. I would win a full bet ($500) while risking only part of a bet ($50).

Lem Banker said he liked seven games. He is betting the Browns, Broncos, Rams, Raiders, Falcons, Chiefs and 49ers. He is betting the Browns and Broncos because he thinks the price is right for tough home teams. This is how professionals think and how I don't think. We'll see.

Lem bets heavily. I met him while covering a fight in Las Vegas last spring and he was driving a Mark IV that was a block-and-a-half long. "We have a saying out here," he said in what I interpreted as a good-natured warning, "that there's nobody as dumb as a smart New Yorker."

There are a half-dozen other bettors I will be following through the season, regularly and irregularly, to try to get an X-ray of the betting public's head. Central Casting has sent me:

Greenwich Village Fats. Fats is a prosperous businessman—he has to be to support an old betting habit. He says he once had $400,000 in gambling debts, reduced now to $150,000. He blew his family, got psychiatric help, now says he bets $100 a game. I am especially interested in Fats because he is betting with information from a professional gambler who bets $250,000 a weekend, for himself and for pros in other cities. He is called a "mover." I want to meet The Mover.

Fast Eddie. Fast Eddie is a salesman in the garment district, where betting is a way of life in and out of business. I met Fast Eddie at the Super Bowl in New Orleans. He said he won $9,000 last season. He says he bets $200 a game. I call him Fast Eddie because he says he never knows who's playing until the weekend and then he bets on instinct.

Mr. Rich. Mr. Rich lives in a Park Avenue duplex. He lives off his investments, as far as I know. He says he bets up to $500 a game. "It's a hobby," he says. His wife and fifteen-year-old son help him handle the phones on Sunday as he shops among a half-dozen bookies.

Frankie the Doorman. Frankie the Doorman says, "I love action. I crave it. My job is boring, betting is exciting." To support his habit he works as a doorman in a Manhattan apartment building, is superintendent of the small apartment building where he lives in Queens, and plays the saxophone in a band on Saturday nights for $50. A tenant in the building where he works loaned him $800 for the final payment of a gambling debt that once was $11,000. Frankie the Doorman says he isn't going to bet for a few weeks because just now he is short. He bets $20 or $30 a weekend, usually on parlays, mostly on television games.

Danny Lavezzo. Danny Lavezzo owns P. J. Clarke's, the society McDonald's, a glorified hamburger joint. He is a horse player and sometime horse owner and rabid Giants fan. This season, he says, he will bet only on the Giants. Bookies and friends, knowing this, always give him the worst of the spread. If the Giants are 7-point underdogs, he has to lay 7½ or 8. "It doesn't bother me," he says with masochistic glee. "I love to beat wise guys." I don't know how much he bets.

Jonathan Schwartz. Jonathan Schwartz is an important New York radio personality, a fiction writer (*Almost Home*), and crazy Boston Red Sox fan. He bets socially with a friend, as many people do, "because it keeps us in touch" and "keeps a nice tension in my life" and "makes a beer taste good." The friend, Kenny Silverbush, bets $20 on the Giants in each of their games at the prevailing spread. In alternate years Schwartz or Silverbush picks a second team, before the season, that another $20 will be riding on. Last year Schwartz picked the Vikings. The Vikings won 7 and lost 7 against the line while the Giants won 6 and lost 8, giving Schwartz a $20 edge. This year Silverbush's second choice is the Dolphins.

I have two social bets myself. I bet Archie Mulligan, a bartender at the Lion's Head, $5 that the Giants don't win half their games. And I gave Dick Snyder, a vice-president of Simon & Schuster, the underbidder on this book, 10–1 odds, $100 to $10, that the Giants win one game. The bet was made impulsively when he was distressed by the trades that made former Giants of Fran Tarkenton and Fred Dryer. This was his way of punishing himself for rooting for the Giants, and I was only too willing to help him work it out.

Best of all, if the Giants win from one to six games, a distinct possibility, I will win both bets—a glorious middle.

SUNDAY

There are times when I wake up Sundays positive that I will win, certain that I have found the soft spots in the line. I lie in bed looking up at the ceiling or feeling a presence beside me or not beside me or surveying the wreckage of the Sunday *Times* I had roared through the night before, hands clasped behind my head, sweetly contemplating a day of good cheer. This attitude usually reflects the type of bets I've made, whether they were the result of methodical handicapping that led to a clear choice or to an indefinite leaning—a hunch.

Felt positive today, felt I was lifting off the pad for a fun-filled tour of inner space. So positive that, as a sporting gesture on the opening day of the season, I gave Mr. Rhodes a $100 play on the Raiders, who were down to 2 points over the Steelers; and to Billy I gave $100 on the Bears, who were up to 7 points under the Falcons, giving me a shot at a middle (since I had earlier given 5½ with the Falcons).

Sportingly, I lost both $100 bets. And the $20 stab on the parlay card. I won the $500 bets.

There was only one misstep and it seemed more like a pratfall. The first score I heard, during a telecast of the Jets and Bills, was 7–0 Steelers—scoring on a blocked kick. All my deep-think unraveled by a freak play. Sweet mystery of life.

But soon came a computer readout: Falcons 31, Bears 7 at the half. The Jets were drubbing the Bills, with the help of a touchdown on a punt return—their first such score in a decade. Then, on the late afternoon show, the Dolphins took command early and never let up on the Chiefs, winning 20–10. I smirked continually. Sweet reason, I toast thee.

But the strongest feeling I was aware of was relief. My approach to exhibitions and my evaluations were sound. My first winning day was out of the way, they have to catch me now. I would have to lose on four of the next five weekends to fall significantly behind. No way I can lose four out of five.

"Think you're hot stuff, don't you?"

"Well, um, yes, I feel pretty good. Might as well feel

good when you win, because you're damn sure going to feel not so good when you lose."

"It's only opening day, and you know how easy opening day can be. Wait 'til the linemaker draws a bead on the situation."

"Screw him. I drew a bead right now."

"Just keep the long season in your sights. And stop throwing $200 bills around. That's money too. Remember what Ted Williams said about wasting at-bats. Don't."

"The trouble with you is you're greedy. I had some fun with those two bets. Have fun and win money, that's the name of the game."

Before the kickoffs I posted a letter to a lawyer with a list of my bets for the week. I will do this all season, and he will keep the letters in a safe, unopened. This will put me on record as having said I'm doing what I'm doing before I do it. Since bookies don't give receipts, there is no way to prove that I actually make the bets.

I also called each of my bettors to get their selections before the kickoffs, as I will each week.

With the exception of Danny Lavezzo, who lost on his beloved Giants, and Lem, who won four (Broncos, Rams, Falcons, 49ers) and lost three (Browns, Raiders, Chiefs), my cast of bettors outdid me. And Greenwich Village Fats reported the first inside-information caper of the season.

Fast Eddie went for the Jets ("fantastic with Namath"), the Lions ("the Giants are terrible"), and the Dolphins ("a terrific team"), three-for-three. Mr. Rich had the Rams and 49ers ("much the better teams"). And Fats tore it all up with six out of seven, including, he said, three "punch" games.

"What the hell are punch games?" I asked.

"A game you double your basic bet on is a punch game," he said. "A double punch is a triple bet."

On the advice of The Mover, Fats bet the Cowboys, 49ers, Steelers, Rams, Bengals, Falcons and Bills, punching the Falcons, Rams, and Bengals. The inside-information caper turned out to be a chapter from the gang that couldn't bet straight. It involved their only loser. Fats said that The Mover knew that Joe Namath didn't have his knee brace in Buffalo.

Namath wears the brace as a precautionary measure. He discovered an hour and a half before the game that it wasn't in his duffel bag. He is responsible for packing it. The Jets chartered a plane to pick it up in New York and fly it to Buffalo where Namath put it on in the third quarter.

Of course I was impressed with The Mover's intelligence sources. But then I am impressed when a gossip columnist tells me what color shorts the secretary of state wore on his trip to Albania.

How did The Mover and friends find out about Namath's knee brace hours before the press did? I don't know. A reporter close to the Jets speculated that one of two travelers with the team, both presumed to be bettors, might have put the news on the inside-information wire. It could have been a team or stadium functionary.

I was equally if not more impressed, however, by the mind-boggling thickness of people who would bet on a football game because a quarterback forgot his knee brace. The information was good, the evaluation awful. Namath could play without the brace. He is as mobile, or immobile, without it as with it. The Bills, a bad team, would have to get to him, and get to him in exactly the right way, before the missing brace would be missed.

I suspect that what inside-information is truly about is the thrill it gives the holder of such dubious marginalia. It is a currency of value in the ego-tripping, chest-pounding world of gamblers who get the same charge out of trying to beat the system with espionage and connivery—an "edge"—as I get from trying to beat it with coachly logic. Lots of luck to them. They'll need it more than I will.

MONDAY

Whatever the cost in dollars, the involved bettor's dues are really paid in time. The time spent thinking, talking and reading about games and betting, the time spent daydreaming of coups and conquest, the time spent second-guessing and giving space to anxieties to wail, the time spent phoning and waiting to phone and waiting for phone calls from bookies. Even those of us who bet as a pastime invest heavily in time. Perhaps it's symptomatic—perhaps we would look elsewhere for a solitary diversion if we weren't betting—but sometimes, when my life-is-too-serious-to-take-seriously pose relaxes, I wonder whether the dues are prohibitive.

At dinner with Gail I made phone calls to Billy the bookie before and after the crabmeat cocktail. We visited friends afterward, and conversation was spotted here and there between TV touchdowns. How many hours did I clock, how many conversations did I tune out on in the bad old days?

We hadn't seen each other in two months. She is beautiful, a young, auburn-haired, hazel-eyed Katharine Hepburn to some, bright, spirited, talented, tense and blue-eyed to me. If she weren't so everything and I wasn't such a perpetual, if winsome, adolescent, we would have called our game on account of it's over ages ago.

Tonight we were like a quarterback and coach reintroduced after a series of trades brought them together again. We were comfortable, we recreated familiar games of affection, but our loving spoke of distance remembered in our tissue. The odds on us were longer than 6–5 against.

I hedged my $500 Redskin bet, playing scared, with $300 on the Vikings. I didn't want to ruin Sunday, lovely Sunday, with a bet I didn't believe in as much as I did the Falcons and Dolphins. The Redskins won 24–21—blocking a kick for one touchdown.

The bottom line on the first week is plus $930. I won $500 on the Dolphins, $390 on the Falcons ($500 minus $110), $170 on the Redskins ($500 minus $330), and lost $110 on the Raiders and $20 on the parlay card.

The closing line (with my bookies) on the games of the first week:

Falcons	8	Bears
Bengals	3½	Patriots
Cowboys	15	Eagles
Lions	10	Giants
Rams	11½	Saints
Colts	8½	Cardinals
Packers	2	Browns
49ers	6½	Chargers
Broncos	3	Oilers
Jets	6½	Bills
Chiefs	3½	Dolphins
Raiders	2	Steelers
Vikings	4	Redskins

The public bet on the Falcons, Cowboys, Packers, Rams, Colts, 49ers, Bills, Steelers and Vikings. You get this by comparing the official opening line to the closing line. The Falcons, for example, started as 5½-point favorites and went all the way up to 8 because they had so much support. The Packers went from 2-point underdogs to 2-point favorites. The public was right on six of the nine games that had line moves. Good day for the public. Good day for gift shops. Bad day for the bookies.

The gamblers who bet into the outlaw line won eight and lost two. Good day for the gamblers. Good day for Cadillac salesmen. Bad day for the bookies.

Seven home teams and six visiting teams won against the spread. Nine favorites and four underdogs won.

Favorite	My Line	Outlaw Line	Opening Line	Closing Line	Underdog
Falcons* (24)	6	3	5½	8	BEARS
COWBOYS (22)	13	14	14½	15	Eagles
LIONS (14)	9	10	10	10	Giants
BROWNS	P	3	2	2	Packers (16)
RAMS (20)	10	9	9½	11½	Saints
COLTS	6	7	7½	8½	Cardinals (7)
49ers (31)	1	5	5½	6½	Chargers
BRONCOS (13)	3	3	3	3	Oilers
Jets (17)	4	6	7	6½	BILLS
CHIEFS	1	5	3½	3½	Dolphins* (10)
Bengals (24)	3	1	3½	3½	PATRIOTS
Raiders*	4	3	3	2	STEELERS (6)
VIKINGS	P	5	3½	4	Redskins* (3)

This chart is a composite of the odds shifts and results for the week. Asterisks denote my bets. The number within parentheses is the margin of victory by that team. Home teams are listed in capital letters. Underscored spreads signify that the opposite team is the favorite or underdog in that line. P indicates "pick," or even, games in which there is no favorite.

The game is on.

THE STANDINGS

AFC

	w	l	t	vs. spread w	l
Eastern Division					
Dolphins	1	0	0	1	0
Jets	1	0	0	1	0
Colts	0	1	0	0	1
Bills	0	1	0	0	1
Patriots	0	1	0	0	1
Central Division					
Bengals	1	0	0	1	0
Steelers	1	0	0	1	0
Browns	0	1	0	0	1
Oilers	0	1	0	0	1
Western Division					
Broncos	1	0	0	1	0
Chiefs	0	1	0	0	1
Raiders	0	1	0	0	1
Chargers	0	1	0	0	1

NFC

	w	l	t	vs. spread w	l
Eastern Division					
Cowboys	1	0	0	1	0
Cardinals	1	0	0	1	0
Redskins	1	0	0	1	0
Giants	0	1	0	0	1
Eagles	0	1	0	0	1
Central Division					
Lions	1	0	0	1	0
Packers	1	0	0	1	0
Vikings	0	1	0	0	1
Bears	0	1	0	0	1
Western Division					
Falcons	1	0	0	1	0
Rams	1	0	0	1	0
49ers	1	0	0	1	0
Saints	0	1	0	0	1

RESULTS

Falcons 37, Bears 21
Bengals 31, Patriots 7
Cowboys 28, Eagles 6
Lions 30, Giants 16
Rams 34, Saints 14
Cardinals 10, Colts 3
Packers 26, Browns 10
49ers 34, Chargers 3
Broncos 30, Oilers 17
Jets 41, Bills 24
Dolphins 20, Chiefs 10
Steelers 34, Raiders 28
Redskins 24, Vikings 21

BETTORS	w	l	pct.
Fast Eddie	3	0	1.000
Mr. Rich	2	0	1.000
Fats–Mover	6	1	.857
Merchant	3	1	.750
Lem Banker	4	3	.571

EXOTICA

Home Teams 7, Visitors 6
Favorites 9, Underdogs 4
Pros 8, Outlaw Line 2
Public 6, Official Line 3

Second Week

TUESDAY

Before I try to analyze the next weekend, I try to analyze the last weekend. This is another of those practices that can be counterproductive, for one of the surest paths to self-destruction is to overreact to week-to-week results. It should take three or four games to get a solid fix on most teams.

To avoid paralysis through analysis, and self-deception through alibiing, I check a few crucial things. It would be simple for me to alibi the loss of the Raiders to the Steelers on the basis of a blocked kick, because the Raiders outgained the Steelers by more than a hundred yards. But a quick read of the game report and glance at the period-by-period score shows that the Steelers had the game well in hand, the Raiders scoring three touchdowns in the last period. The yardage is misleading because the Raiders made much of theirs while the Steelers obviously were playing the clock. The Steelers simply beat them.

Similarly the Redskins simply beat the Vikings, even though they scored on a blocked kick too, and even though the Vikings had more than twice as many first downs as they did. When they fell behind, the Redskins came right back and scored: They controlled the game. But I filed away for future reference the fact that the Vikings with

Fran Tarkenton moved the ball consistently on a rugged, experienced defense.

The Falcons and Bears, Dolphins and Chiefs, went according to plan. I'll take two curtain calls and the ears and tail for that.

In the only other game of significance the winning Cardinals made five first downs to the losing Colts' twenty, and somebody named Tim Van Galder, who I never heard of, quarterbacked them. The Colts marched up and down the field and missed four field goals. My interpretation is that they are going to have trouble getting the ball into the end zone against a decent defense.

Turnovers—fumbles and interceptions—frequently are an accurate gauge of a game's result and, of course, a handy alibi. Only one winning team had more turnovers than the team it beat this weekend. A bettor can always finger turnovers as the cause of his woe—which in some cases they are—but in general good teams turn the ball over less than bad teams or, to put it another way, good teams make the other guy turn the ball over more, especially when it counts. The Vikings and Colts have caused so many turnovers in recent years that their defenses have been offensive forces.

That done, I turn to the new line. In this table I list, from left to right, my line, the outlaw line and the official line:

	My Line	Outlaw Line	Opening Line	
Falcons	16	6½	7	Patriots
Browns	3	3	3	Eagles
Cowboys	13	9	9	Giants
Chargers	3	3	3	Broncos
Dolphins	16	14	14	Oilers
Rams	11	10	10½	Bears
Jets	2	P	2½	Colts
Vikings	6	2	1	Lions
Raiders	4	2½	3	Packers
Steelers	6	2	2	Bengals
Redskins	13	8	10	Cardinals
49ers	15	11	12	Bills
Chiefs	14	10	12	Saints

I am taking stands on several games: the Falcons over the Patriots, the Cowboys over the Giants, the Dolphins over the Oilers, the Vikings over the Lions, the Steelers over the Bengals, the 49ers over the Bills, the Chiefs over the Saints.

I bet $1,000 each on the Falcons and Vikings. It is remarkable how easy it is to say, "Give me the Falcons for a dime." When I was a street urchin, an uncle advised me never to get into a crap game with more than 15 cents "and if you lose walk away." A dime and a nickel are 15 cents. I bet a nickel each on the 49ers and the Steelers.

The Vikings are the standout bet. If I had a brain in my head I would bet only on them, and go to sleep until Sunday. The matchups are perfect: They have the defense to cope with the Sandersless Lions and the offense to move on a limited defense. If every game were this easy, betting wouldn't be any fun.

Theory No. 5 is that you should never bet an underdog unless you think it will win the game. So far I have bet three slight underdogs, but only because I thought they would win. I never bet an underdog with the hope that it will merely cover the spread. A hope is a hunch is not a conviction.

The Falcons should dispatch the Patriots the way the Bengals did, the Falcons and Bengals being teams of similar strengths and weaknesses. I am tempting fate by betting the 49ers, but the Bills are so dreadful on defense I can't resist. The Steelers impress me. They should be able to contain the Bengals if they contained the Raiders; the Bengals don't have the passing to exploit the one Steeler weakness.

I wasn't breathless when I hung up the phone on Doctor this week, but I seemed to be puffing through vestigial gills. I promised myself that next week I would tell him to call me back in a half hour while I studied the line. He won't run away.

WEDNESDAY

Years ago I got to know a football player well enough for him to indicate to me after a game toward the end of his career that the game might not have been all that met the eye. I gave him a quizzical look, he returned a hard look that said he couldn't say anymore. I was reminded of that incident in preparation for this book, deciding I should contact him and see what I could withdraw from his memory bank.

I traced him to the midwestern city where he lives with his family and works for a corporation as a salesman. Told him what I was up to, that I would protect him with anonymity, that I was trying to find out what was going on, and he could make a contribution to truth-seeking. Libel laws being what they are, I couldn't identify him or anyone he identified anyway.

He said he would talk to me. I am supposed to call him next week to get confirmation of a business trip that will take him to the East in a few weeks.

THURSDAY

Had a beer with Mr. Rhodes in a midtown pub. I had the beer. He had tomato juice. Mr. Rhodes is a big shambling man, slightly stooped, as though he were paralyzed in the act of lighting a cigarette with his back to the wind. Sometimes I think he affects this posture to elicit sympathy from bettors. He has a way of making you feel sorry for him as you give him money. Tonight he was stooped in tragedy.

"Has the Supreme Court outlawed pornography?" I asked.

"There'll always be an America, there'll always be a First Amendment, and there'll always be pornography," he replied.

"So why are you so low?"

"Last week was a disaster, believe me. And I'm just a pebble next to mountains. Some guys got killed. Big guys. Annihilated. The worst week in five years."

"You'll win it all back, plus."

"It don't always work that way," Mr. Rhodes said.

"Sometimes they go right out and buy Pucci bracelets for their wives and diamond brooches for their broads. You never see the money again. And if you do win it back, they don't have it anymore, and you have to take a down payment. When you lose, this business stinks."

I think I was supposed to cry.

I bet $5 on an eight-team parlay. Parlay cards, it occurs to me, are the truest expression of the National Football Lottery. They aren't for gambling, they are for taking part. The odds on eight teams are 100–1. I anticipate the exquisite anguish of winning seven games over the fantasy of winning eight. That one game is the difference between the possible and the impossible.

FRIDAY

Got an education in bookmaking tonight. Undergraduate, graduate and postgraduate. Spoke to Billy the bookie for three hours.

He said he "takes leads."

Never heard of it.

He said he "takes positions."

That either.

Taking a lead, he said, is betting early in the week in anticipation of line moves. This week, because he expected a lot of money to be bet on the Vikings on the weekend, he bet $2,000 on them Tuesday, when they were 1-point underdogs.

One of three things could happen, two of them good. The Vikings already had become 1-point favorites, and he thought they might go higher tomorrow. If the game ends in a tie, he would have a middle. He would win the $2,000, because he got a point, and he would win the bets with his customers, because they gave him a point or two. Should the game be decided by a bigger margin, either way, he would have nearly balanced money on both sides, the $2,000 he bet and the $2,000, give or take a few hundred, that his customers bet. He has averted the bookie's nightmare of holding too much money on one team.

The bad thing that could happen is that he might anticipate wrong. The customers might bet on the Lions, in which case he would be holding $2,000 extra on the Vikings.

"You have to know your customers," Billy said. "Fran Tarkenton is with the Vikings, so in New York everybody's going to bet on him. (He is a former Giant.) And they looked good in the TV game. I have to keep an eye on the teams that play in the TV game because the public probably will bet on the team that wins and against the team that loses in their next game.

"Most of the betting from Tuesday to Friday is between bookies taking a lead. You have to do it today because the public is smarter than it used to be. They get more information. They get to know a couple of teams and keep betting them when they win. We have to watch seventy or eighty teams on a weekend (including colleges), a bettor might know nine or ten of them real good."

Taking a position is the practice of deliberately not trying to balance the books by "laying off." There goes another of my myths shattered. I had always been under the impression that the bookie's ideal was to get a perfectly balanced book on a game, which he then couldn't lose, equating him with a customer's man on the stock market who got a percentage of every deal, win or lose. Not necessarily so. According to Billy, the ideal is rarely achieved. A bookie winds up with an imbalance of one degree or another 90 percent or more of the time. In those cases he says he "needs a decision"—is rooting for one team to beat the other.

Further shattering the myth, Billy said he doesn't want the book to be balanced. He prefers to take a position (need a decision) because he can make more money that way. The straight 11–10 means that, on the basis of balanced betting, he makes $1 on every $21 bet—paying $10 to the winner, collecting $11 from the loser—which is less than 5 percent of the total. Given his expenses, bad debts, and whatnot, that is a small margin for a bookie to work on.

Maneuvering to give himself the best of the situation is forced on the bookie by the one-sided, and often perverse, betting habits of the public. Here is an illustration of what he is trying to accomplish.

Say he has an imbalance of $1,000 on ten of the thirteen weekly pro games, $2,500 bet on one side, and $1,500 on the other, the public having ignored three games. When the $2,500 side wins, the bookie pays out $2,500 and collects $1,650 (including the vigorish) for a net loss of $850. When the $1,500 side wins, he pays out $1,500 and collects $2,750 for a net gain of $1,250. The 11–10 odds add up to 3–2 in the bookie's favor.

Let us assume now that five $2,500 sides and five $1,500 sides win. The bookie would clear a profit of $2,000. Had there been equal betting on all games he would have cleared the same amount, $200 per game.

But let us assume that the bookie wins six and loses four games, which is more likely because the public is wrong more often than it is right. (I met a man once who said he gave up betting on his opinion, he simply bet against the public, on the theory that by the end of the season the linemaker will prove more reliable than the public. Last week, as noted earlier, the public was right six times and wrong three times, which is why the bookies took such a pasting.) With a six-four breakdown, the bookie would clear a profit of $4,100. With a four-six breakdown, he would lose $100. That is why he isn't gambling when he gambles, as long as he has some capital behind him to withstand short-term losses. Bookies who take unnecessarily large risks or who don't have some capital behind them become ex-bookies, because nobody goes out of business as fast as a bookie who doesn't pay off.

The above illustration is purely hypothetical and connected, in theory only, to one aspect of the bookie's day-to-day reality. In fact, he is likely to get deluged with action on local and televised games, resulting in so much uneven betting that he must resort to taking leads and encouraging and discouraging bets by moving the line, and by laying off.

The layoff system is the bookie's last resort to control imbalances. Most bookies have arrangements with bigger bookies or with very big bookie offices to lay off their excess bets; in effect to bet their excess money with those bookies, reducing both the risk and the potential for profit. The very big offices at the top of the pyramid have enough capital to withstand occasional pastings until the 11–10 asserts itself. Occasionally even these bookies may get deluged with one side of a game and refuse to take all the excessive bets off a smaller bookie's hands, causing a backlash down to the smallest potatoes.

Mr. Rhodes said he prefers not to lay off, that he'd rather not get involved with the Idahos. He tries to control the flow of money by moving the spread quickly. If that fails, he will take the game down as a betting proposition. When the Falcons zoomed up an 8-point favorite last week, he took a few $200 bets on the Falcons and refused further action.

Doctor spends long vacations in Miami, so it is possible he lays off some money there. It is dangerous to bet interstate—big-syndicate betting and layoff centers were wiped out after Robert Kennedy, as attorney general, got legislation passed in 1961 against interstate trafficking in gambling information. But some interstate betting traffic apparently still exists, on a small scale, because it is impossible to maintain surveillance on independent bookies who have an unlimited supply of dimes and telephone booths, as Doctor does. (I know for a fact that Doctor will handle interstate traffic with his customers, because he has called me in various outposts.)

As a "runner," Billy is a customer's man for a big betting office. He said he didn't know how many runners they had and had never met any of them. He operates out of his home and a small bar in a lower middle-class neighborhood in New York. He said he averages between $30,000 and $40,000 income a year, has gone as high as $70,000. He has anywhere from ten to thirty steady customers, depending on the season and economic conditions. "You could make a good living off six good customers," he said.

I asked him if a single bettor had ever beaten him consistently.

"Two, three guys have done good for a while, but over the long haul I can't think of anyone," he said. "If they win on one sport, they lose on another. If they win, they get greedy. If they lose, they try to win it back in one gulp."

Billy's financial arrangement with his office is a 50–50 split. They give him half the profit after deducting losses. If the losses exceed profits, they mark it down in red ink on his ledger and he doesn't collect until he gets into the black. The umbrella of the big office provides Billy with security and one fine tax-free living. And he can book as much of his action himself as he chooses to. "I'm not looking to get rich," he said. "I do okay."

I asked him if the big office has enough muscle to make sure he works for them.

"Nah, that stuff went out over twenty years ago," Billy said. "If they wanted to, they could clean out the neighborhood and put in their own people in two weeks. They don't bother anyone. There's plenty of business to go around."

He would not tell me who his bosses are. I assume they are dese, dem and dose guys. I have a small pang, the size of a facial tic, about dealing with these characters. I will do my best as a good citizen to take their money from them.

I told Billy I'd like to talk to his wife. He said she had just entered the hospital with an internal disorder.

SATURDAY

Every team has to have a rookie quarterback. I've got one who has all the makings—she's tall, she can run and pass, she reads my defenses well. She was moving up to first string last spring, when the first-stringer, Gail, asserted herself with unexpected authority. The rookie quarterback and I gave it one more try tonight. We did it all, but there was more motion than emotion. A high-wire act. And while I was somersaulting in space, as I extended myself for the climactic catch, I was struck by a sublime vision:

Holy Moley! Tim Van Galder, a rookie quarterback, is quarterbacking for the Cardinals tomorrow! Have to bet the Redskins.

SUNDAY

Sunday, bloody Sunday.

Woke up with premonitions of gloom if not doom, in my love life and sporting life. Loved my $1,000 bets, didn't love my $500 bets. Hedged the three $500 bets for $200 apiece, taking the Bills and 13 (I had taken the 49ers, giving 12), the Lions and 1½ (I had taken the Vikings and 1), and the Bengals, giving 1 (I had taken the Steelers and 2). Getting the best of the line, as I did in these games, gives me a satisfaction of its own. It is a game within a game, like the game between the pitcher and the runner leading off first base. But you still have to pick winners.

I had half a notion to bet the Redskins, but by the time I made up my mind to swing with my phallic intuition it was too late, my bookies' phones were jammed, and I had to rush to Yankee Stadium to see the Cowboys and Giants. For bad measure I had taken the Cowboys, giving 10, convincing myself that not even Craig Morton could keep the Cowboys from romping and that Tom Landry was worth 6 points alone over Alex Webster.

This was my first live game and the prospect of playing

toteboard with the scoreboard tickled me. Somebody once figured that there are ten or twelve minutes of actual playing time in a pro football game, and I can't imagine a better way to entertain yourself between plays than by following the numbered scoreboard lights blinking progress reports. In combination with the game in front of you, it is a multimedia experience that can churn your insides, jangle your nerves, send you scurrying to the toilet, and all sorts of wonderful things.

At 1:30 P.M. I was doing fine, the Cowboys leading 7–0, the 49ers and Falcons leading 3–0.

At 2:00 P.M. the reports were mixed but still hopeful, the Cowboys leading 10–7, and the 49ers still 3–0, neither great, but the Falcons looking safe with a 6–0 lead.

At 2:30 I got my first jolt of the season. The Patriots were leading the Falcons at the half 7–6. The Cowboys were still up by 3, the 49ers were up by 4, the Steelers had moved out 10–3.

At 3:00 I conceded the 49ers, who had lost John Brodie on an injury in the first period and were tied 13–13. The Cowboys were ahead by 6, the Steelers by 7, the Falcons had retaken the lead 13–7.

At 3:30 I began playing catch-up. The Patriots led the Falcons 21–20 late in the fourth quarter. The Cowboys were driving for a touchdown that would give them a 9-point victory; the Giants scored on two long touchdown passes to Rich Houston, who does that once a season. The Steelers were hanging on 10–9. The 49ers had moved out 20–13.

At 4:00 I was in the bowels of Yankee Stadium doing reporter's work. I lost all four games.

The Vikings performed as advertised over the Lions in

a later game 34–10, but it would be unseemly to do a jig over an isolated insight. You can't lose them all.

The football world was buzzing about the Jets and the Colts: Joe Namath passed for six touchdowns and 496 yards, Johnny Unitas added 376 for an NFL one-game passing record. I was buzzing about my bettors, who wasted me. Lem Banker had seven winners (Vikings, Raiders, Jets, Chargers, Giants, Bengals, Redskins) and one loser (Eagles). The Jets were the "hot game," a game many people jumped into because two offensive players, Eddie Hinton and Norm Bulaich, were out for the Colts. This goes to show what you have to know—the Colts scored 34 points without them. Lem went with the Bengals because four or five Steelers had minor injuries and one, halfback John Fuqua, was sidelined. That stood up. He liked the Raiders because "it's on grass and they're a bad artificial turf team." That logic evades me, but they won. Fast Eddie won three (Jets, Vikings, Redskins) and lost two (49ers, Steelers). "Everybody's talking about the Steelers," he reasoned, "so I bet them." Mr. Rich won with the Jets and Vikings. Greenwich Village Fats had four winners (Raiders, Jets, Dolphins, Chargers) and three losers (Falcons, Eagles, Lions).

Sing a sad hometown-fan song for Danny Lavezzo. He got 9 points instead of the 10 that was available on the Giants, for a tie. "I'm getting crucified," he said.

I giggled. Misery loves company.

Monday

Lem bet the Saints against the Chiefs, with 14 points, "because the Saints are triple tough at home." Not wanting to spoil a wretched week I bet $100 on the Chiefs, giving 12½. If I had a reason, I'd give it to you. Straining for a winner probably. A good way to get a financial hernia. The Chiefs won 20–17.

That made me a $1,355 loser for the week. I won $780 on the Vikings ($1,000 minus $220). I lost $1,100 on the Falcons, $350 on the 49ers ($550 minus $200), $350 on the Bengals ($550 minus $200), $220 on the Cowboys, $110 on the Chiefs, $5 on the parlay. The bottom line is minus $425.

This is same as trailing 3–0 early in the first period. If I can't overcome that, my name isn't Pudge Heffelfinger. At this stage of the season the losers can still afford to laugh.

"That was some exhibition you put on, expert."

"Need to create suspense. Wouldn't be any fun if I won all the time."

"Keep this up and you won't create suspense, you'll create bankruptcy. You ramble on about logic and pull stunts like the 49ers, Cowboys and Chiefs. Let me quote my favorite author on the 49ers: 'Can beat anyone, but erratic.' And on the Cowboys: 'They are a bad bet with Craig Morton at quarterback.' And a $100 bet is not a conviction. It's not even a hunch. It's a prayer."

"When you're right you're right, and you're right."

"You were caught with your omnipotence showing. You won last week, so you thought you had it all worked out. How come you bet only six games? Why not go all the way?"

"Lost my head."

"You did that at Monte Carlo. Lots of good Monte Carlo did you. Terrific discipline and self-control."

"Like I said, exhibition seasons are meaningless. And

like Joe Namath said, the game's not supposed to be that easy."

This is how the composite table of the week looks, including the closing line:

	My Line	Outlaw Line	Opening Line	Closing Line	
Falcons*	16	6½	7	9	PATRIOTS (1)
Browns (10)	3	3	3	3	EAGLES
Cowboys* (9)	13	9	9	10½	GIANTS
CHARGERS (23)	3	3	3	3½	Broncos
DOLPHINS (21)	16	14	14	15	Oilers
Rams	11	10	10½	11	BEARS (0)
Jets (10)	2	P	2½	4	COLTS
LIONS	6	2	1	2	Vikings* (24)
Raiders (6)	4	2½	3	3	PACKERS
BENGALS (5)	6	2	2	1	Steelers*
Redskins* (14)	13	8	10	11½	CARDINALS
49ers*	15	11	12	12½	BILLS (7)
Chiefs* (3)	14	10	12	14½	SAINTS

There was one significant switch, from 1 point Lions to 2 points Vikings. The public was right about that, but finished with a six-six record against the line. The professionals were four-four betting against the outlaw line. Home teams won seven and lost six, favorites won eight and lost five.

The line is tightening up. It will get tighter.

THE STANDINGS

AFC

	w	l	t	vs. spread w	l
Eastern Division					
Dolphins	2	0	0	2	0
Jets	2	0	0	2	0
Bills	1	1	0	1	1
Patriots	1	1	0	1	1
Colts	0	2	0	0	2
Central Division					
Bengals	2	0	0	2	0
Browns	1	1	0	1	1
Steelers	1	1	0	1	1
Oilers	0	2	0	0	2
Western Division					
Broncos	1	1	0	1	1
Chiefs	1	1	0	0	2
Raiders	1	1	0	1	1
Chargers	1	1	0	1	1

NFC

	w	l	t	vs. spread w	l
Eastern Division					
Cowboys	2	0	0	1	1
Redskins	2	0	0	2	0
Cardinals	1	1	0	1	1
Giants	0	2	0	1	1
Eagles	0	2	0	0	2
Central Division					
Lions	1	1	0	1	1
Packers	1	1	0	1	1
Vikings	1	1	0	1	1
Bears	0	1	1	1	1
Western Division					
Rams	1	0	1	1	1
Falcons	1	1	0	1	1
49ers	1	1	0	1	1
Saints	0	2	0	1	1

RESULTS

Patriots 21, Falcons 20
Browns 27, Eagles 17
Cowboys 23, Giants 14
Chargers 37, Broncos 14
Dolphins 34, Oilers 13
Rams 13, Bears 13
Jets 44, Colts 34
Vikings 34, Lions 10
Raiders 20, Packers 14
Bengals 15, Steelers 10
Redskins 24, Cardinals 10
Bills 27, 49ers 20
Chiefs 20, Saints 17

BETTORS	w	l	pct.
Mr. Rich	4	0	1.000
Lem Banker	12	4	.750
Fast Eddie	6	2	.750
Fats–Mover	10	4	.714
Merchant	4	6	.400

EXOTICA

Home Teams 14, Visitors 12
Favorites 17, Underdogs 9
Pros 12, Outlaw Line 6
Public 12, Official Line 9

Third Week

TUESDAY

After putting the second week under my microscope, I reached the conclusion that there are no momentous conclusions to be reached yet. The uncertain condition of Roman Gabriel's arm is the most important development for future reference. John Brodie will be back to haunt his supporters. O. J. Simpson and Jim Plunkett were the architects of the two major upsets. Simpson gained 138 yards, his career high. The inability of the 49ers to contain him in a one-dimensional attack surprises me. The Falcons struggled to a two-touchdown lead over the Patriots, then were done in by Plunkett. Simpson and Plunkett, as noted, can do that. Can't say I forgot the note. Didn't think they'd do it when they did it is all. I'm not sure what to make of the Bengals, who beat the Steelers on five field goals. Paul Brown must be assembling, tooth by tooth, a man-eating defense: 17 points in two games.

I was as dazzled as the next fan by Joe Namath's act, but it is bound to cause grief for bettors who believe he can do anything he pleases anytime he pleases—many do. His powerful magic notwithstanding, that ain't so. Looking ahead, it has to be kept in mind that—on the basic cause-and-effect level—such a performance is an indictment of the Colts' pass defense too. And the Jets' defense, such as it is, must be indicted and convicted if it allows the Colts such liberties. There will be money to be made betting against both teams.

This week's lines:

	My Line	Outlaw Line	Opening Line	
Colts	4	9	7½	Bills
Bengals	6	3½	4	Browns
Rams†		no line		Falcons
Redskins	10	10	10	Patriots
Cowboys	8	6½	7	Packers
Lions	6	10½	10½	Bears
Jets	10	10½	11	Oilers
Steelers	3	4	4	Cardinals
49ers†		no line		Saints
Chiefs	7	7½	7½	Broncos
Vikings	P	3½	4	Dolphins
Raiders	7	6	6½	Chargers
Giants	P	6	6	Eagles

† There will be no lines on these games until the condition of Roman Gabriel and John Brodie, both injured, is determined.

Let me congratulate myself: I told Doctor to call back in a half hour after he gave the line to me. Why do bookies intimidate me on the telephone? Is it the urgency in the furtive cadence of their announcements: "The Colts 7½ . . . the Bengals 4 . . . the Redskins 10 . . ."? Secret pronouncements from—where? Or am I intimidated by barbers, headwaiters and bartenders as well? I think not. Yet when I get that first call of the week from Doctor I feel like I'm standing on my tiptoes at the end of a high diving board, my diaphragm suddenly frozen. Ridiculous.

I made three bets: the Dolphins plus 4 over the Vikings for $500, the Chiefs giving 7 to the Broncos for $300, the Chargers plus 6½ over the Raiders for $300.

I like the Dolphins for the same reason I liked the Redskins two weeks ago. Their offense is varied enough to check the charge of the Viking defense. The Broncos don't throw the ball well enough to do the same to the Chiefs, whose limited offense should roll on the Broncos' limited defense. I look for John Hadl to throw the ball on the Raiders, who still don't have a pass-rush, and who can't decide who their quarterback is. (This bet, incidentally, goes against my own line, which is a half-point higher than the opening line. I blew it: It should be no more than 4, Raiders.)

California teams, like California horses, are skittish and unpredictable. I suspect it has something to do with avocados, surf boards and Yvette Mimieux. It's a nice place to visit, but I wouldn't want to bet there.

WEDNESDAY

Billy said his office had been hit by police, gave me a new number to call.

"What happens now?" I asked.

"Nothing," he said. "The second string moved right in, and we go right on."

"And the guys who got hit?"

"Bailed out. They'll be back in action in a couple of days."

THURSDAY

Should betting on games be legalized? If not, why not, since so many people are doing it anyway? If so, should the government run it?

My instinctive response is that betting should be legalized, that I would rather donate my losses or vigorish to the state or to a licensed operator than to illegal and perhaps sinister elements, that it might raise some tax revenue and put a dent in crime and reduce police corruption and save police manhours and alleviate crowded court conditions, and, who knows, lead to a cure for the common cold.

I am willing to be persuaded that all of this is liberal rubbish.

I am eager to be persuaded that the government should license, oversee, take a cut from, but not run, legal betting on football, baseball and basketball.

Which is why I attended a synod on the subject today by the forces of righteousness. Unfortunately I was not persuaded. I came for facts and got Elmer Gantryed. The movie was better.

Featured were Pete Rozelle, Bowie Kuhn and Walter Kennedy, the commissioners of football, baseball and basketball, and two district attorneys, Carol Vance of Houston, president of the National District Attorneys Association, which represents five thousand D.A.s, and William Cahn, chairman of the organization's gambling committee, from Nassau County, a suburb of New York City. They called themselves an educational task force, organized by the sports commissioners to combat pending legislation that would expand legal offtrack betting in the city to all sports.

There were no top law enforcement officials from the city itself because, in common with their kind from many big cities, where the problem is most acute, they favor legalized gambling. Too, Cahn is among the minority of district attorneys in his own state who are on record opposing legalized gambling. And Vance is from one of the states where there is no legal gambling of any kind; twenty-nine states have legal gambling. The synod wasn't loaded, it was overloaded.

The opposition to legalized sports betting by the commissioners is understandable. They feel it is a threat to their going, profitable concerns. Why more of a threat than all the illegal gambling going on? Because, they insist, it would create many new bettors who would be obliged to root for their money instead of their teams and who therefore would contribute to a damaging climate of suspicion. Perhaps a climate for fixes too.

The experience of offtrack betting in New York City suggests that fears of a bettor explosion are greatly exaggerated. After two years OTB officials found that few casual bettors had become serious bettors, that their customers essentially are hard-core horse players. Nor has there been a noticeable escalation of suspicion.

Pete Rozelle cannot be blamed for being overcautious: A disgruntled bettor once punched him in the eye during a game. But his expressed fear that NFL stadia would seethe with traitorous fans, if betting were legal, is spinach. The majority of fans don't and won't bet, and the majority of those who do bet on their team. To support that fear Rozelle gave a gratuitous illustration. "I don't want to see Joe Namath sitting on the ball with a 3-point lead and people booing because he won't go to beat a 6-point spread," he said. Boo on Pete Rozelle. Bettors are often paranoid but not that paranoid.

The district attorneys turned out to be holy rollers, defenders of our virtue and pious asses. Gambling, said Carol Vance, "is not the American Dream." Just what I need, the district attorney of Houston, Texas, telling me what the

American Dream isn't, or is. I live in a place, as most Americans do, that has pari-mutuel betting. This means that I can legally dream the American Dream of hitting a 100–1 shot. And in Texas, which you can paper over with illegal parlay cards every week of the football season, there are folks who dream the illegal American Dream of going 12-for-12 at 1,000–1.

Bill Cahn was first on line when they passed out piety. It developed that he saw betting on horses and drinking whiskey as social evils (immediately disqualifying him from owning an NFL franchise).

Vance and Cahn have the orientation of funeral directors who come to believe there is no life before death. In their jobs they deal with aberrant behavior—the man who is loan-sharked out of business, the woman left without money for food by a gambling husband, criminal heavies —so they assume you can't bet without becoming a degenerate or a victim. And everyone who knocks down a martini is a potential alcoholic and threat to society.

I dwell on this because I do not ask law enforcement officials for moral judgments. Morality is not the question. The question is whether legal gambling can work for the society better than rampant illegal gambling without jeopardizing the games. When the thrust of a reply is moral, I tend to believe that anything that follows will be colored accordingly. A man who says that gambling is original sin and un-American is not likely to give me the facts to weigh a decision.

Vance and Cahn were concerned that legalized gambling would be a "regressive tax" on the poor. That those who could least afford it would squander the biggest percentages of their incomes. Such protecting-the-poor-from-themselves paternalism warms the cockles. But I doubt that gambling makes the poor much less poor. Numbers-playing is largely a ghetto phenomenon, and what it does is provide a quarter's worth of hope for people who can't afford more, and I'll be damned if I'm going to make a moral judgment on that. Legal lotteries and bingo are in the same league. Moralists warned that the advent of off-track betting, like the end of Prohibition, could shred the social fabric. The Republic still stands.

(The irony of the NFL joining a poor people's crusade must be recorded. How many poor people can afford season tickets? How many poor people go to NFL games?)

The district attorneys were concerned too that organized crime actually would benefit from legalized gambling, because it would create victims for loan sharks. Probably it would. The end of Prohibition, after all, did not reduce alcoholism. But people wanted to drink, and the laws prohibiting it were unenforceable. And people want to gamble, and the laws prohibiting it are unenforceable.

Cahn pries himself into the headlines twice a year for allegedly cleaning out multimillion-dollar gambling nests. This farce satisfies everyone. It satisfies citizens who want a fearless district attorney. It satisfies citizens who want to bet. Nothing changes. When I asked him about the absence of headlines on convictions, he mouthed an embarrassed, hurried and tortured run-on sentence about crowded courts, lesser pleas, etc.

I did not have the heart to tell him about the important figure in the Nassau County government who booked games on the side for several years.

Crowded courts and overburdened and corrupt police

are sores on the body politic. In New York City in 1970 there were 9,611 gambling arrests—and ninety-six convictions on felony charges. One out of a hundred. Ninety-five cases out of a hundred were settled for a $100 fine or less. As a result the police are under orders not to waste time with the small potatoes.

This is a green light for betting, because it seems evident that the small potatoes are proliferating while the Idahos remain static. The pro football revolution is not about poor people. It is about businessmen and stockbrokers and professional people who bet. It is about suburbanites who bet. Some of them have qualms about dealing with dese, dem and dose guys. (Not infrequently the dese, dem and dose guys don't want to deal with them either, because heroin, loan-sharking, extortion, numbers, and the like yield a higher return at less risk and require a minimum of improvisational brain power.)

There is a bookmaker in a suburb of Boston whom I hope to get to later. A middle-class bettor can deal with him with a clear conscience. He has a master's degree in business administration.

Vance and Cahn made sense only when they questioned the ability of government to effectively compete against bookies. The government can complete only by providing the same or better service.

This means that you can pick up the phone two minutes before a game and get a bet down at 11–10.

This means that your anonymity will be protected, so that the federal government won't dun you for taxes on your winnings, or detect how much untaxed money you are betting with.

Much is made over the "credit" that bookies give, but I don't think that's much of an obstacle to overcome because

I don't think bookies give credit. As a convenience they let you bet now and pay later, but later is just Tuesday. If you don't pay by Tuesday they will be very upset and your credit rating will be zero, unless you have an arrangement, such as I have, to pay or be paid at a certain figure. All other things being equal, I think bettors would be willing to deposit cash in an account that can be used for betting, as they do now in offtrack betting.

Can all other things be equal? A bookie with twenty or thirty customers has his hands full on Sunday afternoons. I once dropped a bookie because he wasn't available when I needed him. The government is not famous for customer relations.

Taxes are a thornier problem. The federal government has driven most bookies in Nevada underground with a 10 percent tax on bets. Licensed bookies cannot compete legally against illegal bookies, so they book big bets under the table. The government has a curious double standard, because casino betting is not taxed and high rollers are protected. Before city or state government can get into bookmaking, or into licensing bookies (if that's the practical way to do it), the tax problem must be resolved.

I will make a moral judgment on that issue. At this point of the season I am losing. The government will not let me deduct my losses. But if I win they want some of my winnings. The government, like a Mafia extortionist, wants to be your partner only when you win. That's immoral.

FRIDAY

Life sure is exciting in the big city. I'm getting calls from a breather (either homosexual or sexual with a register like Vince Lombardi). The way things are between Gail and me—the lines of communication cut again, camouflaged in the distance between us, obscured in my commitment to the season—a breather is almost welcome. We communicate about the way Gail and I do, one panting, one puzzled, except that Gail and I reverse roles when we reach wit's end. Right now all I can stand from The Breather is ten hot breaths before I hang up. Maybe it will grow into something big, fifteen or even twenty hot breaths. Maybe, God willing, words.

SATURDAY

Weighed myself today. I'm up to 164, two and a half pounds over my best betting weight. Made me so uneasy I wolfed a plum tart.

SUNDAY

Zapped them. Three-for-three.

I was good and I was fortunate. Not lucky, which would imply that I took a few stabs and happened to connect. Fortunate, because none of the games could be worked out on my galactic slide rule, as the Vikings-Lions could. I was comfortable with the bets, but I knew I could blow any or all of them.

The Dolphins scored their only touchdown with a minute and a half left to beat the Vikings 16–14. They had it when they needed it. I had them when I needed them.

I lost last week when John Brodie was knocked out of commission. I won today when Len Dawson was knocked out of commission. His backup, Mike Livingston, put five touchdowns on the board in the second half for the Chiefs, who won 45–24.

The Chargers tied the Raiders 17–17. I'll take the money, but I can't take credit for Buckminster Fuller-type prescience. The Chargers, the team that lives and dies with the pass, lived with the run.

My three-for-three is most impressive, to me if no one else, because I swivel-hipped through a schedule strewn with booby traps. The Patriots upset the Redskins, the Oilers upset the Jets, the Packers upset the Cowboys, the Falcons rolled over the Rams, the Browns rolled over the Bengals.

"Now you're cooking," I told myself.

"Now I'm cooking," I agreed.

"You win more money betting three games than six games."

"Must be a moral there someplace."

"Stay cool and you've got them."

"Two winning weeks, one losing week. Time to change from gin and tonic to Irish whiskey, neat."

There are two professionals in my stable of bettors, Lem Banker, who is a loner, operating on his wits and knowledge of betting percentages, and, through Greenwich Village Fats, The Mover, who apparently operates only on information he gets from other gamblers. Lem bet the Rams today because, he said, he had heard that Roman Gabriel would start. Fats and The Mover were on the Falcons because their information was that Gabriel would not start. Something had to give. It was Lem.

Lem won two (Oilers, Chiefs) and lost three (Bills, Cowboys, Rams). He bet the Chiefs despite a rumor Len

Dawson would be sidelined with a rib injury. The rumor was half right, Dawson aggravating the injury in the first half, but the Chiefs covered the spread anyway. Lem bet on the Bills because of Colts' injuries, but the Colts covered too. Fats had five winners (Colts, Lions, Steelers, Chargers, Falcons) and one loser (Bengals).

Mr. Rich split two games, winning with the Oilers ("Namath lets down against bad teams"), losing with the Rams. Fast Eddie split too, winning with the Steelers and the Oilers ("I don't trust Namath"), losing with the Vikings and Bengals.

Frankie the Doorman swung into action this week with a winning parlay on the Dolphins and Oilers. "I don't like Namath," he explained. "I don't like guys like (Cassius) Clay and (Tom) Seaver who think they're so hot."

MONDAY

I wouldn't miss a Giants-Eagles game. I view them as titanic struggles between Utter Chaos and Total Anarchy. Went to Philadelphia for the game tonight.

First the good news: The Giants won 27–12. I win that $100-to-$10 bet from Dick Snyder, and he has a victory to celebrate. I'm going to have to give more thought to social betting. It really gives me a bigger kick to beat a friend out of a couple of bucks than it does to win a couple hundred on some silly game out there that I couldn't care less about. I won $7 from a friend at 7–1 on the Jets-Colts Super Bowl and that probably is the highlight of my career. Even if I never collected.

Now the bad news: I bet $100 on the Eagles with 7

points, because their defense is only half bad and because the Giants shouldn't be favored by a touchdown over dear old Lafayette High. I didn't count on Ron Johnson scoring four touchdowns, three on passes.

I won $1,000 this week. I won $500 on the Dolphins, $300 on the Chiefs, $300 on the Chargers. I lost $110 on the Eagles and got back $10 on my social bet. The bottom line is plus $575.

While I was in Philadelphia I stopped off at Jimmy the Salad's restaurant for a salad and a hello. Jimmy the Salad is a degenerate gambler of the first order. He'll bet on anything. What I like about him is that he's made his peace with his addiction, accepting it for what it is. His wife accepts it too, taking over the restaurant in the evening so he can ensconce himself at home in front of a television set and with three short-wave radios blaring play-by-play reports of basketball or baseball games at him from all over the country. He looks, sitting there in a soft armchair, as though he is undergoing shock treatment, cathodes attached to his temples and buttocks and navel. His eyes roll back in his head, his pelvis jerks, he agonizes and vaults, curses and cheers. Sex in an electric chair. I never saw a happier-looking man.

Tonight, he said, he had a parlay on the Giants over the Eagles and the Detroit Tigers over the Boston Red Sox. I was reminded of the fellow who parlayed Truman over Dewey and the Rangers over the Canadiens in 1948. I was glad to see Jimmy win one.

He offered one observation about the local scene that fascinated me. "There aren't as many bookies as there used to be," he said, "and they're very careful about customers. They don't want deadbeats. They used to get rough if a guy didn't pay off; now they're like businessmen. They don't want trouble."

That isn't the Philadelphia I used to know and love.

The composite chart for the week looks like this (including the line on the Falcons–Rams and 49ers–Saints posted Sunday morning):

	My Line	Outlaw Line	Opening Line	Closing Line	
Colts (17)	4	9	7½	9	BILLS
Bengals	6	3½	4	6	BROWNS (21)
FALCONS (28)	0	0	0	2	Rams
Redskins	10	10	10	12	PATRIOTS (1)
Cowboys	8	6½	7	9½	PACKERS (3)
Lions (14)	6	10½	10½	11	BEARS
Jets	10	10½	11	13	OILERS (6)
Steelers (6)	3	4	4	6	CARDINALS
49ers (28)	0	0	0	12½	SAINTS
Chiefs* (21)	7	7½	7½	7	BRONCOS
VIKINGS	P	3½	4	4½	Dolphins* (2)
RAIDERS	7	6	6½	7½	Chargers* (0)
Giants (15)	P	6	6	7	EAGLES*

The pros turned the gold of the outlaw line into fool's gold this week. They were blitzed—zero and six. The public was four and seven against the opening line. (Once the opening line is posted the pros are part of the public, insofar as these reckonings are made, so they may have recouped losses later in the week.) Favorites and visiting teams won eight games and lost five.

Moral of this story is that the linemaker isn't as dumb as he sometimes looks.

THE STANDINGS

AFC

	w	l	t	vs. spread w	l
Eastern Division					
Dolphins	3	0	0	3	0
Patriots	2	1	0	2	1
Jets	2	1	0	2	1
Colts	1	2	0	1	2
Bills	1	2	0	1	2
Central Division					
Bengals	2	1	0	2	1
Browns	2	1	0	2	1
Steelers	2	1	0	1	1*
Oilers	1	2	0	1	2
Western Division					
Chiefs	2	1	0	1	2
Raiders	1	1	1	2	1
Chargers	1	1	1	2	1
Broncos	1	2	0	1	2

NFC

	w	l	t	vs. spread w	l
Eastern Division					
Cowboys	2	1	0	1	2
Redskins	2	1	0	2	1
Cardinals	1	2	0	1	1*
Giants	1	2	0	2	1
Eagles	0	3	0	0	3
Central Division					
Lions	2	1	0	2	1
Packers	2	1	0	2	1
Vikings	1	2	0	1	2
Bears	0	2	1	1	2
Western Division					
Falcons	2	1	0	2	1
49ers	2	1	0	2	1
Rams	1	1	1	1	2
Saints	0	3	0	1	2

* Tie

RESULTS

Colts 17, Bills 0
Browns 27, Bengals 6
Falcons 31, Rams 3
Patriots 24, Redskins 23
Packers 16, Cowboys 13
Lions 38, Bears 24
Oilers 26, Jets 20
Steelers 25, Cardinals 19
49ers 37, Saints 2
Chiefs 45, Broncos 24
Dolphins 16, Vikings 14
Raiders 17, Chargers 17
Giants 27, Eagles 12

BETTORS	w	l	pct.
Mr. Rich	5	1	.833
Fats–Mover	15	5	.750
Lem Banker	14	7	.667
Fast Eddie	8	4	.667
Merchant	7	7	.500

EXOTICA

Visitors 20, Home Teams 19
Favorites 25, Underdogs 14
Pros 12, Outlaw Line 12
Public 16, Official Line 16

Fourth Week

TUESDAY

I never knew a man intimately who bet $5,000 on football. I do now. I shave him every other morning.

I bet $5,000 on two games today. I can't believe I bet the whole thing.

Four factors were involved.

First, the games are right—Dolphins vs. Jets, Lions vs. Falcons. I've been lying in ambush for the Dolphins-Jets. The Dolphins are favored by 4½. I make them 10. They are playing in New York. I wouldn't care if they played in Grand Central Station, I'd make them 10. There is no way the Jets' defense can contain the Dolphins. And halfback Emerson Boozer is hurt for the Jets, a critical loss against a team of this caliber.

The Falcons should be able to control the ball on the Lions. I can't believe Norm Van Brocklin won't be able to take it right to this defense, five-yard it into Lionburger. Without Sanders the Lions don't have the long ball threat to make their running go against a fairly solid defense.

I bet $2,000 on the Dolphins. I bet $2,000 on the Falcons, giving 1 point, another $1,000 when the game went to pick.

Factors two, three and four have to do with timing. There comes a time when you have to make a move, when you have to step out because the coordinates seem right. Perhaps I am getting impatient for a decisive strike. And

I am not unmindful of the fact that this is the second time I have opened up after a solid confidence-building week. But I'm winning enough so that I can't get disemboweled by a split, and I love both games, and that's the stuff of a bettor's dreams. If you can't make a move under these conditions, you need a strong laxative.

There was only one result last weekend that puzzled me: the Browns over the Bengals by three touchdowns. The Bengals threw the ball forty-three times, indicating that the Browns ganged up on the run and dared them to throw, indicating that the Bengals might not throw very well. Mike Phipps broke it up with a long touchdown pass in the last quarter. Maybe it's him. I don't know. The Oilers beat the Jets because they were able to sustain an offense against that defense I've been putting down. Chester Marcol, who kicked four field goals in a previous game, kicked three as the Packers upset the Cowboys. File that for future reference. Jim Plunkett did unto the Redskins as he did unto the Falcons. Can't bet against Jim Plunkett.

The lines this week are:

	My Line	Outlaw Line	Opening Line	
Falcons	7	2	1	Lions
Patriots	3	3	3	Bills
Bengals	9	9	9	Broncos
Chiefs	6	6½	6½	Browns
Giants	7	10	10	Saints
Redskins	13	17	16	Eagles
Colts	6	5	5	Chargers
Packers	9	8	8½	Bears
Cowboys	10	6½	6½	Steelers
Vikings	14	14	14	Cardinals
49ers	4	4	4½	Rams
Raiders	9	8	9	Oilers
Dolphins	10	P	4½	Jets

Apparently I'm not alone in my opinion on the Jets and the Dolphins. The outlaws put it up as a pick proposition, and the high rollers kept banging at it until the line shot to 4½. Interesting how they bet the Redskins from 17 to 16 against the Eagles. On general principle, I guess. Seventeen, as they say, is a lot of wood to chop.

WEDNESDAY

Five thousand dollars is a lot of bread. Five thousand dollars. That number has been caroming around my insides like a pinball all day. And yet it hardly seems like money at all, and won't, I imagine, until it is amputated from or grafted onto the bottom line. I don't think of it in terms of what it might buy, what good it might do, what security it would give me, what anguish it would cause me if I lost it. It is something to play with and I am playing with it in a dangerous game. It gives me pleasure to know that I am willing to take such a risk, but since I have not won or lost yet, and since the games seem distant, the money is an abstraction. The idea of betting $5,000 is, right now, more real than the money. Perhaps it will remain so until I feel it coming into or leaving my hands.

THURSDAY

I spoke to a former NFL player today who said that he—himself, personally—had taken part in "six or seven" point-fixing conspiracies. In one of them, he said, eleven teammates were involved.

I believe him. His revelations have the quirky ring of truth.

I consider myself neither naïve nor cynical about these

things. It would be foolish to ignore the possibility of larceny when there is so much money at stake. I suspect that there have been, are, and always will be isolated incidents.

Having said that, I must admit that I was startled by what I was told. The NFL has never uncovered a single case of a fix, at least for public consumption. I was now getting chapter and verse on fixes plural.

I was getting it in Boston, in an airport restaurant. We met there because he had spent his career in the NFL before the merger with the AFL, and we felt that, since he was relatively unknown to begin with, the chances of anyone recognizing him in an AFL city were none or less than none. He is big but not huge. A broken nose is the only physical clue to his past.

He said that he began by betting on his own team when it was a very bad team and was listed as a big underdog. "I was dumb," he said. "I always bet on myself. I always thought we would win. We always lost. We'd be a 14-point underdog and lose by four touchdowns."

I asked him where and with whom and how much he bet.

He said that he hung out with other players at a bar. He bet with a bookie. "Never more than $300." He said he didn't know whether other players were betting.

How did he get started betting against himself?

"I was making six, eight, ten thousand a year. I hated the owners. They treated you like shit. They were wearing $200 suits, and I was wearing a beat-up sport jacket. My motivation was to get back at them. At the end of the season I'd have a few hundred bucks if I was lucky, and no job. I was susceptible to anything that came along."

"What came along?"

"This guy I was betting with said he'd bet $350 for me if I made sure we went under the points."

"Just you?"

"Me and two others. A cornerback and a halfback. I think we were underdogs by a touchdown. We lost by about 24 points."

"What did you do to lose by that much?"

"That's the crazy thing. I didn't do anything. I wasn't in a position to do anything. I never felt I was deliberately playing to lose. Maybe, subconsciously, I was. But I never felt that I was trying to lose. I wouldn't know what to do. I wasn't going to let my man beat me, because my job depended on that. I always played my man honest. I just didn't do anything extra."

"How often did you do that? Was $350 all you ever got?"

"Four or five times in a couple of seasons. Always after we were out of the race, or at the end of the season when the games didn't count. I got $1,000 for one game, the last one. I didn't have to do anything, but I was prepared to try something. A fifteen-yard penalty at a crucial point. I don't know what. We might've gotten into big money, but the halfback was cut, and we lost out. I was traded after the season."

"Did you do anything with the new team?"

"Before the last game of the season my roommate (an All-Pro) told me I'd get $300 that Sunday if I did what he told me to do. I wasn't even sure I was starting. He said, 'If you get in late in the game, listen to me.' I found out ten other guys were in on it. I didn't play, but I got the $300."

The player finished his career with a third team, which was a contender.

"Did anything go on there?"

"I never did anything. I was making the most money in my life, $15,000. I was treated fairly. I had a job in the off-season.

"But I was still dumb about it. We had a shot at the playoffs one season. We had to win the last game. A few days before the game a cornerback asked me if I knew where he could bet. He wanted to bet $500 against us. I told him I'd make the bet for him, and kept the money myself. I was booking the game. Can you imagine anyone being so dumb that he would bet on his own team even though he knew a guy on the team was trying to lose? He was right. We didn't stand a chance. But I thought we could win. I always thought my team could win."

I asked him if he ever rejected an opportunity to make money at his team's expense.

"Once. They asked me to sprinkle a powder on some food at the training table before a game. It would have given everyone the runs. I could have made $5,000, but I didn't have the nerve. I would have done it, but I was afraid of getting caught."

I asked the player how, as an athlete, he justified his involvement with gamblers?

"When you become a professional—and even when you're in college—it's not a game anymore," he said. "It starts in college. A football scholarship is a joke. Anyone who wants to get through college can work his way through. You're paid to play football. By the time you're a senior you realize it's a business. When I turned pro I was treated like an athletic bum. If they treated me decently, if they helped set me up in a community, I would have played my heart out for them."

"Do you think they're fixing games today?"

"I don't think it goes on like it did. The organizations are better. The pay is better. The outside money is better. But if a guy was offered $10,000 tax free, it might be the same as me taking $1,000. I wouldn't condemn a guy who did it. It's strictly business, and that's how business is done. I don't think the game is crooked, but one or two guys might be doing business."

"Do you do that in your business? Do you cheat your boss?"

"No. Because he treats me decently. When business is good he gives bonuses. He talks to me. He treats me like a human being. I take pride in the organization."

"Do you bet?"

"No. A few years ago a guy I knew as a player called me up and said he had information. I followed him for a while and we won. Then we lost, so I quit. I still can't pick winners."

On the jet shuttle back to New York I thought about a game I once saw in Boston between the Patriots and Raiders. I decided to sleep on the interview and the game.

Friday

In the clear light of high noon, the traffic honking and screeching at me from eleven floors below, $5,000 in bets beginning to drum a soft beat in my medulla oblongata, I made a gallant attempt to put yesterday in perspective.

My first concern was protective—toward the book. I can't be sure if these anonymous revelations will be deemed newsworthy by my colleagues, but if they are I'm afraid that they might distort my intentions. I'm not writing an exposé. I don't want the world to see this as a cousin to Bernie Parish's *They Call It a Game,* in which he suggested that coaches might signal each other across the field in order to arrange the outcome of a game. That degree of paranoia is self-destructive. It destroyed his credibility.

Like my confessed fixer, I believe that pro football is basically honest. Proof being that bookies book it. The way to make money on a fix is to bet it, big and often. Unless a bookie is in on the fix himself, this makes him, first, unhappy, because it costs him, and second, suspicious. If a pattern is detected—unusually large bets on one team that are consistently right—the bookies stop booking that team. This has not happened in six years.

Going back to a year before that, 1966, I was at a game between the Raiders and Patriots that had a postmortem typical of pro football. The Patriots were favored by a field goal. The Raiders dominated them for three and a half periods, leading 21–10. A second-string quarterback then sparked the Patriots to two late touchdowns with scrambling antics that the defense, which was playing loosely to stop the pass, wasn't prepared for. On their last play the Raiders tried a medium-range field goal, going for a tie, and it hit the goalpost.

Later in the week I was informed by a bettor that somebody was doing business in that game.

I have been covering pro football for fifteen years and, like every sportswriter, I've heard that refrain so often that if it were true 10 percent of the time we should be giving Academy Awards instead of Most Valuable Player Awards.

I don't think professionals are so professional that they can hit the goalpost from thirty yards to win a bet. Nor are they so unprofessional that they would wait until the last few minutes to do their swoon.

This illustrates why pro football bettors are so suspicious, while the same bettors, betting and losing on baseball, accept the freakiest bounces, the weirdest strategy and the wildest finishes with fatalistic resignation. They understand baseball. They don't understand football. They can accept the error-prone humanity of baseball players. They cannot accept the mental and physical fumbles of cogs in a machine.

I have a scenario on the direct connection of pro football and gambling that goes something like this:

Many of the sport's pioneers were so-called sportsmen. That is, they were involved with horse racing, as owners, track entrepreneurs, and, in the case of Tim Mara of the Giants, as a bookmaker. They were not virgins in the world of angles, edges and odds.

In the late forties and early fifties the game began to flex its muscles. A winning team could be a smash at the box office. But losing teams, which were most teams, still struggled on a marginal financial basis. Players' salaries were low, the stars rarely exceeding $10,000, even on winning teams. This in the wake of the post-World War II social revolution of higher expectations by the workingman, and booming attendance in some cities. (Paralleling baseball after World War I, when the Black Sox and other less publicized scandals erupted.)

The situation was ripe for an owner to bet on his team and for a player to bet on, or against, his team. I make that distinction not because I think that owners are a better class, but because they could afford to indulge a preoccupation while players often could not afford their occupation.

The situation ripened for skulduggery in the next decade. The boom now had to be measured in megatonnage (in attendance and television revenue), yet salaries lagged farther and farther behind profits. The players were America's new darlings, they were feted and fawned over by the high and mighty, and meanwhile at the supermarket their wives had to ponder margarine or the more expensive spread.

It shouldn't surprise us, then, that some owners and some players were betting, especially on themselves. Betting on oneself is as American as tramping across a continent in search of gold. Paul Hornung was treated as a conquering hero after Alex Karras and he were suspended for a year for betting on themselves. But, as my confessed dumper demonstrated, betting against oneself is the logical sequence to betting on oneself. It shouldn't surprise us that there was some of that too.

I'm convinced that there is very little betting going on in the football community today. The owners have multimillion-dollar properties to protect. The players cannot plead poverty anymore.

But people, like footballs, take funny bounces. Where money is at stake, now and then someone is going to do a backflip.

SATURDAY

Got a curious call from Mr. Rhodes.

"You give me a bet, and I take it," he said. "Right?"

"Right."

"You don't see the game and I don't see it, it's not on television. Right?"

"Right."

"And I pay you or you pay me."
"Right."
"So how do we know they really played the game?"
And he hung up.

SUNDAY

Shitfuck.

I give unqualified endorsement to that transcendental double expletive, originated by baseball manager Joe Schultz and immortalized in Jim Bouton's *Ball Four*.

Shitfuck.

The Dolphins won, by 10 points. The Falcons lost, in the last half minute.

Woke up with a sore back. Attributed it to the drumming in the back of my neck. I had found my nervous price: $5,000.

Even my noble kidney betrayed me. I did not mind when the Jets went ahead 7–0. I was merely miffed when Garo Yepremian missed four field goals in the first half, because the Dolphins were asserting themselves, 14–7. But the Lions were leading 13–3, and good old kidney did not take kindly to that. And with two minutes left in the game, with the Dolphins in charge 27–17, the Jets were driving into their territory, threatening my money if not the Dolphins; and the Falcons had come back from 17 points behind to tie the Lions 20–20, and my kidney damn near burst. The game ended with a crumpled play-by-play sheet in my left hand, my jaws clenched, and my legs striding briskly toward the men's room.

I did not know the outcome of the Lions–Falcons for several hours. I took a long slow walk in the Village, making an offering of $1 to the gods at a future construction site where my neighbors have planted a garden and were asking for donations. I hope it does the garden some good. Me it didn't help.

I got the gory details on television. The Lions, down 23–20, got an interference call on the Falcons' three-yard line with thirty-nine seconds remaining. It was, the film showed, a tough call. The ball looked like it was out of bounds when the defensive back hit the receiver. Where I come from, that's a hanging offense for the defensive back. The Lions scored on the next play.

So I lost $1,300. I won $2,000 on the Dolphins and lost $3,300 on the Falcons. My bottom line is minus $725.

That interference cost me $6,300. Had the Falcons won, I would be plus $5,575.

Shitfuck.

Greenwich Village Fats said that The Mover lost $20,000 on the Falcons. I was not consoled. He still won four (Chiefs, Chargers, Bears, Rams) and lost two (Falcons, Cowboys). Lem Banker said, "I'm going back to my old ways of betting" after getting bruised by injury reports last week, and he won four (Bills, Eagles, Bears, Rams) and lost four (Falcons, Cowboys, Saints, Jets). His old ways include betting on the Rams "because it was their whole season" and on the Jets "because they're never underdogs at home."

Mr. Rich kept rolling with three winners (Giants, Lions, Dolphins) and one loser (Packers). "The Lions are a very good team," he said, and while I don't want to argue with him, and can't after today, I'd like to. Fast Eddie won two (Dolphins, Chiefs) and lost three (Colts, 49ers, Cowboys). Frankie the Doorman lost a parlay (Saints, Browns). Danny Lavezzo got his second straight win with the Giants and gave me a detailed analysis of Alex Webster's genius as a coach.

I am not exactly thrilled with my performance against this field.

MONDAY

The Raiders beat the Oilers 34–0. I didn't watch the game. I watched six news shows, and everyone showed the interference play in the Falcons-Lions game, and every call went against me. The number caroming inside me now was $6,300. I am not a violent man, but I contemplated violence on the TV set. The set was lucky. It belongs to Gail.

This week's composite chart:

	My Line	Outlaw Line	Opening Line	Closing Line	
FALCONS*	7	2	P	2	Lions (3)
Patriots	3	3	3	3	BILLS (24)
BENGALS (11)	9	9	9	9	Broncos
Chiefs (24)	6	6½	6½	7	BROWNS
GIANTS (24)	7	10	10	11	Saints
REDSKINS (14)	13	17	16	16½	Eagles
COLTS	6	5	5	5½	Chargers (2)
PACKERS (3)	9	8	8½	8½	Bears
COWBOYS (4)	10	6½	6½	6½	Steelers
VIKINGS	14	14	14	14½	Cardinals (2)
49ers	4	4	4½	6	RAMS (24)
Dolphins* (10)	10	P	4½	5	JETS
Raiders (34)	9	8	9	9½	Oilers

The pros won four and lost two against the outlaw line, the public won four and lost five against the opening line. Everyone went down with the 49ers, on the basis of Gabriel's sore arm. The favorites won six and lost seven. The visiting teams won nine and lost four.

Pardon me while I go ask an astrologist what all this means.

THE STANDINGS

AFC

	w	l	t	vs. spread w	l
Eastern Division					
Dolphins	4	0	0	4	0
Bills	2	2	0	2	2
Patriots	2	2	0	2	2
Jets	2	2	0	2	2
Colts	1	3	0	1	3
Central Division					
Bengals	3	1	0	3	1
Browns	2	2	0	2	2
Steelers	2	2	0	2	1
Oilers	1	3	0	1	3
Western Division					
Chiefs	3	1	0	2	2
Raiders	2	1	1	1	3
Chargers	2	1	1	3	1
Broncos	1	3	0	1	3

NFC

	w	l	t	vs. spread w	l
Eastern Division					
Cowboys	3	1	0	1	3
Redskins	3	1	0	2	2
Giants	2	2	0	3	1
Cardinals	2	2	0	2	1
Eagles	0	4	0	1	3
Central Division					
Lions	3	1	0	3	1
Packers	3	1	0	2	2
Vikings	1	3	0	1	3
Bears	0	3	1	2	2
Western Division					
Rams	2	1	1	2	2
Falcons	2	2	0	2	2
49ers	2	2	0	2	2
Saints	0	4	0	1	3

RESULTS

Lions 26, Falcons 23
Bills 38, Patriots 14
Bengals 21, Broncos 10
Chiefs 31, Browns 7
Giants 45, Saints 21
Redskins 14, Eagles 0
Chargers 23, Colts 21
Packers 20, Bears 17
Cowboys 17, Steelers 13
Cardinals 19, Vikings 17
Rams 31, 49ers 7
Dolphins 27, Jets 17
Raiders 34, Oilers 0

BETTORS	w	l	pct.
Mr. Rich	8	2	.800
Fats–Mover	19	7	.731
Lem Banker	18	11	.620
Fast Eddie	10	7	.588
Merchant	8	8	.500

EXOTICA

Visitors 29, Home Teams 23
Favorites 31, Underdogs 21
Pros 16, Outlaw Line 14
Official Line 21, Public 20

Fifth Week

Tuesday

Bedded down with fever as a boy, at night my room turned into a chamber of exaggerated cube and shadowy rectangular shapes. The ceiling seemed as high as the dark sky. The top of the window narrowed in the distance like a skyscraper. The far end of the room disappeared over the horizon. I had to shut my eyes tight to banish the distortions of light and fear.

The walls closed in on me last night. I went from living in a shoebox to a shoe.

I don't want to melodramatize the illusion. My head is screwed on: at least I think it is. But I have never lost money while living in a garret before. It seems smaller, crowded, unlivable today. It seems insane to stay here when I don't have to. I attribute this to the smaller, crowded, unlivable condition of my head. Losing jars my focus back to reality. No garret is small enough to close the distance between Gail and me. This is a very crummy place for a forty-one-year-old man with a column in a New York newspaper to be living. Paying $1.29 a pound for cherries remains beyond my depression-born powers of imagination, but I'm getting out of here.

I'm still annoyed over the Falcons and Lions, and annoyed at being annoyed, and annoyed at being annoyed at being annoyed. I need a moderator for the conversations I've been having with myself. I speak with a forked tongue of ambivalence.

I know now, for example, that I was wrong on the game. Wrong to make it the biggest bet of my life. The biggest bet of one's life should win by three touchdowns, easing up. If it goes down to the last half minute, it's a bad bet. You might win and you might lose, but you don't risk rent money (even garret-rent money) on a might-win-might-lose proposition. The Falcons tore the ass out of the Lions in the second half, as I thought they would from the start, but I underestimated the ability of Greg Landry to create an offense by himself, and I didn't take into account the inability of the Falcons to throw the ball well and how that might enable the Lions to play respectably on defense. Those factors made it a closer game than I handicapped it. The Falcons were the right pick, they weren't the cinch I made them.

I'm not going to dive out the window over that, and in fact the victory of the Dolphins and the self-control of betting only two games whisper to me that I may be getting grooved into the proper frame of mind at last. Betting too many games can be a sign of weakness, indecisiveness. Betting two games makes me feel virtuous, morally superior, like a glutton on a diet, depriving myself of whipped-cream things. A bettor can find the silver lining in hell's own fire. If I bet one game, I would see Saint Francis of Assisi in the mirror. If I divined no game worth betting, I would don my sandals and walk on the Ganges.

What annoys me is that I'm still clenching my jaws over the fool game. That is perfectly human, but it bugs me. It bugs me because it announces to me that I am taking this more seriously than I intended. Which is embarrassing coming from a purist who maintains he would rather be right than rich.

The problem is that when you bet as much as I am you have to care, deeply, for the money rather than the game. I've always felt that betting was a benign stimulant—which in moderation it is—and now I'm putting my heart, my lungs, my liver and my small intestine into it. To say nothing of my faithful kidney.

This annoys me because I am horrified by the weekend tennis player who is a snarling killer on the court, the sailboat skipper who browbeats his crew in a club race, the fan whose life is wrapped around his alma mater's football team or hometown baseball team. That, to me, is grotesque. I like to think it's possible to play hard and root hard without taking defeat like there's been a death in the family. That isn't possible when you're betting enough to call it gambling.

The intensity of the experience has roiled my competitive juices as well—it isn't a frivolous pastime anymore. Winning and losing has become personalized, as though I have stared all week at a photograph of Sunday's opponent to get myself psyched up for the confrontation. I want to beat my bookies, beat each of them. Not because they are agents of the system, which would depersonalize them, like blackjack dealers, but because I want them to respect what I'm doing. Let *their* diaphragms get taut when we do business. I want to beat my bettors too, because I'm matching my background and wits against the computer-like approach of professionals and the buckshot approach of amateurs.

Pass the greenies. I'm a player again.

WEDNESDAY

Took yesterday off. Returned to the line and the bets and the madness today.

	My Line	Outlaw Line	Opening Line	
Falcons	14	14	13	Saints
Raiders	12	14	13	Bills
Browns	6	4½	5	Bears
Chiefs	7	7	7½	Bengals
Cowboys	4	3	2½	Colts
Steelers	10	11	13½	Oilers
Rams	10	13	13½	Eagles
Vikings	14	10	10½	Broncos
49ers	10	8	7	Giants
Jets	7	7	7½	Patriots
Dolphins	10	10	9	Chargers
Redskins	7	5	6	Cardinals
Lions	3	7	6½	Packers

The pros bet the Steelers up to 13½ over the Oilers. I made four $1,000 plays: Dallas giving 2½ to the Colts, the Redskins giving 6 to the Cardinals, the Vikings giving 10½ to the Broncos, the Packers taking 6½ against the Lions. The Cowboys and the Colts are a mismatch; I probably would bet higher, but Sunday slowed me up. The Colts don't have the firepower to budge the Cowboy defense. Sonny Jurgensen is starting his second game for the Redskins, who should have no trouble smothering an offense that already has started three quarterbacks. The Vikings managed to lose to the Cardinals Sunday, I'm not sure how. Throw that result out. The Vikings should crush the Broncos, who have allowed 30 points per game and have a one-pronged offense. The Packers–Lions Monday night looks like a wrist-wrestling stalemate in Petaluma; I have to take the Packers and their ground game with a touchdown.

Called Billy the bookie for his line. He said he'll be out of action for a few days. His wife died. She had cancer.

I didn't know her, of course, but I heard Joe Schultz's double expletive sigh in me.

THURSDAY

Realized today that I neglected to subtract $10 from the bottom line for a five-team parlay card last week. That's the last one for the season. When you're betting thousands, betting $10 is a shrug, it has no meaning. Champagne to grape soda.

Realized this as I talked with Ernie the Postal Clerk, the great grid accountant.

Ernie spends all his spare time during the football season, at home and on the job, poring over parlay cards. He collects twenty-five or thirty each of half a dozen different cards, picking them up in bars in New Jersey. He plays a hundred or more of them a week, four teams on each card, for a total of $400 to $500. He isn't crazy either. He says he can't pick winners, and it's hard to find reliable bookies where he lives, and "this gives me something to do in the football season."

What Ernie does is collate the spreads on the various games, which frequently differ drastically from card to card, because these cards can be put out by anyone with a child's printing press. Generally they are put out by the people who bring you the numbers and other quick and high-profit capers. They are also put out, like raffles, by American Legion posts and fraternal organizations.

This week one of the cards lists the Lions as a 1-point favorite over the Packers, and another has them at 7. Ernie wires the best of both lines (Lions minus 1, Packers plus 7) with the best of both lines on three other games. He works his selections and cross-bets on a mathematical basis, so he has a shot at a big score if he catches a few middles—the Lions, say, winning by 3 or 4—while theoretically risking negligible losses.

Ernie said he is behind a couple hundred dollars this season, but he was confident that his numbers game would prove out. He said he won $2,000 last season, busting one hustler in the process. "I beat him out of $2,000, and he paid me half of it," he said, grinning. He didn't seem upset over getting short-ended. It was proof positive that he could beat the system.

Friday

Visited Frankie the Doorman late tonight. He works the lobster shift, alone, accompanied by a portable radio that sits on an antique table in a glumly lit lobby.

Frankie is probably younger than he looks, which is about fifty. He has, as far as I can see in the light, no teeth. But he smiles continually, a bushy mustache lending a bittersweet jauntiness to his litany of woe. I imagine he is one of those backbench musicians to whom spectators are attracted because he is having such a good time.

"I used to bet big money," Frankie said, smiling. "I was a big deal bocce player, believe it or not. Sundays big crowds would come to see me play. They'd bet hundreds on me.

"But it got into my blood, you know. And it's like a disease. The bad thing about gambling is that it turns you into a cheat and a con man. Borrowing money, writing bad checks, lying to your friends. I'm not like that. Now I bet a few bucks, go to the track on my day off. Look at this place. I'd go nuts if I didn't have some action."

Frankie's blue doorman suit fits him like a quilt. I see him bucking the headwinds of life with a street-wise grit, every once in a while catching the zephyr of a winner and soaring and dancing like a kite.

SATURDAY

The rookie quarterback quit the team. Can't say I blame her. Must be hundreds of teams who'll give her a chance to play more. It grieves me deeply though, because I may have discovered the handicapping equivalent of the lost chord and the missing link—the Tim Van Galder connection—and let it slip through my hands.

Aggrieved, I hatched a seduction plot to get inside information that might really be useful. Had drinks with the daughter of an NFL executive. No feedback.

The horny dwarf has to punt again.

SUNDAY

Won—you won't believe this—fifty big dollars. Had nearly $5,000 going and won $50, a 1 percent return. At this rate I'll break even by the Super Bowl. I'd be better off investing in municipal bonds.

Frustrating is what it is. I feel I'm beginning to get there, but when I check the landmarks I'm going nowhere. Am I swimming against a surging tide? Losing thousands,

I might be desperate and my thrashing might seem heroic. Losing hundreds is absurd, comic. There are no surging tides in kiddy pools. I'm playing with an inner tube and a rubber duck.

Having bet four games, I indulged my gluttony with three more. I took the Cardinals and 7 over the Redskins for $500; I had the Redskins giving 6. I took the Broncos and 13 for $200; I had the Vikings giving 10½. I took the Dolphins giving 8 to the Chargers for $500. I thought the Dolphins would wear down the old men on the Chargers' defensive line. I took the Bengals and 8 against the Chiefs, for $100, to support a feeling that the Chiefs would suffer traditional breakdowns against a good defense. I took the 49ers for $1,000, giving 7 to the Giants, who haven't beaten a playoff team in years. The 49ers, I thought, should pass them silly.

My handicapping was good, my money management was dreadful. I had four solid winners. The Colts couldn't budge the Cowboys, losing 21–0. The Redskins smothered the Cardinals 33–3. The Dolphins were so much better than the Chargers that they survived an ankle break by Bob Griese early in the game, winning 24–10 with Earl Morrall stepping in. The Bengals defensed the Chiefs 23–16. The four winners held their opponents to a total of two touchdowns.

The two losers were deserving losers. The Vikings' defense again collapsed in the fourth quarter, mysteriously, and a touchdown pass with seconds left bailed them out 23–20. The Giants beat the 49ers 23–17 in a downpour. I don't like to bet games in bad weather because there is no way to handicap them. These are might-win-might-lose propositions too, and I can cut cards or flip coins if I want to gamble like that. I'm pissed because I was careless: I didn't check the weather. I know bettors who call NFL cities long-distance Sunday mornings to check the weather. I glance at the weather map in the *Times*. Apparently I missed a barometric blitz meeting a low pressure screen. Come to think of it, I don't read the map very well.

I was happy for Danny Lavezzo anyway. "I'm betting my house on the Giants," he said. What's he going to do with two houses? Mr. Rich and Fast Eddie had the Giants too. Mr. Rich went three-for-three again (Giants, Bengals, Jets). "The Giants," he said, "have an excellent football team, but I couldn't analyze it." Fast Eddie also went three-for-three (Giants, Jets, Cowboys). "I heard there was bad weather in San Francisco," he reported. Why didn't I hear that? Frankie the Doorman had the Giants, but the Patriots ruined his parlay.

The swing of my four amateurs to the Giants churned at me. I tried to make sense out of it.

"I haven't said much lately. Time to face up to a few things."

"Shoot."

"This is the fifth week and you haven't reevaluated the league. The amateurs see that the Giants are improved, why don't you?"

"There aren't that many teams to reevaluate. The Bengals are the only team in the AFC exceeding expectations. The Colts are floundering as advertised. The Packers are doing well, and I've got them tomorrow night. The Vikings and 49ers have cost me. The Vikings mystify me. The 49ers are as erratic as ever, I should be locked up for betting on them."

"You left out the Giants."

"I can't believe Norm Snead. Give him enough rope and he'll hang anyone who bets on him. They beat two bad teams and a good team in a monsoon. I still don't believe them."

"It's your money. What about betting seven games? Were you tired of feeling morally superior? If you loved the Cowboys so much, why didn't you make one bet and do your Saint Francis of Assisi number?"

"Because I'm so bloody involved. I can't pass a game up if it works out to a clear choice in my head. I'm playing every one of these games in my head. What about the Redskins and the Dolphins? I've gone right down the line with them."

"Except when you killed a good bet on the Redskins by buying back half of it on the Cardinals. You're behind only $725. Calm down. There are twelve weeks to go."

"If I wanted to calm down I'd try titwillows. I'm going to bear down, not calm down. Not finding out about the weather in 'Frisco tells me I'm not bearing down hard enough."

"It's your money."

"It's my money."

"Fight, team, fight."

"Win, team, win."

MONDAY

Went to Chicago on impulse. Impulse Airlines. Took an hour to get off the ground. Fly the friendly ground of Impulse. Gail was in a designer fashion floor-length swivet when I showed up. Doctor the bookie had called, as planned, and I wasn't there yet. The call announced my imminent arrival. Unenthused by my impulsive imminence, she took herself out of the lineup with a headache. I watched the Packers and Lions on television.

The Lions led 17–0 in the third quarter. For the first time I considered the possibility of losing money for the season: I might be out more than $1,500 after the game. Yet, strangely, it did not seem like an impending disaster. If anything, I felt relieved. I would know where I stood, what I had to beat, where the opponent was, whether he had flames shooting out of his nostrils, and that seemed like a game that was vastly more interesting—to a bookwriter if not to a bettor—than drifting aimlessly. It would be a test. The year after I lost control I went back to betting $100 per game and, betting one game per week, won seven straight bets. I couldn't afford to lose.

These musings were abruptly sent to the sidelines—by bettor and bookwriter—when the Packers returned a punt for a touchdown and seized the initiative. They went on to win 24–23.

The bottom line now reads plus $325—I'm still drifting but I'm drifting in the right direction. (Amazing how little it takes to give a bettor the jollies.) I won $1,000 on the Cowboys and Packers, $500 on the Dolphins, $450 on the Redskins ($1,000 minus $550), and $100 on the Bengals. I lost $1,100 on the 49ers, $900 on the Vikings.

Winning can jar you into unreality. After a late dinner with Gail I found myself wondering whether a Tim Van Galder film festival would appear on the back of my eyebrows this night. It didn't, and I believed, wanting to believe, that we made contact.

The week's betting chart:

	My Line	Outlaw Line	Opening Line	Closing Line	
Falcons (7)	14	14	13	13½	SAINTS
RAIDERS (12)	12	14	13	13½	Bills
BROWNS	6	4½	5	6	Bears (17)
CHIEFS	7	7	7½	8	Bengals* (7)
Cowboys* (21)	4	3	2½	3	COLTS
STEELERS (17)	10	11	13½	13	Oilers
Rams (31)	10	13	13½	13½	EAGLES
Vikings* (3)	14	10	10½	13	BRONCOS
49ers*	10	8	7	8	Giants (6)
Jets (28)	7	7	7½	9½	PATRIOTS
DOLPHINS* (14)	10	10	9	7½	Chargers
Redskins* (30)	7	5	6	7	CARDINALS
LIONS	3	7	6½	6	Packers* (1)

The pros won eight and lost five against the outlaw line, the public won five and lost seven against the opening line. There were three line shifts of 2½ points (Vikings, Jets, Chargers), two of which proved wrong. The home teams won four and lost nine. The favorites won nine and lost four.

Statistics, frankly, drive me nuts.

THE STANDINGS

AFC

	w	l	t	vs. spread w	l
Eastern Division					
Dolphins	5	0	0	5	0
Jets	3	2	0	3	2
Bills	2	3	0	2	3
Patriots	2	3	0	2	3
Colts	1	4	0	1	4
Central Division					
Bengals	4	1	0	4	1
Steelers	3	2	0	3	1
Browns	2	3	0	2	3
Oilers	1	4	0	1	4
Western Division					
Raiders	3	1	1	1	4
Chiefs	3	2	0	2	3
Chargers	2	2	1	3	2
Broncos	1	4	0	2	3

NFC

	w	l	t	vs. spread w	l
Eastern Division					
Cowboys	4	1	0	2	3
Redskins	4	1	0	3	2
Giants	3	2	0	4	1
Cardinals	2	3	0	2	2
Eagles	0	5	0	1	4
Central Division					
Packers	4	1	0	3	2
Lions	3	2	0	3	2
Vikings	2	3	0	1	4
Bears	1	3	1	3	2
Western Division					
Rams	3	1	1	3	2
Falcons	3	2	0	2	3
49ers	2	3	0	2	3
Saints	0	5	0	2	3

RESULTS

Falcons 21, Saints 14
Raiders 28, Bills 16
Bears 17, Browns 0
Bengals 23, Chiefs 16
Cowboys 21, Colts 0
Steelers 24, Oilers 7
Rams 34, Eagles 3
Vikings 23, Broncos 20
Giants 23, 49ers 17
Jets 41, Patriots 13
Dolphins 24, Chargers 10
Redskins 33, Cardinals 3
Packers 24, Lions 23

BETTORS	w	l	pct.
Mr. Rich	11	2	.846
Fats–Mover	22	11	.667
Fast Eddie	13	7	.650
Merchant	13	10	.565
Lem Banker	20	14	.588

EXOTICA

Visitors 38, Home Teams 27
Favorites 40, Underdogs 25
Pros 24, Outlaw Line 19
Official Line 28, Public 25

Sixth Week

Tuesday

Crucial bet: the Redskins over the Cowboys, giving 2 points, for $1,200. The Redskins are clearly the better team. They are more likely to find a way to win, the Cowboys are more likely to find a way to lose. Without Duane Thomas and Roger Staubach, the Cowboys have to grind out their offense and you can't grind the Redskins consistently. Craig Morton—poor Craig Morton, nothing personal intended—loses this kind of game. With Sonny Jurgensen in harness, with Larry Brown and Charley Taylor, the Redskins have the people who can make exceptional plays. I regard this game as easy pickings because all you have to do is pick the winner.

The lineup:

	My Line	Outlaw Line	Opening Line	
Jets	7	7	8	Colts
Giants	6	7	9	Cardinals
Redskins	6	2	2	Cowboys
Vikings	10	7	7	Bears
Packers	P	P	2	Falcons
Lions	3	4½	5	Chargers
Rams	7	6	7	Bengals
Dolphins	13	13	13	Bills
Browns	3	1	2½	Oilers
Steelers	13	13½	13½	Patriots
49ers	10	13	12½	Saints
Chiefs	14	18	16	Eagles
Raiders	10	10½	10½	Broncos

Four more bets: Browns giving 2½ to the Oilers for $500, Chargers taking 5 over the Lions for $500, Cardinals taking 9 over the Giants for $200, Patriots taking 13½ over the Steelers for $200.

The Browns are an interesting bet for me because I am going on intuition. They play the Broncos next week and the Oilers again the week after that, so they can win three in a row and get back into the playoff picture, which is just the sort of thing they might do because they always seem to. A team with Leroy Kelly and a coming-on Mike Phipps ought to beat a team like the Oilers. Simple as that.

I look for the Chargers' offense to score often on the Lions. The Steelers haven't shown me that much yet, though they finally got around to starting Franco Harris last week. The Cardinals can move the ball on a team, like the Giants, without a physical defense.

The Colts fired Don McCafferty, who won the Super Bowl and went to the AFC championship game in two seasons as head coach, and replaced him with line coach John Sandusky. I like McCafferty, because another thing I inherited from my great-grandfather, the people handicapper, was a tradition of humanism. McCafferty is good folks, he has a tolerance for individuality as long as the player does his job, and he has shown that he can win. These are not universal qualities in football coaches. McCafferty was fired because a new management wants to play with its toy. That is its privilege. It will be my privilege to bet against them when they play the Dolphins next week.

In the right situation I'd bet the Dolphins with Earl Morrall, because they are so strong and well-balanced that they can take him with them, but I don't know what to make of the 49ers without John Brodie, who sprained an ankle severely and will be replaced by Steve Spurrier. Of course I didn't know what to make of them with Brodie. Betting on the 49ers gives me the anxious sensation of tiptoeing through a patch of poison ivy. I always ask myself afterward, "Why did I do that?" And I always do it again.

WEDNESDAY

Like Newton, the apple and gravity, Theory No. 7 crystallized this afternoon quite by accident, when I saw the street and the new apartment where I am going to live. It is the theory of emotional betting.

Contrary to professional wisdom, Theory No. 7 holds that betting emotionally can be good for you—provided you admit to yourself what you're up to so you don't get carried away, or out. It is an escape valve for pent-up commitment or hostility, warm-blooded feelings that must be appeased, tickled and conned if we are to achieve the judicial detachment necessary for cold-blooded handicapping.

The trick is to pick your spots. If one has a favorite or unfavorite team, one should bet on or against it only when intuition tugs like a Great Dane on a leash. Winning such bets brightens one's outlook on life, puts spring in one's step, swells the heart with self-congratulatory sweetness or venom. Losing such bets fills the bettor's need for self-abuse and the fan's need for suffering. Denying these basics reduces homo sap to a computer whose arterial circuits will dry up or burn out like an old toaster.

I, for example, hate the Giants. Hate meaning love when they lose. Not the team, not the players, the organization. The Giants.

Now to make it pay off. So far it hasn't. So far it has cost me $1,200.

I may also be hung up on Norm Van Brocklin, in the opposite direction, wanting to see him win, but I'm not sure how much of it is emotional and how much of it is judgment. It has cost me, I know that much.

The street where I am going to live is paved with the gold of ginkgo tree leaves. The trees form an autumnal arch that gets a close nod over the Sistine Chapel. Mayor Jimmy Walker lived on this street in the Village, and Theodore Dreiser and Sherwood Anderson and Marianne Moore, and. On one side of the street is a park with a swimming pool that in summer is sweetened with an exotic melting-pot blend of ethnic-racial urine. Looking down the street there's a giant cargo ship tied up at a Hudson River pier. My four-story brownstone is unlike other brownstones I have lived in because it is owned by a marvelous old lady, Alice Constable, who already has regaled me with tales of Messrs Walker and Dreiser, Presidents William Howard Taft and Woodrow Wilson, and Starr Faithful, a society beauty who lived on the top floor and was found murdered in 1931. (John O'Hara's *Butterfield 8* was based on her, and Elizabeth Taylor did the movie.) In the hallway is a replica of the warrant pronouncing the death sentence on King Charles I in 1648, signed by an ancestor of Alice Constable's husband and Oliver Cromwell. My apartment has a two-story studio with a skylight and a balcony and a trapdoor leading to a cellar that was built to make bathtub gin during Prohibition.

I tripped along these streets at age ten, delivering packages for my father, who had a laundry and dry cleaning store. It was America's only bohemia then, and I was titillated by the oddball characters, by Fourth Street crossing Tenth Street, by cobblestoned mews where George Washington slept, by a plaque where Mark Twain lived, by glimpses of sexual assignations, in airy apartments like my new one, that ten-year-old dwarfs were not supposed to understand. ("Thank you, sir," accepting a dime tip while quickly surveying a pile of clothes on a chair, the corner of a rumpled bed, a shapely calf and ankle.)

There are shoots of grass that peep up through some cracks in the pavement. My roots are down there. This is my city, these are my streets, my shops, my friends. I dig its brawling energy, I despair over its climate of fear, I embrace it good and bad. I am a New Yorker. And now, when the city is in trouble, as it has been periodically for more than a century, as cities all over are, the Giants, who made their fortune here, are abandoning it. Screw them.

The best thing about the Giants is that they were founded by a bookmaker. His son, Wellington Mara, who makes much ado about the virtue of loyalty, defended the city jealously as his and his alone when the Jets invaded, got $10 million in the AFL–NFL merger because he happened to be in New York, and now, at a psychologically damaging time, he has joined the exodus to the suburbs. He got rich here, he had automatic sellouts for years, the city offered to enlarge and engineer Yankee Stadium to meet the competition, and he took his loyalty across the river, to another state of mind.

This sort of ingratitude is rampant in the NFL. Betting against the Giants is the only tangible way I can register a protest. It is a game-within-the-game that enlivens my betting season.

Norm Van Brocklin is another matter. He is one of the few athletes I have ever gotten personally involved with. When the Eagles reneged on their promise to make him coach after he nearly single-handedly won the championship in 1960, I wrote a series of columns attacking them. They denied the truth through a lackey on another Philadelphia newspaper and tried to put heat on me through my editors. At an annual sports banquet at the time of the brouhaha Van Brocklin got up and said that what I and a colleague had written was the story. It was a rare act of responsibility by a public figure. Three years later, when he was coaching the Vikings, the Eagles came under new management, and my colleague, Jack McKinney, and I allowed ourselves to be used as negotiating conduits to get him back to Philadelphia. Van Brocklin was eager to return to Philadelphia, and that was no rare thing either. The deal was set, but Pete Rozelle vetoed it.

In common with much of the football community I regard Van Brocklin as something of a football genius. A large segment of the community doesn't believe he will ever be a winner as a coach because of his temperament. They doubt that he can handle modern players with his slashing tongue and unshakable 1950 values. I am not enchanted with his values, but I like his cantankerous spirit and think he'll win. His biggest problem is that people and he expect too much too quickly from him. He was with the expansion Vikings for their first six years; this is the seventh year of the expansion Falcons. Perhaps I am pushing him with high expectations too. I damn sure wouldn't have bet $3,000 on the Atlanta-mother-Falcons if Joe Kuharich coached them.

That game still galls me, but perhaps it has sobered me,

acted as ballast for my enthusiasm, the way a touchdown pass brings down a gambling cornerback. I am, as always, optimistic, else how could I rent this rainbow pad for $450 a month, more than three times my previous rent?

Pressure. Now I must win. Thoroughbreds perform under pressure.

THURSDAY

Raids! Subpoenas! Arrests! Indictments! Headlines in the newspapers this week are trumpeting massive roundups of dese, dem and dose guys and a hundred police allegedly on their payroll. The district attorney of Brooklyn, Eugene Gold, and the FBI, in separate actions, claim to have blitzed the central headquarters and main outposts of the local Mafia, all in Brooklyn.

It is interesting to me that the FBI said it smashed a gambling ring that netted from $10 to $50 million a year. That's a very wide net. Which is why I look with jaundiced eye at all figures on gambling. They are guesses. Nobody knows what the actual figures are, locally or nationally. The FBI's candor is commendable. Law enforcement agencies tend to give bloated figures because they make big headlines. Gold estimated that organized crime clears $1.75 billion annually on gambling in this country. Somewhere between $50 million and $5 billion would be a more accurate guess.

I don't mean to denigrate serious efforts to flush underworld scum and corrupt public officials. And I sympathize with the strategy of grabbing the face mask of public attention with overstatement. But I do wish that the law enforcers would stop telling me that there is a national gambling conspiracy afoot when there is no substantive evidence to support it. And I do wish they would stop insulting my intelligence by suggesting that gambling revenue finances all other organized criminal activity. The profits from heroin traffic, extortion, stealing, and the like pay very nicely for themselves, I imagine. If they didn't, the Mafia, as a free enterprise conglomerate, wouldn't engage in them: Unprofitable subsidiaries would be ruthlessly dissolved.

I asked Billy the bookie if he knew anything about the Brooklyn busts, my ulterior motive being to find out if "Marine for No. 6" was recorded for posterity on FBI bugging tapes.

"The guys in Brooklyn are maniacs," he said. "My wife got me out of that, otherwise I'd be in the can or the river by now. They're like cowboys in chaps. They're living in another world. They still disappear people. We're gentlemen. Bookmaking is a business."

He said his office was not run by dese, dem and dose guys. He said a small percentage of the bookies he knew in New York outside of Brooklyn were directly affiliated with criminal elements. He said independent bookies may use Mafia offices to lay off bets, but strictly on a business basis.

Gold's investigation turned up the valuable information that the Mafia had infiltrated some two hundred legitimate businesses. Loan-sharking usually opens the door to infiltration. Businessmen who can't get money from banks go to loan sharks and pay exorbitant rates of interest. Loan sharks exist because they fill that need. They do the same for gamblers who have gone over the brink—and for bookies. Bookies who suffer heavy weekend losses are considered good lending risks.

I asked Billy if his office has a referral service that sends customers to loan sharks.

He said, "The runners are responsible for the money. I've got about $40,000 owed to me now. I give a friend 25 percent of what he collects. I tell him to take it easy, be a gentleman, you get just as much in the end. I don't want any trouble. If a guy can't pay I cut him off. After he pays I don't let him bet as much."

I don't take Billy's testimony to be gospel, to reflect Everybookie's modus operandi. But, as Mr. Rhodes once said to me, "There's a revolution in everything else, why shouldn't there be a revolution in bookmaking?"

Earlier I referred to a public official in Nassau County who booked games. I phoned him. He said he had a small operation out of his home that brought him up to $40,000 a year from ten to fifteen customers. He said he laid off his excess bets with two bigger bookies. "There are other guys like me," he said. "They hire housewives in the suburbs to be their answering services." He said he gave it up because it took too much time, and he had all the money he could use without the government becoming suspicious.

"The biggest aggravation is bad debts," he said. "I once co-signed a loan for $4,500 to get paid. But you're going to lose some. It's like supermarket pilferage."

I also referred to a bookie in suburban Boston who has a master's degree. An informant reported, "There are no more sleazy 'Godfather' types here anymore. Today's bookie calls himself a sports bookie. He's a sophisticated guy with numbers and percentages."

The bookie with a master's degree pays a suburban couple $300 a week to use a room in their home as an office (from noon to 2:00 P.M. and 6:00 to 8:00 P.M., the traditional working hours of bookies). The bookie has two clerks. In 1971 he grossed approximately $7,300,000, handled $4,645,000 himself and laid off $2,655,000. He furnished these approximate figures (bookies ordinarily don't keep books) on the bets he personally handled:

	Volume	*Profit*
College basketball	$ 225,000	$ 20,000
Pro basketball	770,000	61,000
Football (college and pro)	1,240,000	97,000
Hockey	280,000	51,000
Baseball	2,000,000	−12,000
Horse racing	130,000	−2,500
Total	$4,645,000	$214,500

He said that his operating costs, including $20,000 in bad debts, came to about $60,000. He made $155,000 in profit.

The $12,000-loss he took on a volume of $2 million bet on baseball is instructive. Baseball is a very tough game to beat, but bettors know more about it than any other game and, since they don't have to give or take runs, they can pick winners. Usually they are done in by the odds, but things weren't usual last year in Boston. Which jibes with reports that some mobsters have no patience with a sure thing that isn't sure for 365 days a year. (Baseball is opposed only by spotty action on horses for three months and by a handful of playoff games in basketball and hockey and by exhibition football for two more months.)

I phoned a newspaperman in Washington, D.C., Morrie Siegal, who is familiar with the betting scene there. He said, "Years ago you could bet anything from 50 cents to $50,000. Today you're lucky to find a bookie who'll take a thousand-dollar bet. The big bettors are betting each other."

Boston, New Jersey, New York, Philadelphia, Washington, suburbia. Though far from a scientific sampling, every interview I've conducted points toward a change, if not a complete changeover, in betting and bookmaking habits. The new breed of sports bettor and bookie is deftly sidestepping old-fashioned cops-and-gamblers chases.

FRIDAY

The Breather called. After three hot breaths I said that he had better speak now or forever hold his breath, because I was moving on the morrow.

I assumed it was a he—living in the Village and all—and it was. He breathed three more times and launched into a feverish description of the wonderful things he was going to do for, and to, me. I mean, he was going to make *Deep Throat* seem like *Mary Poppins* and the Marquis de Sade a Pat Boone.

"If you do," I said, borrowing a line from an old joke, "and if I hear about it. . . ."

SATURDAY

Spoke to Lem Banker. Told him I was still brooding over the Falcons and Lions. "That's last week's news," he said. "Forget it. It's a new week, a new battle."

That's a pro.

Late at night I checked the weather reports by phone.

Raining in Milwaukee, intermittently raining in Detroit, clear in Washington, etcetera, etcetera. My dialing finger turned blue. No way I can do that every week.

That's not a pro.

SUNDAY

Maybe it's the age of the gifted amateur. Despite another money management blunder, I beat them.

I did some odds things. I hedged my $500 bet on the Chargers by taking the Lions giving 6; then I took the Chargers and 7 (having originally taken them with 5). The practical effect of that high-finance juggling was that I had 2 more points with the Chargers, but I was laying $270 to $200 on the game. Those 2 points, from 5 to 7, were worth it to me. I bet the Bengals and 7 over the Rams for $200, because it occurred to me that Roman Gabriel would be severely restricted by that defense. And —the blunder—I took an additional $200 on the Patriots with 14 over the Steelers. I called Mr. Rhodes back immediately and said I'd like to cancel the bet (it was stupid to have $400 on a bad team), and he refused.

"You want to cancel that bet," he said, "it'll cost you $20. You have to bet the Steelers."

"It's nice to do business with you," I said.

"Sorry, my friend."

"Let it stand," I said, biting off my nose.

It was a splendid day nonetheless, starting with a breakfast of champagne at Jonathan Schwartz's, where we watched the Reds and the Athletics, listened to snatches of the Giants–Cardinals on radio, and then took in the Cowboys–Redskins on the big television set (a $1,200 game) and the Bengals and Rams on the small set (a $200 game). I got a headache, was sent scurrying to the toilet by my nervous kidney four times, laughed a lot, and won. It was better than sex.

Jonathan's hate for the Giants is much more fully developed than my own, like a muscle enlarged through use, owing to his long-standing social bet against them. He was already $160 in arrears, the Giants having won four of five and the Dolphins five of five games against the line. "I hope Ron Johnson breaks both legs," he said. I would have settled for two weeks of whooping cough, sensitive and fair-minded as I am.

While listening to the frantic cadence of Marty Glickman, the Giants' announcer, Jonathan informed me that he had bet him a case of scotch that I would win money betting this season. I liked that, in fact I double-liked that. Not only did it give me another whack at the Giants, through Glickman, whom I have nothing against, though he has now taken sides against me, but it suddenly deposited a responsibility on me that I could feel osmose through my side and attach itself to my rib cage. Now I had a cause: friend vs. foe.

"I want to know just one thing," Jonathan said. "If you win money every week from now to the end of the season, will you bet it all on the Super Bowl?"

"Possibly," I said. "I don't know."

The Athletics won the World Series, the Giants won but didn't cover the spread, as did the Dolphins, reducing Jonathan's debt to $120, and the Cowboys were leading the Redskins and me 13–0 when I settled down to do some serious squirming and flinching and rooting. The Redskins roared back, Larry Brown having an exceptional day even for Larry Brown. My only worrisome moment came late in the game when Craig Morton was shaken up. "Oh, God, no, let him play," I said. Sure enough he got up and threw two interceptions. The Redskins dominated the last three quarters—meaning they controlled the game when they had to, which is the mark of this team—and won 24–20. It was a close game that really wasn't that close, the way a 2–1 game in baseball is close but not close when a Bob Gibson is protecting the lead in the eighth inning.

The favored Browns and underdog Bengals won for me too. The Browns won on finesse and experience, giving up yardage but not points to the Oilers. The Rams won on a last-play field goal after the Bengals missed three short ones in the last quarter. I lost two games. The Steelers overwhelmed the Patriots, the Lions overwhelmed the Chargers. Where were you, Jim Plunkett, when I needed you?

Fats and The Mover had their poorest day, winning two (Bills, Browns) and losing five (Giants, Chargers, Chiefs, Cowboys, Raiders). Lem Banker won four (Redskins, Colts, Cardinals, Falcons) and lost two (Patriots, 49ers). He liked the Colts because of the coaching change, the Falcons because they played the Packers in Milwaukee instead of Green Bay, the 49ers because it was a "must game" for them. Mr. Rich won three (Colts, Saints, Eagles) and lost two (Cowboys, Giants). Fast Eddie won two (Redskins, Browns) and lost one (Packers). "The Browns have nothing," he reasoned, "but the Oilers have nothing at all." Frankie the Doorman lost two parlays (Patriots and Giants, Cardinals and Cowboys). Danny Lavezzo was afraid of the points, but loyal fan that he is he went down with the Giants. He got a measure of satisfaction, he said, because he didn't get diddled on the points. The Giants diddled to him this time.

MONDAY

The Vikings were favored by 9 over the Bears tonight. I thought the Bears would score once, maybe, by accident, twice. I thought the Vikings would score a lot more than that. Wrong. Wrong for $660. I couldn't believe the first half. The Bears had the ball for twenty-five minutes. I give Abe Gibron, rookie coach of the Bears, former all-everything offensive lineman, credit for ball control. But what happened to the Viking defensive line? Have to cogitate on that. The Vikings had a touchdown called back and missed a field goal at the end, but that was after the bear got out of the barn. The Bears won 13–10.

	My Line	Outlaw Line	Opening Line	Closing Line	
JETS (4)	7	7	8	8	Colts
GIANTS (6)	6	7	9	9	Cardinals*
REDSKINS* (4)	6	2	2	2	Cowboys
Vikings*	10	7	7	9½	BEARS (3)
PACKERS	P	P	2	2	Falcons (1)
LIONS (14)	3	4½	5	7	Chargers*
RAMS (3)	7	6	6	7	Bengals*
DOLPHINS (1)	13	13	13	13½	Bills
Browns* (6)	3	1	2½	2½	OILERS
STEELERS (30)	13	13½	13½	14	Patriots*
49ERS	10	13	12½	13½	Saints (0)
CHIEFS	14	18	16	15½	Eagles (1)
RAIDERS	10	10½	10½	10½	Broncos (7)

The pros were four and three against the outlaw line, the public was three and three against the official line.

The home teams won four and lost nine again. The favorites won four, the underdogs nine.

I won $530 for the week, winning $1,200 on the Redskins, $500 on the Browns, $200 each on the Cardinals and Bengals, losing $440 on the Patriots, $270 on the Chargers, $660 on the Vikings. The bottom line is plus $855.

Maybe I should be doing handsprings because I'm slightly ahead of the game, and very much alive, after six weeks. But I feel that I still can't get out of my own way. Choose one: I'm (a) hungry, (b) a grouch, (c) both.

THE STANDINGS

AFC

	w	l	t	vs. spread w	l
Eastern Division					
Dolphins	6	0	0	5	1
Jets	4	2	0	3	3
Bills	2	4	0	3	3
Patriots	2	4	0	2	4
Colts	1	5	0	2	4
Central Division					
Bengals	4	2	0	5	1
Steelers	4	2	0	4	1
Browns	3	3	0	3	3
Oilers	1	5	0	1	5
Western Division					
Raiders	3	2	1	1	5
Chiefs	3	3	0	2	4
Chargers	2	3	1	3	3
Broncos	2	4	0	3	3

NFC

	w	l	t	vs. spread w	l
Eastern Division					
Redskins	5	1	0	4	2
Cowboys	4	2	0	2	4
Giants	4	2	0	4	2
Cardinals	2	4	0	3	2
Eagles	1	5	0	2	4
Central Division					
Lions	4	2	0	4	2
Packers	4	2	0	3	3
Bears	2	3	1	3	3
Vikings	2	4	0	1	5
Western Division					
Rams	4	1	1	3	3
Falcons	4	2	0	3	3
49ers	2	3	1	2	4
Saints	0	5	1	3	3

RESULTS

Jets 24, Colts 20
Giants 27, Cardinals 21
Redskins 24, Cowboys 20
Bears 13, Vikings 10
Falcons 10, Packers 9
Lions 34, Chargers 20
Rams 15, Bengals 12
Dolphins 24, Bills 23
Browns 23, Oilers 17
Steelers 33, Patriots 3
Saints 20, 49ers 20
Eagles 21, Chiefs 20
Broncos 30, Raiders 23

BETTORS	w	l	pct.
Mr. Rich	14	4	.778
Fast Eddie	15	8	.652
Fats–Mover	24	16	.600
Lem Banker	24	16	.600
Merchant	17	13	.566

EXOTICA

Visitors 47, Home Teams 31
Favorites 44, Underdogs 34
Pros 28, Outlaw Line 22
Official Line 31, Public 28

Seventh Week

TUESDAY

A piece of sculpture I have been eyeing in a Village gallery for several weeks is mine. Put a deposit on it today as soon as I got the line and made my bets.

The sculpture appealed to my sense of irony and whimsy, color and vitality. The irony and whimsy were not intended by the artist, Anna Thornhill. Using Styrofoam building blocks and cutout figures, she constructed a fanciful urban sprawl as big and wide and dynamic as Mean Joe Greene. It is New York.

That's where the irony and whimsy come in. The Giants are going to pay for it. I hope. Or, as a baseball manager once said of a traded player who rapped him, "That's vindictive of the kind of person he is."

The Redskins are favored by 6½ points over the Giants. I favored the Redskins by $2,000. I've lost $1,000 on the Giants this season, so if I win I will be $1,000 ahead. The sculpture cost $800.

The Redskins should beat the Giants because the Redskins are a very good team and the Giants are something less. Largely because Ron Johnson is such a threat to run with and catch the ball, allowing the offense to function and the defense to stay off the field a lot, the Giants are doing better than expected. But the Redskins' defense will control him and them, and the Redskins' offense will do whatever it must to score. The Giants are in the same division as the Redskins but not in the same league.

I made three other bets. I took the Lions and 6 over the Cowboys for $1,000. Charlie Sanders is returning for the Lions. The Cowboys, averaging 20 points per game, may run over the Lions but they shouldn't run away from them. I bet $200 each on the Chiefs, giving 3 to the Chargers, and on the Bears at pick over the Cardinals. The Chiefs should outmuscle the Chargers, who are groping through a change of philosophy from pass to run. The Bears are another admittedly intuitive play. They aren't much of a team, but they have a core of toughness, a Bearish malevolence emanating from Dick Butkus and Abe Gibron, that should scatter the Cardinals bowling-ball fashion. The Bears shut out the Browns earlier, the Browns resembling the Cardinals (except at quarterback) in that they have more skill than kill; their other defeats also were administered by physical teams, the Packers and Chiefs.

I like the Vikings over the Packers, but I have lost confidence in them. Theory No. 8 may explain why, if losing confidence in a team that is two and four needs explaining. Theory No. 8 holds that every football team has an inner balance, as delicate as the equilibrium in your ear, and that when it gets thrown off—for a game or a season—so does the team. Something happened to the inner balance of the Vikings with the appearance of Fran Tarkenton, through no fault of his, much as something happened to the Colts with the disappearance of Bubba Smith.

Every team plays one part of the game better than the other part (although you would be hard pressed to find which part is which in teams like the Eagles and Saints).

No team is perfectly balanced. Jimmy Jacobs, the great handball player, five times national champion, is totally ambidextrous at his game. You and I could not distinguish between the quality of his right and left hands. Yet, he insists, he is right-handed; there are certain shots that could be taken with either hand that he always hits right-handed. In football the preference usually is determined by the coach, by what aspect of the game he stresses, however imperceptibly. When questioned about the difference between Vince Lombardi and George Allen, for example, Larry Brown said that Lombardi was more involved with the offense, Allen with the defense. I handicap Allen as a defensive coach who usually thinks defensively (i.e., conservatively, resourcefully) on offense. He'd rather let the opposition take chances and make mistakes. This is why the Redskins play so many superficially close games (and why they are a good bet when the points are such that all you ask them to do is win).

The Vikings have been defensive-oriented: Their coach, Bud Grant, is a defensive man; their stars, Alan Page and Carl Eller, are defensive players. I used to prefer to see the Vikings on defense when I bet on them. Two things have happened to that defense, I think. One, it was assembled primarily to neutralize the pass, but NFL offenses have gradually recycled toward the run, and this season, with the hashmarks moved toward the center of the field, the cycle has come full. Defenses must cope with the pass and the run. Two, Tarkenton's presence seems to upset the team's balance somehow, as though it had learned to walk with a tilt in one direction and now must compensate in the opposite direction. Last season the Vikings were awesome on defense, allowing an average of 10 points, shutting out three opponents, yielding more than 13 points just twice. The same personnel are now allowing 17 points per game, the extra touchdown frequently coming in the fourth quarter. Possibly they'll get together for the second half of the season. Until they do I can't trust them with my money.

That's also vindictive of the kind of person I am.

This week's lineup:

	My Line	Outlaw Line	Opening Line	
Jets	17	14½	14½	Patriots
Redskins	9	4	6½	Giants
Cardinals	P	3	P	Bears
Broncos	4	5	5	Browns
Bengals	13	13½	13½	Oilers
Chiefs	4	1	3	Chargers
Rams	3	1	1	Raiders
Dolphins	6	2½	4	Colts
Vikings	P	3½	1	Packers
Saints	P	3	P	Eagles
Steelers	6	7½	7½	Bills
Falcons	6	7½	7	49ers
Cowboys	4	6	6	Lions

The pros made strong moves on the Redskins, Bears, Chiefs, Raiders, Packers and Eagles. The move toward the Raiders is based on Roman Gabriel's performance against the Bengals. He threw the ball like Helen Twelvetrees.

WEDNESDAY

Mr. Rhodes summed up the tenets of betting for me, as passed down by Moses from God, who whittled them between Commandments.

"Wait for a close game and bet against the team with injuries," he said. "The public made millions that way last year. The public loves to hear the crack of bones. The public's saliva flows every time a player writhes on the ground with his fibula sticking out. They don't want to read stories about a player's childhood. They want to read about a player on the operating table."

"Bullshit," I said. "If it was that easy, bookies would be bettors. You have to pick winners."

"My friend, you can't Einstein the game."

Nobody ever called me that before.

THURSDAY

Where there's money there are people who, if you give them some of the money, will tell you what to do with the rest of it. In the stock market they are called analysts, customer's men, brokers. In sports they are called handicappers, or, in words of one syllable, touts. Football touts are proliferating too.

There are said to be two hundred tout sheets and services in the country that specialize in football (and basketball). They range from plebeian newsstand hustles for a dollar-and-up to an elite telegram hustle from Texas for $100 a week.

Tout sheets proliferate because there are bettors who wisely recognize that they don't know the thirty-yard line from pork chow mein and other bettors who foolishly prowl for seers who have solved the riddle of creation. This is sad because the whole point, through my purist's looking glass, is to pick winners yourself. The chances of the inexpert layman beating the odds are minuscule. Picking some winners is the primary sensual pleasure, as well as solace, of the mania.

The point is made sharper by the fact that touts don't pick that many winners. They strain to pick 50 percent. Fifty percent is better than nothing though, which apparently is their attraction. The country is overpopulated with bettors who, picking heads or tails, would be wrong nine out of ten times. For them the touts serve a useful if melancholy purpose. Useful because theoretically they keep bettors solvent. Melancholy because to merely stay solvent—die a slower death—with someone else's expertise is like jogging with someone else's legs. Surely there must be another pastime that would provide more fulfillment. I know this fellow who raises titwillows.

Earlier I mentioned that to stay even you have to pick fifty-three winners in one hundred bets, assuming the bets are for the same amount. A tout would have to pick about 55 percent winners to accomplish that, the added percent being his fee (depending on the size of the bet). The key to winning is money management—knowing when to sock it in—and that is something no tout can advise.

What they are doing is skimming a few dollars off the top, much as I did as a teenage bellhop in resorts when I set up card games. Seven guests would play quarter-and-a-half poker twice a day for a week, cutting $20 to $25 out of every game for my services. Invariably at the end of the week two or three losers would accuse each other of being secret winners because they couldn't account for all the winnings and losings. I, cleaning out ash trays, fetching drinks, all diligence, would say nothing. I, of course, had the money.

The question arises: Why, if they are so smart, don't the published touts bet themselves and retire to Acapulco with nubile servants at age thirty-five? There are two answers.

First, theoretically, it is easier to handicap dispassionately when money and emotions are lobotomized from the equation, although touts obviously have a stake in winning and losing. A psychiatrist told me a story about a compulsive gambler who was given several thousand dollars by a widow to bet for her. He went to the track every day for a week and, with the care and discipline of a professional, won a tidy sum. She gave him a generous reward, and he rushed to the track and blew it in four races.

Second, as Mort Olshan, proprietor of *The Gold Sheet*, says, what he does is no different than what Kiplinger and many stock market newsletters purport to do—furnish inside information to a specialized audience.

The Gold Sheet, according to Lem Banker, is used widely by professional gamblers for reference material. It is crammed with records, schedules and statistics, folds neatly into a jacket pocket, sells for $2. It is valued less as a tout sheet than a fact sheet. Linemakers and handicappers, according to Banker, respect its "power ratings."

Power ratings are arbitrary numerical weights determined by a formula that includes records and statistics and whatever factors the power-rater deems appropriate. This week, for example, Olshan gives the Jets a rating of 6 and the Patriots 21 (the better the team the lower the rating). Adding 2 points for the Jets' home field advantage, he picks them to win by 17. The ratings are adjusted from week to week, depending on results. The Jets retained their rating from the week before by beating the Colts in a close game. The Patriots declined from 20 to 21 after getting buried by the Steelers.

Olshan and other handicappers aren't absolute slaves

to their ratings—they will make further adjustments for the conditions of a particular game as they perceive them—but it is a framework they seldom stray far from. Reason being that without a statistical framework they would be as lost as groundhogs on artificial turf. They don't know the terrain that well. Their numerical calculations are substitutes for imagination and judgment, in effect a guide to determining the point spread. For a linemaker interested in consistency that's fine. But a bettor must use the weapons of imagination and judgment, opinion, to joust successfully with the line. This is accomplished by anticipating rises and declines of teams and by envisioning the interreaction of two groups of people instead of two collections of data.

The touts rarely are successful in that area, if success is defined as picking enough winners to win money. Olshan runs a thorough operation, a model of responsibility in an irresponsible crowd. He has three employees. He has correspondents reporting to him on every game, on every team. He clips newspapers from every NFL city. He keeps records, does computer studies, is a font of information and history, understands the odds and ends of betting. These prodigious labors have brought him a prosperous business in a competitive field. I wish they brought him more winners in pro football.

Olshan's credo, like that of every tout I've come across, is emblazoned on one of his flyers: "The difference between winning and losing is not luck. It's information." Wrong. It's having a good opinion. But they are selling hocus-pocus, and there is a big market for hocus-pocus, and only an old sourpuss would dump on them for that.

Olshan, who works out of Hollywood, sells a pro football telephone service for $50 a month. With that he says he has had winning seasons four of the last five years. He is under 50 percent this season.

In New York the Reed Harris *Sports Newsletter* has the widest circulation. Harris is more typical of the breed than Olshan. He is a carny barker. "I'm going to let you in on a secret. This is the place to be. The games listed in this publication are all very solid selections and the games listed in this week's phone service are even more solid. This is going to be a great week of winners and doesn't everyone love a winner?" He charges $5 an issue. This season he is picking about 50 percent winners in the newsletter (prepared Sunday night for printing and distribution during the week) and under 50 percent in his phone service (given out Sunday mornings, after a whole week of collecting and weighing inside information). He offers a free week of selections if he has fewer winners than losers. From bargains like that you can go broke.

I've hit 56 percent and I'm so mortified that I haven't hired a skywriter to tell the world about it.

FRIDAY

I am having irrational thoughts on the Broncos and Browns. It's brainbending when you think about it. Irrational thoughts on the Broncos and Browns.

I'd like to bet the Browns. The Browns should beat the Broncos, that's all there is to it. But it's their first game in Denver, and though I'm not supposed to care about such things I do. If the Browns are going to collapse, as I thought they might before the season started, this is a likely place. On the other hand it's Floyd Little Day and that, historically, could spell disaster. But for whom? It was Ace Parker Day, Giants vs. Brooklyn Dodgers, when the Japanese bombed Pearl Harbor.

No tout's brain ever bent like that.

SATURDAY

And then there's George Kimball. George Kimball writes sports for the Boston *Phoenix*, a radical weekly. George is best known around the Lion's Head for dunking his glass eye in Mayor Lindsay's ginger ale at a book party. George is batting zero in his pro picks this season, but he showed up at the Head tonight because he has bet his week's salary on the Patriots and 14 over the Jets tomorrow. "The players are up for the game," George assured me. "They think they have a chance to win."

Listening to players. Poor George. I knew him well.

SUNDAY

The Giants haven't qualified yet to sit on the Board of Trustees of the Museum of Modern Art, but they have my endorsement. I shot off this imaginary letter of recommendation today:

> Dear Sirs:
>
> This is to inform you of an untapped source of revenue for new acquisitions. I purchased a handsome sculpture with the sure knowledge that a $2,000 bet I made against the New York Football Giants would be won. This afternoon these unsung patrons of the arts succumbed to the

Washington Redskins. I suggest that your financial advisors keep a sharp eye on them.

Sincerely,
Larry Merchant

The Redskins beat the Giants by a touchdown—giving me a half-point victory—but it was, at once, tougher and easier than the score indicated.

It was tougher because George Allen's brand of football makes you sweat for your money, and because Sonny Jurgensen ruptured an Achilles tendon without being hit on the second series of downs. Billy Kilmer replaced him and moved the team smartly to a field goal and a touchdown, but the extra point was missed, and they had a 9–6 edge at the half, and it was making my kidney behave badly. The Giants tied them in the third quarter, by which time my molars were grinding to dust. Then Chris Hanburger, an all-pro linebacker, turned the game and my nervous system around by stealing the ball from Ron Johnson. Larry Brown bolted thirty-eight yards for a touchdown on the next play. The good team asserts itself in the fourth quarter, and the Redskins did. With their defense in total command, they scored again. With the defense playing loosely to avert the big play and use up the clock, the Giants put together a time-consuming drive for their only touchdown. That says more about the essential control of the game than the final score does, though the score got most Giants' supporters off the hook because the line had moved to 7 in midweek. The game was superficially close.

I've gone into some detail on the tempo of the game because it was a laboratory specimen of Theory No. 9: A team that is clearly superior and is favored by a touchdown or less is very bettable.

I had three other winners, one of which was another laboratory specimen. I bet the Dolphins giving 3½ to the Colts for $500. I could not bring myself to bet more because Earl Morrall is quarterbacking the Dolphins these days. As much as I respect his professionalism, I respect my money more. I feared the Colts, as his former team, might be able to exploit his limitations, but I was wrong because they have too many limitations of their own. It was no contest—23–0.

There was an intuitive aspect to the bet also, but I discount it now, perhaps stubbornly, because I disavow mind-reader stuff. I had the feeling that the Dolphins would rouse themselves after having to come from behind to beat the Bills by a point last week. It's possible, I concede, that team personalities are beginning to take shape in my head to supplement the matchups. I'll have to grill myself about that, but at the moment I'm distracted by the sweet smell of a breakthrough. With the Bears and Chiefs winning I won $2,900 for the day.

Next week: Picassos.

The correct evaluation of good information on Roman Gabriel—information that was common knowledge in California but got scant attention in the rest of the country because the saga of Gabriel's sore arm was starting to pall—resulted in a big win for my pros. Lem Banker reported early in the week that Gabriel "has a dead arm and can't throw more than thirty yards." The Raiders took an early lead and Gabriel, forced to throw, was impotent. Lem won six games (Raiders, Dolphins, 49ers, Redskins, Chiefs, Vikings) and lost two (Bills, Cards). Fats and The Mover won three (Raiders, Redskins, Dolphins) and lost two (Broncos, Bills). Mr. Rich won four (Raiders, Bears, Vikings, 49ers) and lost two (Chargers, Colts). Frankie the Doorman lost his parlay (Redskins-Patriots). Fast Eddie went two-for-two (Vikings, Dolphins), getting a push, as did Jonathan Schwartz and Danny Lavezzo, on the Giants-Redskins.

MONDAY

Gail arrived early in the morning. We drove a rented car up to the painted foothills of the Berkshire Mountains. I had in mind a get-away-from-my-head day of fingertip touching and it was very much like that. We had lunch in a restaurant on the Hudson River. We browsed in antique shops. I thought of football once, stuck behind a Hess oil truck. Mr. Hess is a part-owner of the Jets. Click, my head switched to the Redskins-Jets next Sunday. Could be a big bet on the Redskins.

I did some frantic juggling to get the best of the Cowboys-Lions line when we returned to my new apartment late in the afternoon. Billy had the Cowboys favored by 7. Doctor had them by 6, the spread I had bet earlier. I hedged the bet with Doctor for $1,000 and took the Lions and 7 from Billy for $1,000. The net effect was that I now had the Lions and 7, laying $1,200 to $900. Linus doesn't feel any more secure with his blanket than I do with 7 instead of 6.

As we were about to step out for the evening I got a call—from The Mover. He introduced himself as Fats' friend. I knew immediately who he was and what he wanted and I was elated.

"I need a winner," he said. "Who do you like tonight?"

"The Lions."

"Why? I bet the Cowboys."

"Sanders is back. The Cowboys don't score that much."

"Isn't Owens out for the Lions?"

"They won't miss him that much for one game," I said. "Farr can do the job."

"But Owens is a terrific player."

"I can only give you my opinion. I could be wrong."

"My people tell me the Cowboys should run all over this team," he said.

"They probably will," I said. "Your people are probably right."

"I'm going with the Cowboys. Give me a call. We'll get together."

A Lincoln-Douglas debate it wasn't. It was one of those small triumphs of recognition that hypes the adrenalin of a minor celebrity. I felt that winning this game could be significant.

I did not watch the game. Gail and I went to see *Pippin,* a Broadway musical of spun magic, and then we joined Jonathan Schwartz at a jazz club, the Half Note, to listen to his friends, Jackie and Roy, a husband-wife duet, spin more magic, and then we had a nightcap at the Lion's Head where the magic of another winner—the Cowboys, I learned, won by 4—hyped me still higher into the New York night.

For a great fall. We have been down so long that we couldn't summon the marrow-deep magic between us to equal that up. Exposed, by my expectations, we fought bitterly. Knots inside me unraveled as I planned, or perhaps dreamed of, a coup on the Bears and Lions.

	My Line	Outlaw Line	Opening Line	Closing Line	
JETS (24)	17	14½	14½	14	Patriots
Redskins* (7)	9	4	6½	7	GIANTS
CARDINALS	P	3	P	P	Bears* (17)
BRONCOS	4	5	5	6½	Browns (7)
BENGALS (23)	13	13½	13½	14	Oilers
Chiefs* (12)	4	1	3	3	CHARGERS
Rams	3	1	1	3	RAIDERS (28)
Dolphins* (23)	6	3½	4	5	COLTS
Vikings (14)	P	3½	1	P	PACKERS
SAINTS (18)	P	3	P	P	Eagles
Steelers (17)	6	7½	7½	7	BILLS
FALCONS	6	7½	7	7	49ers (35)
COWBOYS (4)	4	6	6	7	Lions*

The pros won six and lost two against the outlaw line, the public won two and lost six against the official line. Everybody got rich betting on the Raiders, who went from 1-point underdogs to 3-point favorites. Seven favorites and three underdogs won (there were three pick games). Visiting teams won eight, home teams won four (with one tie).

I won $3,800: $2,000 on the Redskins, $500 on the Dolphins, $200 each on the Bears and Chiefs, $900 on the Lions ($2,000 minus $1,100). The bottom line is plus $4,655.

Never in doubt.

THE STANDINGS

AFC

	w	l	t	vs. spread w	l
Eastern Division					
Dolphins	7	0	0	6	1
Jets	5	2	0	4	3
Bills	2	5	0	3	4
Patriots	2	5	0	2	5
Colts	1	6	0	2	5
Central Division					
Bengals	5	2	0	6	1
Steelers	5	2	0	5	1
Browns	4	3	0	4	3
Oilers	1	6	0	1	6
Western Division					
Raiders	4	2	1	2	5
Chiefs	4	3	0	3	4
Chargers	2	4	1	3	4
Broncos	2	5	0	3	4

NFC

	w	l	t	vs. spread w	l
Eastern Division					
Redskins	6	1	0	4	2*
Cowboys	5	2	0	2	5
Giants	4	3	0	4	2*
Cardinals	2	5	0	3	3
Eagles	1	6	0	2	5
Central Division					
Lions	4	3	0	5	2
Packers	4	3	0	3	4
Bears	3	3	1	4	3
Vikings	3	4	0	2	5
Western Division					
Rams	4	2	1	3	4
Falcons	4	3	0	3	4
49ers	3	3	1	3	4
Saints	1	5	1	4	3

* Tie

RESULTS

Jets 34, Patriots 10
Redskins 23, Giants 16
Bears 27, Cardinals 10
Browns 27, Broncos 20
Bengals 30, Oilers 7
Chiefs 26, Chargers 14
Raiders 45, Rams 17
Dolphins 23, Colts 0
Vikings 27, Packers 13
Saints 21, Eagles 3
Steelers 38, Bills 21
49ers 49, Falcons 14
Cowboys 28, Lions 24

BETTORS	w	l	pct.
Mr. Rich	18	6	.750
Fast Eddie	17	10	.629
Merchant	22	13	.628
Lem Banker	30	18	.625
Fats–Mover	27	18	.600

EXOTICA

Visitors 55, Home Teams 35
Favorites 51, Underdogs 37
Pros 34, Outlaw Line 24
Official Line 37, Public 30

Eighth Week

TUESDAY

As Tom Mix used to sing on his cereal-sponsored radio serial, "It's roundup time on Ralston." We're halfway through the season. Time to round myself up.

The most important thing I've extracted from a review of my bets is that I should be tied to a mast and flogged whenever I list toward a heavy favorite. I've made six bets on teams favored by more than a touchdown—and won one of them. My 62 percent winning average would be 70 (which would be worth hiring a skywriter about) without those bets.

In contrast I've won eleven of the fifteen bets I've made on teams favored by a touchdown or less. I have won ten of fourteen bets on underdogs.

There's a moral here, and it is this: My strength is picking the winner of the game on the field. That is what I'm really trying to do when I bet on short-priced favorites and underdogs. I will never ever make another bet on a team favored by more than a touchdown.

This makes sense, for me, because my handicapping is based on the assumption that the teams will play the best football they are capable of for sixty minutes. But if the team I favor is winning by more than a touchdown for fifty-five minutes, it may decide to play protectively for the last five minutes, giving up a tactical touchdown, and that can't be handicapped. If that team is favored by more than a touchdown, I can lose a game I have handicapped correctly. And I will brood and turn to plum tarts for consolation.

The casual bettor may find that picking the winner of close games is what he does least best. The solution for that problem obviously is not to bet close games. Obviously too, that may be, like laying off whiskey for an alcoholic, easier said than done. Every man to his own poison.

I've kept track of the teams I've been most and least successful with, betting on or against them, and that aspect of my betting profile is inconclusive. On a games-won-and-lost basis I've had most success with the Dolphins (5–0), Redskins (4–0), Chiefs (4–1), Cardinals (3–0), Cowboys (3–1); and least success with the Steelers (0–2), Raiders (0–2), 49ers (0–2). On a money-won-and-lost basis I've had most success with the Redskins (plus $3,820), Dolphins (plus $3,550), Cowboys (plus $2,980), Jets (plus $2,000), Colts (plus $1,500); and least success with the Falcons (minus $4,010), Patriots (minus $1,540), 49ers (minus $1,470), Lions (minus $1,070).

The money won and lost is more pertinent than the games won and lost because that is a litmus test of where my strongest convictions lie. Convictions ultimately lead to the decisions to make double and triple and quadruple bets. Which is where the money is.

That is why statistics on betting are misleading. The professionals have a decided advantage in betting limited amounts into the outlaw line—an advantage not unlike that of the insider in the stock market—but they must still know when to up the bets after the official line comes out. The money the pros and the public sent in on the Raiders last week may have equaled or surpassed the volume of betting on four or five games combined, rendering games-won-and-lost academic.

Similarly the public's inevitable wrongheadedness betting into the official line is, up to now, offset by its tendency to bet favorites, who have won fifty-one times to the underdogs' thirty-seven. Underdogs have been backed just eleven times in ninety-eight games. The public has been wrong thirty-seven times and right thirty times challenging the line. (The discrepancy in the number of favorites that have won and the number of times the public has been wrong lies in the number of times that favorites have won without a line change.) A $100 bet against the movement of the money on every game would have netted a $400 profit to date.

The man who must have action and knows nothing about football and can exercise iron discipline in betting the same amount in every game—a contradiction in terms because anyone who must have action won't have iron discipline—is advised to follow this trend. It won't make you rich and it won't make you poor and there is no romance or intellectual stimulation to it, but you can't have everything. Touts promise more and are fortunate to deliver as much, for a price.

Computer surveys have been made on every conceivable betting statistic, and this is the only one that seems to be built into the system. Statistics on favorites vs. underdogs, home teams vs. visitors, et al., fluctuate from year to year. There seems to be a minor trend favoring high-priced underdogs at home (9 to 6), but that would be included in the wrongheaded trend because the public generally bets high-priced favorites to higher-priced favorites (twenty-one out of twenty-four 10-point-or-higher favorites have been bet up so far). Should the trend toward visiting teams hold up, the linemaker presumably will absorb it into his formula by reducing or eliminating home team credit.

All of which proves that there may be a substitute for picking losers, but there is no substitute for picking winners.

Speaking of which, I made three bets today. I bet $2,000 on the Lions to beat the Bears, giving 5½ points, and another $500 giving 4½ points (indicating that money is coming in on the Bears). The Bears don't have the secondary to cope with the threat of Charlie Sanders. Nor do they have the offense to exploit the softness of the Lions. Every matchup factor points to an easy win for the Lions.

I bet $1,000 on the Redskins giving 3 to the Jets and an additional $500 when the line slipped to 2½. If the Jets win this game I will have to relearn all the eternal verities of football. One of which is that you can't beat a good team without a defense, which is something the Jets don't have. If I had the guts of my convictions I'd hock the family jewels on this one, if there were any family jewels. I'm intimidated more than I should be—just as the linemaker is—by Joe Namath.

I bet $1,000 on the Bengals taking 2 from the Steelers. The Steelers have yet to demonstrate that they can move the ball consistently on a firm defense, and the Bengals have yielded less than two touchdowns a game.

The lineup:

	My Line	Outlaw Line	Opening Line	
Rams*	0	0	0	Falcons
Lions	7	7	5½	Bears
Steelers	3	3	2	Bengals
Cowboys	7	7½	7½	Chargers
Giants	6	6	7	Broncos
Browns	7	10	10	Oilers
Dolphins	10	8	10	Bills
Vikings	14	14½	16	Saints
Chiefs	P	1	1	Raiders
Cardinals	3	3	4	Eagles
49ers	1	1	1	Packers
Redskins	6	3	3	Jets
Colts	7	7	7	Patriots

* No line yet, pending medical report on Gabriel.

Wednesday

Midterm report on my weight: 165½ pounds, up 4½ since opening day. I asked a psychiatrist if I was being driven to food and drink by my anxieties. He said that the gambling experience can be so intense that it can increase metabolism which makes you hungrier.

I hope it doesn't make you shorter.

Thursday

It occurs to me that I am betting $1,000, one thousand whole dollars, on the Bengals to beat the Steelers, and I have not seen either team play a play. This occurs to me too: How much am I betting on a symbol of victory, Paul Brown, against a symbol of defeat, the Steelers?

Pittsburgh newspapers have had a standing headline for thirty years—"SOS, Same Old Steelers."

Also methinks I am beginning to hallucinate. I have the absolute clearest visions of interviewing George Allen after the Redskins lose Sunday. Allen is an alibi artist after his rare defeats and it is as morbidly fascinating to coax alibis from him as it is for small boys to pull the wings off flies.

"What happened, George?"

"Breaks went against us."

"What about that fumble you recovered on the one-yard line?"

"The Washington papers made us overconfident by downgrading the Jets."

"Do you give them credit for winning when they upgrade the opposition?"

"Two of our players had bruised ribs."

"Yes, George, but they had six guys out with lung cancer."

Mind trips like these are breaking warts out all over my self-image of mildly off-center reasonableness. I have lived with my neuroses and obsessions for quite a while and I expect to keep doing so until death do us part, but suddenly I see them, as no doubt others have all along, in the full flower of dottiness. I am possessed. An eccentric laser beam of energy, in my work, in my betting, as in all things, even in procrastinating and sleeping. I have fallen asleep on a toilet in Monticello, New York, and in a ditch in Camp Gordon, Georgia, and while the Tri-Delt spring dance went on without me at Oklahoma, and in an abandoned service station in Harrisburg, Pennsylvania, and in a Model-T Ford coughing through Twenty-Nine Palms, California, and in a bombed-out building in Frankfurt, Germany. And I read, voraciously and absent-mindedly, in circumstances imaginable and unimaginable: Captain Cook's *Logbook* in my host's library, *The New Yorker* between plays of football games and pitches of baseball games, a Red Smith column or the ingredients on a Sara Lee chocolate cake tin as milady disrobes for bed, *The Rolling Stone* while a seaplane swoops Jonathan Schwartz and me toward a summer weekend, he screaming, "We're twenty feet from the UN building!"

I have never stopped running-reading-sleeping long enough for my inward eye to telescope its myopia into focus, but suddenly I see a fierce battle joined by the id, kid and yid in me. I am pleased to report that they applauded each other when I admitted my irrational hate of the Giants, and they gave a standing ovation when, relieved to have made a clean breast of it, I applied rational action by betting against them, and winning.

"Feel better?"

"Better."

"Now what are you going to do about the Falcons?"

"If you don't let me alone I'm going to call mother."

FRIDAY

Met The Mover finally. He is tall, fiftyish, foppish and he has mod-length white hair that could be a powdered wig. We talked in a midtown coffee shop, near his penthouse apartment.

He said he didn't want to be quoted because the

courts, under new legal precedents, might force me to reveal his identity. I assured him that, if pressured by the law, I would develop amnesia or claim the interview was fiction. Researching an illegal activity, one can't be choosey about sources and methods. Besides that, I don't know who he is.

He said he still had trepidations. I agreed not to quote him directly.

The Mover then introduced me to the world of "betting groups" and "point scalping." And to the role of Las Vegas in pro football betting.

There are betting outfits or groups around the country who pool their resources and bet large sums, up to $25,000 a game in a few cases (but, The Mover emphasized, nowhere near the bets of $50,000 and up that were fairly common fifteen years and more ago). The groups usually are assembled by a handicapper, who works on a percentage or salary or both. The handicapper may be an expert in a particular sport rather than in all of them. He is, in effect, a private tout. He has contacts on the inside-information network of handicappers. He may have contacts in Las Vegas to bet into the outlaw line. The biggest groups have men working for them in Las Vegas, placing bets for them, reporting on changes in the line.

(A lawyer I know in the South recently told me that a client of his, a mother of two children, was a "bag woman" for a betting group. He said she flew regularly to Las Vegas to pick up and deliver money.)

The Mover said the line used to originate in Minneapolis, that the biggest lay-off office in the country was in Cincinnati, that there were major offices in Miami, New Orleans, Chicago, New York, Boston, Detroit, Los Angeles. The laws banning interstate traffic in gambling information have wiped out most of the major offices. As a result Las Vegas has become the center, the New York Stock Exchange, for what remains of interstate betting. The official line now originates in Las Vegas.

The Mover said he does not deal interstate as much as he once did, but he still "moves money" for groups in the Midwest, upstate New York and New England. (All interstate calls are initiated on public telephones; most of his are incoming.) He said that in many cities it is difficult to get a big bet down, especially as game-time approaches, so groups funnel money through him to big offices in New York. When there is a consensus of opinion or a hot handicapper, he adds his own money to the bet. (He spoke contemptuously of young hustlers—obviously raised by permissive parents—who won't put in the phone time necessary to coordinate such an effort. They have it too easy, he said.)

The Mover provides his service in return for money-backed handicapping—an opinion isn't worth beans, he said, unless it's backed by money—and for the opportunity to scalp points.

Scalping points is another sophisticated money-manipulation technique to skim a piece of the action. A handicapper in Buffalo calls The Mover and says he'd like to get down for $8,000 on the Redskins giving no more than 4 points to the Jets. The Mover, being in constant touch with bookmakers, knows that there is 2½ and 3 available. He tells the man in Buffalo that he has a bet and he himself bets as much as he can at 2½ and the rest at 3. Should the Redskins win by 3 or 4, The Mover wins a free bet. During the course of a football and basketball season

The Mover may make a thousand bets and he is bound to cash in some of those free bets. (The handicapper may be doing the same thing on the other end, telling his clients that he has made a bet at a half or full point difference than he actually has, providing himself a free bet.)

The Mover said he does not work on a percentage, as some such money men are said to. He said the bulk of his income is accumulated betting.

I asked him how he was doing this season.

"You can quote me on this," he said. "Terrible. Guys in Vegas have gone to the vault fourteen times. We're breaking even in the pros and getting murdered in the colleges."

The Mover said he can bet into the outlaw or early line, but he prefers to wait until the end of the week when all the information and opinions are digested by the handicappers he relies on. He said that he himself knew nothing about sports. He said he made money on horse racing, college basketball, college football and pro football in that order. He does not bet baseball.

He asked me who I was betting Sunday. I told him the Lions and the Redskins. He said we would have to meet again soon. "Maybe we can pool our luck," he said.

Saturday

The Rams got on the board as 3½-point favorites over the Falcons. I took the Falcons for $1,000. As bad as the Rams' offense is going, this looks like no more than a field goal game. If Gabriel experiences a miracle of healing I can always blame the Red Chinese conspiracy. He has been taking acupuncture treatments.

Jonathan Schwartz called, said he was down $160 on his social bet and getting short-tempered with his friend about it and they had agreed to let him make one big bet to try to get even. I advised him to bet $100 on the Lions and join Gamblers Anonymous, not necessarily in that order.

Also got a call from Greenwich Village Fats. "You can take the professionals and shove 'em," he said. "I never saw so many goddamn losers. They lost seven out of eight college games today."

SUNDAY

Credit where credit is due: I won an extra thousand dollars today because I had a good momma and poppa and solid football teachers.

Between my hallucinations on George Allen and the week-long drumbeat of Jet talk in the media—we are all susceptible to that—I managed to convince myself that I should hedge $500 of the $1,500 I had on the Redskins. But when I spoke to Doctor, the bet order came out the other way around. I took another $500 on the Redskins.

I choose to believe that the switch was implanted in me, seeds of unchanging principle, somewhere between puberty and Bud Wilkinson. The Redskins are a good team without a significant weakness. The Jets are a mediocre team because they have significant weaknesses on defense. The Redskins had beaten the Vikings and Cowboys. The Jets had not beaten a team with a winning record.

Of course if the Jets won I would curse my fumbling tongue. But as Joe Namath is fond of saying, if a frog had wings it wouldn't bump its ass so much. The Redskins won 35–17. It was such a mismatch that my kidney remained smugly serene throughout.

The Lions beat the Bears just as easily 14–0. They beat them easily despite four interceptions by the Bears to none by themselves. Charlie Sanders caught six passes.

Now the dumbkopf awards. I hedged $500 on the Rams giving 2½ to the Falcons, leaving me with a possible 3-point middle. But the Rams won 20–7 because their offensive line overpowered the Falcons to such an extent that Roman Gabriel had to throw only eleven times. Nothing like a terrific ground game to cure a sore arm. Beats acupuncture.

I did some weird things with the Bengals and Steelers, but nothing helped. I hedged $500 on the Steelers, giving 2½, and took it back on the Bengals with 3. I needed 23. The Steelers wore out the Bengal defense 40–17. Franco Harris must make a difference.

I won $2,750 for the day: $2,500 on the Lions and $2,000 on the Redskins, minus $1,150 on the Bengals ($1,650 minus $500). The bottom line is now plus $7,405.

He said modestly.

There were no startling upsets, but there was pandemonium in New York at the end of the Giants-Broncos game. The Broncos, underdogs by 7 and losing by 12, tried four passes from inside the Giants' ten-yard line on their last series. The game was over, but the point spread wasn't. You never heard such screaming. They didn't make it.

Guess I haven't made an impact with The Mover yet. He bet the Lions but went with the Jets instead of the Redskins. The Namath syndrome has the pros bamboozled too; Lem Banker also went for him. The Mover won three (Lions, Steelers, Chiefs) and lost one (Jets) anyway. Lem won five (Giants, Steelers, Lions, Vikings, Rams) and lost four (Jets, Oilers, 49ers, Cardinals). Mr. Rich won three (Steelers, Rams, Giants) and lost two (Jets, Raiders). Why did everyone have the Steelers but me? Another blind spot? Fast Eddie had one winner (Giants) and three losers (Jets, Cards, Raiders). Frankie the Doorman lost his parlay (Redskins, Raiders). If Frankie could match his contempt for Joe Namath with an equally productive emotion, he might make some money.

MONDAY

Mr. Rhodes called to ask if I had any interest in the Colts and Patriots. I did not. He said, "You can take a pass. McGovern should take a pass tomorrow. Would you like to bet the election?"

I asked what he had in mind.

"I'll give you Pennsylvania, Ohio and Illinois with McGovern—and 8–1 odds."

I said I might consider it if he threw in New York, California and Texas.

"I'll bet you even money McGovern don't win four states."

I said I'd take a pass.

"You know why Nixon will win a landslide?" Mr. Rhodes said. "Because with Nixon the point spread would be 5–12. If you want the underdog, you get 5; if you want the favorite, you lay 12. Nixon don't give away nothing. McGovern would take 5 with the favorite and give 12 with the underdog. Nixon is my kind of bookmaker."

I said, feebly, that I would take that 4:00 A.M. walk through Harlem now, thinking of nothing else that could shut him up.

"I take it five times a week myself," he said, hanging up.

	My Line	Outlaw Line	Opening Line	Closing Line	
RAMS (13)	P	0	3½	2½	Falcons*
LIONS* (14)	7	7	5½	5½	Bears
STEELERS (23)	3	3	2	3	Bengals*
Cowboys (6)	7	7½	7½	9	CHARGERS
GIANTS (12)	6	6	7	7	Broncos
BROWNS (20)	7	10	10	10	Oilers
Dolphins (14)	10	8	10	10	BILLS
VIKINGS (31)	14	14½	16	16½	Saints
CHIEFS (13)	P	1	1	1½	Raiders
Cardinals	3	3	4	5	EAGLES (0)
49ers	1	1	1	1	PACKERS (10)
Redskins* (18)	6	3	3	2½	JETS
Colts (7)	7	7	7	8	PATRIOTS

Home teams won eleven and lost two, favorites won nine and lost four. The pros were three-four against the outlaws, the public was two-six against the official line. Once again the performance of favorites may have offset the public's wrongheadedness.

My father hit a four-teamer on a parlay card for a dollar. As I suspected, it's in the genes.

THE STANDINGS

AFC

	w	l	t	vs. spread w	l
Eastern Division					
Dolphins	8	0	0	7	1
Jets	5	3	0	4	4
Bills	2	6	0	4	4
Patriots	2	6	0	2	5*
Colts	2	6	0	2	5*
Central Division					
Steelers	6	2	0	6	1
Bengals	5	3	0	6	2
Browns	5	3	0	5	3
Oilers	1	7	0	1	7
Western Division					
Chiefs	5	3	0	4	4
Raiders	4	3	1	2	6
Chargers	2	5	1	4	4
Broncos	2	6	0	3	5

NFC

	w	l	t	vs. spread w	l
Eastern Division					
Redskins	7	1	0	5	2
Cowboys	6	2	0	2	6
Giants	5	3	0	5	2
Cardinals	2	5	1	3	4
Eagles	1	6	1	3	5
Central Division					
Lions	5	3	0	6	2
Packers	5	3	0	4	4
Vikings	4	4	0	3	5
Bears	3	4	1	4	4
Western Division					
Rams	5	2	1	4	4
Falcons	4	4	0	3	5
49ers	3	4	1	3	5
Saints	1	6	1	4	4

* Tie

RESULTS

Rams 20, Falcons 7
Lions 14, Bears 0
Steelers 40, Bengals 17
Cowboys 34, Chargers 28
Giants 29, Broncos 17
Browns 20, Oilers 0
Dolphins 30, Bills 16
Vikings 36, Saints 6
Chiefs 27, Raiders 14
Cardinals 6, Eagles 6
Packers 34, 49ers 24
Redskins 35, Jets 17
Colts 24, Patriots 17

BETTORS	w	l	pct.
Mr. Rich	21	8	.724
Lem Banker	35	22	.626
Merchant	24	15	.615
Fats–Mover	30	19	.612
Fast Eddie	18	13	.580

EXOTICA

Visitors 57, Home Teams 46
Favorites 60, Underdogs 41
Pros 37, Outlaw Line 28
Official Line 43, Public 32

Ninth Week

Tuesday

If betting is a hobby for Mr. Rich, politics is a hobby for Richard Nixon. I spent election night at Mr. Rich's duplex. He won too.

The mysterious Mr. Rich, according to one of the guests, is a consummate gamesman. Cards, backgammon, sporting propositions, you name it, he'll try you out. The son of one of the wealthiest men in America tried him out in backgammon and got an expensive lesson.

According to this guest, Mr. Rich bet $100,000 on the Jets over the Colts in the Super Bowl. That's a heap of zeroes even if you knock one off for hyperbole. It certainly is more than he told me he was betting before the first week of the season—up to $500 a game.

Modesty becomes him. He is an unprepossessing man of about fifty who could be taken for a haberdashery clerk. The ego of the gambler is suppressed behind thin lips and a retiring but amiable manner that blends into the quiet game-room furniture like air. "I've been gambling since I was seven," he said. "I have a feel for it." I was reminded of Peanuts Lowrey, the baseball coach. Lowrey is one of the great golf hustlers. He deliberately shot double-bogeys on the last two holes of a practice round once because he was breaking the course record, and there was no sense letting that get out.

Mr. Rich let one thing out that revealed the seriousness of his hobby (if his 72 winning percent hasn't). He said he has access to the outlaw line, which he called the service line. Whatever it's called, hobbyists don't bet into it.

Earlier in the day I had made my bets. The Bears have been so good to me that I bet another $2,000 against them, taking the Packers giving 3 and 3½ for $1,000 each. The Bears are going to have trouble scoring on any defense with muscle and the Packers can bench-press Wrigley Field. I'm not excited about the Packers' offense, but they ought to be able to beat this team with Chester Marcol alone.

I bet $500 each on the Lions with 7 over the Vikings and the 49ers giving 6½ to the Colts. These are all what might be termed negative bets. I'm betting against teams as much as for teams. Asking the Vikings to outscore a scoring team by a full touchdown is asking too much. They don't have the runners to swash through the buckling Lion line. The Colts don't score on the better teams, and despite all the grief the 49ers have brought on themselves and me I must still rank them among the better teams on the basis of their personnel. I can't give up on all that high-grade beef yet.

For Monday I took 3 points with the Browns over the Chargers for $500. I made the Browns, who do well against unphysical teams, the favorites by 3. They are coming, the Chargers are going.

The lineup:

	My Line	Outlaw Line	Opening Line	
49ers	9	6½	6½	Colts
Jets	7	11	11½	Bills
Rams	7	11	10	Broncos
Vikings	7	7	7	Lions
Packers	6	1	3½	Bears
Steelers	P	P	1	Chiefs
Dolphins	17	17	18	Patriots
Falcons	14	13	14	Saints
Redskins	9	10	10	Giants
Raiders	3	2	P	Bengals
Oilers	P	2	3	Eagles
Cowboys	13	17	17	Cardinals
Chargers	3	4	3½	Browns

WEDNESDAY

"Hello, foe."

It was Doctor. When he has to give you money, you are the foe. When he has to collect money from you, his greeting is "Hello, friend."

I set up a meeting with Doctor in the lobby of the Biltmore Hotel. He handed me a manila envelope that I slid into my inside jacket pocket without opening. We small-talked for a few minutes as we strolled outside. He said, "The favorites are killing me." Bookies cry a lot.

When I got home I counted out fifty-nine $100 bills and two $50s. (Billy owes me $1,480, I owe Mr. Rhodes $110—$35 was lost on parlay cards). I stood in the middle of my studio considering the hiding places. The fireplace? No, too obvious. Under the trapdoor? Ditto. Inside the tennis racket cover? Not bad, but findable. My column? Yes, my column. I have a column, which no columnist should be without. It is a foot square and eight feet tall, made of wood, and it disassembles into three hollow parts. Actually it is a four-sided painting, and it increased in its original value sixfold when I deposited my booty in it.

THURSDAY

Didja ever get the feeling thatcha wanted ta go? And then ya got the feeling thatcha wanted ta stay? And then ya got the feeling thatcha wanted ta go? And then ya got the feeling thatcha wanted ta stay?

Jimmy Durante sang it. Gail and I have been enacting and reenacting it for more than a year now. This is not unique in the annals of the love and war between men and women, but a part of the solution we have agreed to may indeed be revolutionary.

She is going to see a psychiatrist.

That is standard operating procedure for a quintessential modern romance.

I am going to help pay for it by betting for her.

They don't teach that in Psychology 101.

I have agreed to go to a psychiatrist myself, after the season. I am scared stiff that in the process of taking my head apart like a watch, he or she will misplace the twenty-four-jewel mechanism that picks winners. I'd rather be dotty, even if it means sleeping through the Super Bowl and reading the *Air Force Exercise Manual* while Liv Ullmann strokes my hair.

Our decision, put off until now because we usually were apart geographically as well as emotionally, was arrived at circularly.

Gail asked me to bet for her.

"That's crazy," I said.

"No crazier than me losing money on stocks," she said.

She had a point there. I said that since we were both crazy why didn't we go for outside help.

Agreed. Agreed although I think I already know what the final solution will be.

"Get rid of this bum," the shrink will say. "He's a gambler." At least the suspense will be over. We'll have a result. Two winners or two losers.

Meanwhile $100 worth of sanity is riding on the Packers against the Bears.

FRIDAY

The bets I made this week, as I look back, seemed to make themselves. I've won four weeks in a row, six out of eight. I am so into the game that I think I'm inside the football looking out. This is a good place to be because the fifty-yard line is wherever you are and because you know that at any moment you may be dropped, kicked or deflated.

The bets haven't been divinely inspired or intuited. I'm hot, hot, hot because a series of games have come up that are like pitches into a hitter's power. I am winning because my projections on the Redskins and Bears were right. No mystery about it.

But success, like failure, does funny things to the head. I am not bedeviled by doubts and other hobgoblins of the mind. After I make my line and am read the official line I feel impelled along as though I am a character in a book with no free will. The bets seem automatic. The Packers are 3 over the Bears—bop, zip, zam—give me a thou on the Packers. The Vikings are 7 over the Lions—no way—give me the Lions for a nickel. Were I losing I think I would bet the same teams, but probably for lesser amounts, certainly with less assurance. Well, no. Were I losing I would be somebody else. *That's* what success does to you.

But hubris was tackled for a loss by that old reliable, experience. There is a sudden twitch of caution in me. It signals:

Nobody wins forever.

Winning isn't going to change your life.

Be cool, have fun, enjoy.

I've been having conversations about that with myself.

"You're playing with their money, why not send it in, let it rip?"

"Because I've got them where I want them. If I start betting $5,000 a game I've got them where they want me."

"Maybe that's why you're a sportswriter and Norman Mailer is Norman Mailer. You won't go all the way, even when you have a running start."

"You really know how to hurt a guy. I am what I am. If I had my druthers I'd druther be Olga Korbut."

"I was just testing you."

"Don't forget the $8,000 I lost. That's alive somewhere in my cells. Remember the tortoise and the hare?"

"But the hare went to sleep."

"I'm not going to."

"I have inside information that the hare left its knee brace home and passed out because he was drugged."

"But the tortoise kept plugging away because buried in

its subconscious was the humiliation of having once lost to a mollusk."

SATURDAY

I can think of swell things to do with money, but right now I'm more concerned that the house might burn down with my $6,000 than with the possibility that it might burn a hole in my pocket. Nevertheless, under the urging of my ever-helpful agent, I went shopping. He insists that spending winnings is such a joyous dividend of the betting game that it should be practiced regularly. He'll be disappointed that I have no extravagant desires, no ambitions to own a Maserati, a Cessna, a Lollobrigida.

After eliminating a $6 red velvet bow tie and cherries at a scandalous $1.49 a pound, I reduced my options to a green velour shirt for $20 and a Mickey Mouse wall clock for $17.95.

This was a heavy decision, burdened with fraughtful implications. I have never owned a green anything except for plant life and a partially green scarf crocheted by Gail. A green shirt represented a daring departure for me.

A Mickey Mouse clock represented turning the clock back. When I was seven or eight, my kid brother and I crept out of our rooms before daylight on Christmas day to see what Santa had brought down the kitchen stove, under which our presents always were piled. My brother found big, promising, jangling boxes and I found none. I crept back to bed in abject misery and confusion.

Later my parents pulled a Mickey Mouse watch out of one of the socks we ritually hung from the stove handles. I was thrilled, for about fifteen minutes. Perhaps it was then I first sensed what growing up might mean. You got presents you couldn't play with. A stiff price to pay for the right to stay up late.

I don't own a watch or clock today.

I do own a green velour shirt.

SUNDAY

That's another reason why I love Doctor. One of his services—and I seriously question whether a government agency would provide this one—is the wake-up call on Sunday morning. Since he calls by appointment I have him call when my beauty sleep must end.

"Get out of the gondolier!" Doctor cries.

This is Doctorese for "Get your feet wet with a bet."

I accommodated him by hedging the Bears with 4 points (I had the Packers giving 3 and 3½) for what Doctor sometimes calls a "jaspar." A jaspar is old poolroom talk for $500; a "stick" is $1,000. You can see that Doctor had the proper schooling.

Then I raced to the airport to get the shuttle to Washington for a rerun of the Giants-Redskins. As we were taxiing onto the runway I was informed by a stewardess that I was on the way to Boston. With my customary last-minute sprint I had sprinted onto the Boston plane, the plane I had sprinted onto a month earlier when I went to see the dumper.

Is this an omen? Should I bet the Patriots? Should I turn all my bets around? Is that how Wrong-Way Corrigan got famous?

I went to sleep, got off at Boston, boarded a shuttle back to New York, read the Boston papers, boarded a shuttle to Washington, slept, and got to the game in the middle of the first quarter—with no score. Or sweat. Figure it cost me $48 in vig for extra fare. I once got fogged out of Dallas, rerouted to Memphis, where I watched the Cowboys play the Cardinals on television, then flew to Dallas after the game and got a great story. But I paid vig for it too. Afterwards I ate dinner in an Italian restaurant. Anyone who goes to an Italian restaurant in Texas deserves anything he gets. What I got was lousy spaghetti sauce accidentally spilled on my brand-new black stetson, from which it never recovered.

I didn't bet the Redskins this week because they were favored by 10 points. The Giants played them tougher than they did in the first game, but the Redskins again played as well as they had to. The Giants scored three times, the Redskins scored on the following possession each time. Then they scored when they didn't have to, with a few seconds left, and there was a lovely uproar and a promise of more to come.

Leading by a touchdown, the Redskins called a time out with twenty-four seconds on the clock so Larry Brown could score again. There was bad blood between the teams, a fight breaking out moments before, and there was a confusion of information on whether Brown could reach the 1,000-yard mark for the season by scoring from four yards out (he couldn't). From where I sat it looked as though Billy Kilmer called the time-out himself without any signal from the sidelines. He explained later that the Redskins did indeed want to knock the Giants' jocks off and that he thought Brown did have a shot at 1,000 yards. But why take even the slightest chance that the Giants might recover a fumble and score a touchdown?

The result was that bettors who backed the Giants lost a bet they had almost surely won. The Giants fueled the uproar in New York by complaining bitterly about the ethics of rubbing it in. Pete Athas, a cornerback, blurted, "I think George Allen was trying to cover the spread," adding a qualifier that revealed the depth of feeling that had gone into the game. "I would have done the same thing," he said. Meaning beat them by as much as you can.

George Allen said he didn't even know what the point spread was, which was laughable because George Allen knows everything. When it is to his advantage he uses the spread as a psychological weapon on his players. He also said, making more sense, that the Redskins took many a humiliating beating for many a year, so what's wrong now that the shoe is on the other team? Anyone who understands how Allen plays on the emotions of his players like the strings of a harp understands that such an ending is in perfect character. Just as, two weeks ago, it was in perfect character for him to order the Redskins to play a prevent-type defense so that the Giants could score a meaningless-but-meaningful touchdown that tied the game with the points.

That of course would be forgotten in the uproar, as would the conservative game the Redskins played for 59½ minutes, because here was a curious and dramatic turn of the screw that would loose the paranoia of losers.

I laughed through the whole thing, glad I hadn't bet the game, my kidney behaving like an obedient poodle. I thought the Giants were the bet and I don't bet them. The Giants were the bet, but they lost.

I won. The Packers got by the Bears 23–17, capitalizing on fumbles to overcome a stubborn defense that held them to eight first downs. The Lions lost to the Vikings 16–14, covering the spread. The 49ers won but didn't cover 24–21, the Colts scoring on a long pass at the very end.

Dinner with a couple of friends was on me. Last of the big spenders. My agent would have been proud.

Lem Banker made a big play on the Oilers over the Eagles, giving 2 and 3 points. He said it was one of the outstanding bets of the year. I would feel lucky to win and dopey to lose with either team. The Eagles won by a point by kicking six field goals. Lem won five for the day (Falcons, Jets, Cardinals, Packers, Colts) and lost three (Oilers, Chiefs, Rams). Fats and The Mover won four (Lions, Raiders, Falcons, Packers) and lost three (Chiefs, Cowboys, 49ers). Mr. Rich won four (Steelers, Lions, Colts, Jets) and lost one (Giants). All three of the pros, incidentally, are betting the Chargers tomorrow. So is Fast Eddie, who won two (Raiders, Packers) and lost three (Giants, 49ers, Vikings). Frankie the Doorman won his parlay (Redskins, Lions). Danny Lavezzo, poor man, had the Giants.

MONDAY

Doctor laid the big one on me tonight.

I was juggling points. During the day I took the Browns for an additional $500 with 4 points and another $200 with 5. I had $1,200 on the game and that was too much, so I hedged $500 on the Chargers, giving 5. The juggling required a number of fast moves and two "Call-me-back-in-five-minutes" orders to Doctor.

The second order inspired Doctor.

"Yakapoola," he said.

"Yakapoola?" I repeated.

"Yakapoola means I'll bet you," he said.

"What?"

He was chuckling. "It means I want to bet you, but call me back in five minutes because I have to check with another book. Fooling around with the points. Yakapoola."

Point-juggling, Doctor said, is yakapoola. The term vigorish is said to have originated in England in the eighteenth century. Where did yakapoola come from? The poolroom? The Polynesian for masturbation? It's a magnificent word, a great word, a euphonious word that makes me want to shout:

> Boola boola yakapoola,
> Fool with the points
> And you're no foola,
> Yakapoola.

Doctor said he didn't know where it comes from. Doctor said it just came from him.

"You just made it up?"

"I don't know," he said. "I just said it."

I'll probably find out that Shakespeare put it in King Lear's mouth first, but for now I am satisfied that I midwifed a fabulous word into the language.

It is especially gratifying because by yakapoolaing around I made a few more dollars. The Browns won 21–17 on a late touchdown pass.

The weekend ledger showed a profit of $2,050. I won $1,450 on the Packers ($2,000 minus $550), $500 on the Lions, $650 on the Browns ($1,200 minus $550), and lost $550 on the 49ers. Subtract $100 for love sweet love (having given my former woman a piece of my Packer bet) and the bottom line is plus $9,355.

Well, actually a Lollobrigida might be useful around the house.

	My Line	Outlaw Line	Opening Line	Closing Line	
49ERS* (3)	9	6½	7	7	Colts
JETS (38)	7	11	11½	11	Bills
RAMS	7	11	10	10	Broncos (6)
VIKINGS (2)	7	7	7	7	Lions*
Packers* (6)	6	1	3½	4	BEARS
STEELERS (9)	P	P	1	P	Chiefs
DOLPHINS (52)	17	17	18	19	Patriots
ATLANTA (16)	14	13	14	14	Saints
REDSKINS (14)	9	10	10	9	Giants
Raiders (6)	3	2	P	1	BENGALS
OILERS	P	2	3	5	Eagles (1)
COWBOYS (9)	13	17	17	16½	Cardinals
CHARGERS	3	4	3½	5½	Browns* (4)

One of the more fascinating footnotes of the season was written in Cleveland, where the Browns, according to The Mover, dropped to 6½-point underdogs, meaning smart Cleveland money was on the Chargers. Smart money outsmarts itself again.

The pros won seven and lost three betting into the outlaw line, the public won four and lost five. Favorites won six and lost six, home teams won five and lost eight.

And the password is yakapoola.

THE STANDINGS

AFC

	w	l	t	vs. spread w	l
Eastern Division					
Dolphins	9	0	0	8	1
Jets	6	3	0	5	4
Colts	2	7	0	3	5
Bills	2	7	0	4	5
Patriots	2	7	0	2	6
Central Division					
Steelers	7	2	0	7	1
Browns	6	3	0	6	3
Bengals	5	4	0	6	3
Oilers	1	8	0	1	8
Western Division					
Raiders	5	3	1	3	6
Chiefs	5	4	0	4	5
Broncos	3	6	0	4	5
Chargers	2	6	1	4	5

NFC

	w	l	t	vs. spread w	l
Eastern Division					
Redskins	8	1	0	6	2
Cowboys	7	2	0	2	7
Giants	5	4	0	5	3
Eagles	2	6	1	4	5
Cardinals	2	6	1	4	4
Central Division					
Packers	6	3	0	5	4
Lions	5	4	0	7	2
Vikings	5	4	0	3	6
Bears	3	5	1	4	5
Western Division					
Rams	5	3	1	4	5
Falcons	5	4	0	4	5
49ers	4	4	1	3	6
Saints	1	7	1	4	5

RESULTS

49ers 24, Colts 21
Jets 41, Bills 3
Broncos 16, Rams 10
Packers 23, Bears 17
Vikings 16, Lions 14
Steelers 16, Chiefs 7
Dolphins 52, Patriots 0
Falcons 36, Saints 20
Raiders 20, Bengals 14
Redskins 27, Giants 13
Eagles 18, Oilers 17
Cowboys 33, Cardinals 24
Browns 21, Chargers 17

BETTORS	w	l	pct.
Mr. Rich	24	9	.727
Merchant	27	16	.628
Lem Banker	40	26	.606
Fats–Mover	34	23	.596
Fast Eddie	20	17	.540

EXOTICA

Visitors 65, Home Teams 51
Favorites 66, Underdogs 47
Pros 44, Outlaw Line 31
Official Line 48, Public 36

Tenth Week

TUESDAY

Byron Nelson had a phenomenal streak during the forties when he won every golf tournament in sight for weeks on end. The pressure in him built to such a crescendo that he began to wish he would blow up and lose. "And then," he once said, "I'd go out and shoot another 66 or 67."

Moral being that pressure is what you make it. I have been shooting 66s and 67s for the last five weeks, winning-winningwinningwinningwinning. Fourteen reds in a row came up in Monte Carlo; if red didn't yield why must I? Because, I suppose, I am homo sap and homo sap knows that you can't hit higher than .438, run a 3.30 mile, buy a stock at $2 that zooms overnight to $200. Yet the pressure I had early symptoms of last week (second-guessing myself on the size of my bets) has no noticeable effect on me. I seem to function with my normal abnormality, game-playing being my normal state. Visibly, the pressure restrains my enthusiasm to a sappy smile that announces my success among friends like a neon Carvel sign. I believe, truly, that I have the game whipped, brought to its knees, pleading for mercy. But the pressure reminds me that the 10s can beat the 11s only if we play our game. I have no desire to bet $5,000 to prove my homo sappiness.

And so Byron Nelson tees off again, yelling not "fore" but "yakapoola!"

I made four bets. Undaunted, or stubbornly, I went with the 49ers again, giving 3 and 3½ for $500 each to the Bears. If anyone can break my slump with the 49ers it is the Bears. Steve Spurrier has been playing well. The Bears don't have the secondary to stay with Gene Washington and Ted Kwalick, his receivers, a significant mismatchup.

I took the Bengals giving 4 to the Colts and the Steelers giving 7 to the Browns for $500 each. The Colts still haven't shown to my satisfaction that they can score on good defenses. The Steelers should overpower the Browns, defensively and offensively. I made a token $200 bet on the Oilers with 10 points over the Packers because defenses are beginning to pinch in on the Packers' run-run offense. The Oilers' defense isn't that bad. They could win the game.

There are two other games I may go with. The Redskins are 7 over the Falcons Monday. The way Allen and Van Brocklin play, this figures to be a very tough low-scoring game. I lean to the Falcons, but I'm not sure I think they can win. I also like the Jets and 7 over the Dolphins because, off their last game, Griese and Warfield are out with injuries, and Boozer is back. I'm hesitant because the Jets' already weak defense may have to play without its three firststring linebackers. Perhaps that's a blessing though. When a college coach complains after a losing season that he lost seventeen starters and twenty-nine seniors I always consider him blessed.

The lineup:

	My Line	Outlaw Line	Opening Line	
Bengals	7	4	4	Colts
Bills	6	3	3½	Patriots
Cowboys	13	13½	14	Eagles
Packers	6	9	9	Oilers
Vikings	P	3	3½	Rams
Lions	13	17	16½	Saints
Giants	4	4	4½	Cardinals
Dolphins	7	7	7	Jets
Raiders	4	6	6	Broncos
Steelers	10	7	7	Browns
Chiefs	7	7	7½	Chargers
49ers	6	3	4	Bears
Redskins	3	7	7	Falcons

No game shifted more than a point, suggesting that the outlaw bookies are zeroing in on the same wavelength as the professionals.

WEDNESDAY

I asked all my people about the Redskins and Giants. The newspapers have been strident with charges, countercharges, suspicions. It's the first time this season, interestingly enough, that a game evoked a really passionate post-mortem.

"I believe anything can happen in a game," Fast Eddie said. "It didn't look kosher, but it's bettors beware in anything."

Fast Eddie sung out his response gutterally with the no-bullshit patois of the city, as though a taxi driver stuck in traffic was asked to summarize the Watergate scandal in twenty-five words or less. He was willing to accept anything from caprice to depravity. He is, I am sure, no stranger to either.

I haven't seen Fast Eddie since New Orleans. When I call him Sunday mornings at his home in the suburbs I can hear the bawling of kids in the background. He gives me his picks rapid-fire, always ending with "and that's the story." The owner of the firm he works for, a friend of mine, tells me he is a crackerjack salesman who deals with buyers in the same no-bullshit fashion. Four or five members of the firm give the thirty-year-old Fast Eddie money to bet for them. He said that the World Series and college football have been rough, but they're "about even." And that's the story.

Greenwich Village Fats, who bet the Redskins, said of the game, "They're men but they get psyched up like high school kids. You see a $100,000-a-year executive diving after a baseball at the ballpark. It's human nature."

Mr. Rich, who had the Giants, said, "Nothing untoward happened. But it's possible that George Allen knows that his fans bet."

"It was incredible," said Danny Lavezzo, "but I don't see anything wrong if Allen wanted to make the fans happy. I wouldn't complain if Alex Webster did that for me."

Jonathan Schwartz, ecstatic over the outcome, said, "You should win by as many points as possible. I don't believe in that sportsmanship crap. You should kick the other guy when he's down and be prepared to suffer the consequences in the future."

Frankie the Doorman, another winner, was cynical. He said, "I was lucky. But I think maybe the players might have had something on the game. I can't believe it was on the up-and-up."

Billy, Mr. Rhodes and Doctor offered expert testimony from the bookie's perspective.

Billy said, "I had more money on the Redskins than the Giants; I needed the Giants to win. The reaction I get from my bettors is that Allen wants to rub it in. I look at it as one of those things."

Mr. Rhodes thought of something I hadn't. "They're after the wrong guy. It was Webster who was wrong. Why was he content to lose 20–13? Why didn't he take a time-out and hope for a fumble? Isn't a coach supposed to go all out until the gun goes off? In my opinion he's trying to save his job by playing the game close. Allen definitely was wrong for calling a time-out, but Webster was wronger."

Doctor said his clients were boiling. "They say the game's crooked. What do I know? I'm innocent. I didn't even watch the game. The only thing that matters to me is the final score. Who's Allen?"

"George Allen, the Redskins' coach," I said.

"The only Allen I know," said Doctor, "is Fred."

THURSDAY

Bettors, my survey indicates, aren't as universally paranoid as Pete Rozelle would like us to believe, and bookies are saner than most. But the NFL reported that there were many telephone calls on the Giants–Redskins game and a few letters. Following are excerpts from the letters, followed by Rozelle's reply:

> Your office's alleged contention is that pro football is free from gambling influences. Supposedly your office takes great pains to insure the integrity of the sport. How then do you account for the atrocious behavior of the Washington Redskins Sunday?

I wonder how many games are influenced by point spread considerations? My disillusionment is not just colored by a wager on the game. I feel that those people who wager aren't sports fans at all, but gamblers. Yet they may have the right outlook. Since it appears that this particular game was not a sport endeavor but a gambling endeavor. Otherwise, why would the Redskins jeopardize their victory? The only logical answer is that they were trying to beat the point spread.

We feel that the Redskins and Mr. George Allen were betting. We also feel that this might be the reason why the Rams let Allen go.

As a graduate student in business who is desirous of your job, I am left totally speechless by the Giants–Washington game. Having bet on pools in high school, I understand the meaning of the spread. Reading Kilmer's mind is obvious. He was trying to beat the spread.

Last Sunday's game between the Redskins and the Giants exemplifies everything we have always known to be true about most football games these days—the bookies are in control. How much did George Allen have on the game, and can you prove it, and if you could, would you?

Yesterday's decision by Billy Kilmer leaves an unexplainable void in his thinking. Your staff should make him explain his thinking.

I had hoped that professional football was beyond that type of innuendo.

It is fascinating to this partial viewer that all but one of the letters disavowed any interest in gambling. It is interesting because Pete Rozelle tells us that the gamblers cast suspicion on the game.

This is the letter that Rozelle sent to all his disturbed correspondents:

> This office is thoroughly familiar with all the facts of the New York Giants at Washington Redskins game of November 12, and there is nothing to investigate.
>
> To call a time-out and score a touchdown at any time is clearly the prerogative of the individual coach and team, as long as the actions are taken and achieved within the rules of the game. There are, in fact, rules within the tie-breaking procedures for the division playoff positions which take into account the number of points scored by a team during a season.
>
> If there were no such thing as a point spread our mail on the game would be minimal, and the public furor reflecting the frustration of the losing bettors would not have occurred. This is the precise point we have been making for more than a year now in rebuttal to those who would favor an extension of legalized gambling to professional team sports.

This is the sort of stuffy rationalization one would expect from the telephone company after a computer bills you incorrectly for six months. It is a stupid letter. Everyone knows what the Redskins did was within the rules. Making no effort to intelligently discuss the incident and all its surrounding shades and oddments, no effort to get across the fact that football players and coaches, just like people, often do inexplicable things, some of which may affect the point spread, Rozelle uses the occasion merely to electioneer. As for letters "reflecting the frustration of the losing bettors," I asked the NFL for all their correspondence on the matter. What you have seen is what

I got. Since my attitudes about gambling are not unknown to Rozelle and his aides, I assume these letters are all they received or a typical batch.

Makes you wonder who's paranoid and who isn't.

FRIDAY

Call from Gail.

"Who are we betting this week?"

"You're betting on the 49ers to beat the Bears. Root for them to win by a touchdown."

"Poor Bears."

"They're paying your bills."

"Why don't we bet two games?" Giggles.

"Because one's too many. Freud is spinning in his grave."

"No, he's sitting behind a desk. Misha talks with a Viennese accent and has a goatee."

"Misha? He's probably a Bears' fan. Just what we need."

More giggles. At least we have giggles.

SATURDAY

Is it possible that by winning I am botching the show? Who's going to identify with a book about a bettor who wins? A bettor who wins and turns slightly giddy instead of wildly euphoric? A bettor who wins but doesn't outline a system to lead losers to untold riches and dancing girls?

Wouldn't bettors and moralists be better entertained

and reinforced if I lost and was degraded below degradation, stripped to whimpering failure, transformed into a guide to the netherworld of loan sharking?

I had a dream of guilt. Phil Esposito bet someone $100,000 that he would win the hockey scoring championship again. He won, collected the money, and walked up a hill. He came to a clearing where there were a half-dozen gravestones.

But I'm going to win.

SUNDAY

Like I said, nobody wins forever. But the way I lost today will be enshrined in my personal Hall of Infamy, betting division.

I spent the afternoon with Billy. Five minutes before post time I called Fats to get his bets. Fats said The Mover was going to bet the 49ers, but he had just gotten word on the inside-information wire that Steve Spurrier wasn't going to play because he had bad ankles. Earlier in the week Lem Banker mentioned the same rumor.

As noted, I don't think the inside-information wire is worth the spoor of a diseased hyena. The information usually is reliable, but seldom if ever is it crucial; more often than not it has already been published in the sports pages. Here, however, was a bald statement of fact—Steve Spurrier wasn't going to play—that I could evaluate myself. And my evaluation was that I'd better hedge all or part of my $1,000 bet. Conditioned in skepticism, fortunately, I hedged only half of it, taking the Bears and 3.

Result: Steve Spurrier threw five touchdown passes. The 49ers all the way 37–21.

"There's so much fucking information," The Mover said

when I spoke to him later, having lost all his bets, "it can drive you crazy."

I won $200 on the Jets, with 8, when they lost to the Dolphins 28–24, but I lost everything else. The Browns upset the Steelers 26–24 and the Colts upset the Bengals 20–19 on last-play field goals. The Browns' win is a shocker, their first win over a playoff caliber team. As in the Lions–Falcons game six weeks ago, the team I figured to control the game didn't assert itself until the second half, when it was too late. That's what upsets often are made of. The Packers beat the Oilers 23–10 in the kind of game you can deceive yourself into thinking you were right about. The Oilers did give the Packers more trouble than was generally anticipated, but the Packers scored one touchdown on a pass off a punt formation on the last play of the first half and another touchdown on a punt return. File that away under good-teams-find-a-way-to-win-and-bad-teams-find-a-way-to-lose. File me away under bad-thinking.

Fats and The Mover lost three out of three (Chiefs, Steelers, Bengals). Lem Banker liked the Jets, not only for the reasons I cited, but because "Namath has girl friends in Miami and likes to look good there." He won three (Jets, Browns, 49ers) and lost three (Cardinals, Oilers, Rams). Mr. Rich won two (Packers, Jets) and lost one (Steelers). Fast Eddie won four (Raiders, Packers, Giants, Cowboys) and lost four (Steelers, Bengals, Vikings, Dolphins). Danny Lavezzo got a push with the Giants and said he started betting other teams. I didn't ask him for those bets. I can't stand the sight of blood.

The afternoon with Billy was instructive. They don't write short stories and musicals about the Billys of bookmaking. He lives in a spacious five-room apartment, furnished plainly, linoleum on the floors. The absence of his wife is still a presence. His teen-aged children by a former marriage wander in and out, poking into the refrigerator. The seventeen-year-old boy helps him out sometimes, Billy said. Billy's breakfast was an eggnog with applesauce in it.

This exotic concoction is Billy's only concession to individuality. He guards his anonymity like a herd animal. As precautions against predatory police, he doesn't carry a pencil or paper, doesn't own a car, doesn't dress flashily. He seems to have ordered his medium height and clean features from a Sears Roebuck catalogue.

Billy sits at a small kitchen table taking calls. The telephone has a tape recorder hooked up to it. "This way I have no arguments about bets," he said. "If a guy tells me he bet the other team, I say, 'Come over to my house, we'll play the tape.' It cost $40 and saved me thousands, and a lot of arguments."

Billy marks the bets on a schedule sheet. He said he had about $18,000 bet for the week in all sports. There were nine calls from noon to the 1:00 P.M. kickoff of the first game. When someone would bet a parlay, Billy would shrug, as if to say, What are you gonna do? They want to give me their money.

He said he was holding about $3,000 in bets himself, the rest being processed by his office. He said he was holding a few hundred dollars extra on the Jets (a loser for him), Steelers, and Bengals (winners) and Cardinals (push). "I have no opinion," he said. "I bet against the public." The outcome of the Vikings–Rams would determine whether he had a winning week. Between his office and himself he had about $4,000 riding on the television game, half favoring the Vikings at 4 points, half at 4½. "An old-timer told me when I was starting out in this business never to watch the games—go to a movie, take the family out, anything but watch," Billy said. "But I watch. I have to watch."

Chain-smoking, sitting tensely in an armchair, Billy watched the Vikings and Rams exchange touchdowns as though they were playing tennis. He squirmed, jerked, leaned this way and that in eloquent body English. When Fran Tarkenton threw an unexpected touchdown pass with three minutes left to put the Vikings ahead by 11, he cursed. The Rams, hopelessly out of the game, then put a drive together that brought them deep into Viking territory. On the last play Roman Gabriel threw a touchdown pass, the extra point was good to make the final score 45–41, and Billy won the bets favoring the Vikings by 4½. He let out a whoop. "You got to suffer those out," he said.

At night Billy hangs out in a bar, where he takes bets from his regulars, but his basic place of business is as domestic as a housewife's: at a kitchen table and in front of a television set. The modern bookie, contrary to Runyonesque legend, has all the glamour of the newspaper rewriteman, the traffic cop, the insurance salesman, the collection agent. He provides a service much in demand, pays promptly, works long hours. And he is, as a devoted adherent of free enterprise and the work ethic should be, well rewarded.

The decision of New York police to harass only those bookies who are involved in deadlier games merits three cheers and an I'll-drink-to-that.

MONDAY

I tackled a kid in a high school game so hard with my head that my neck quivered like a tuning fork. As I got up, slowly, I saw the kid wobbling toward the sideline. Immediately I felt better.

Felt like that tonight.

Having lost $670 yesterday, I bet $2,000 on the Falcons with 7 and hedged $1,000 on the Redskins giving 6½. I was trying to salvage a winning weekend out of it. Instead I sunk deeper. But it only hurt for a minute, when Larry Brown was credited with a hotly disputed touchdown on a pass. The Falcons led at the half, had a shot, blew it 24–13, and as Fast Eddie would say, that's the story.

Of the game. I watched it with The Mover, in the loft where Greenwich Village Fats lives with his girl and his dachshund. That's another story. The Mover moaned and groaned so much that I forgot about my own troubles. I rather enjoyed his suffering, in fact.

After the Falcons took a 7–0 lead, The Mover said he could settle for half of his $10,000 bet right then. A half hour later he was wishing he had. As the Redskins came back, his pink complexion turned milky and sour, his manicured posture slumped scruffily. He gave up on winning long before anyone else did, the classic form of reverse rooting: Maybe if I admit I was dumb to bet on them they'll prove I'm dumb again and win.

Unfortunately he was dumb just once. Fats said he lost $50,000 for the weekend. "It's unbelievable, unreal," The Mover whined. "The worst ever."

For a man who moved a quarter million dollars a weekend, wasn't he taking this one defeat a bit hard?

"When you're losing, every defeat hurts," The Mover whined on. "It's like been going on for months. I've lost, but never this bad. I could pick up a half dollar off the street and it would turn to lead. I feel it in my gut. It's turning my stomach."

The Mover looked at me with a pained expression, grinned feebly, and said, "Would you like to buy my girl for $100,000?"

Spoken like a true gambler. Yakapoola means he'd bet his girl too.

The week that was:

	My Line	Outlaw Line	Opening Line	Closing Line	
BENGALS*	7	4	4	5	Colts (1)
Bills (3)	6	3	3½	5½	PATRIOTS
Cowboys (21)	13	13½	14	14½	EAGLES
Packers (13)	6	9	9	10½	OILERS*
Vikings (4)	P	3	3½	5½	RAMS
LIONS (14)	13	17	16½	17	Saints
Giants (6)	4	4	4½	6	CARDINALS
DOLPHINS (4)	7	7	7	8	Jets*
Raiders (17)	4	6	6½	6½	BRONCOS
Steelers*	10	7	7	7½	BROWNS (2)
CHIEFS	7	7	7½	7	Chargers (10)
49ers* (13)	6	3	4	3	BEARS
REDSKINS (11)	3	7	7	6½	Falcons*

The pros won six and lost two, the public won four and lost eight. The favorites won six and lost six, the visitors won nine and lost three (there was one push). The Bills had the most one-sided play, and lost to the spread.

I lost $1,970, winning $350 on the 49ers ($1,000 minus $550 minus $100 for Gail) and $200 on the Jets, losing $550 on the Bengals and Steelers, $220 on the Oilers and $1,200 on the Falcons ($2,200 minus $1,000). The bottom line is plus $7,385.

"They say championships are won in November and December," I told myself.

"What they don't say is that they are also lost."

"You can only win if you aren't afraid to lose."

"That's what I'm afraid of."

"Do I detect a note of uncertainty after all your bluster?"

"No, you detect a note of unbluster after all my certainty."

THE STANDINGS

AFC

	w	l	t	vs. spread w	l
Eastern Division					
Dolphins	10	0	0	8	2
Jets	6	4	0	6	4
Colts	3	7	0	4	5
Bills	3	7	0	4	6
Patriots	2	8	0	3	6
Central Division					
Browns	7	3	0	7	3
Steelers	7	3	0	7	2
Bengals	5	5	0	6	4
Oilers	1	9	0	1	9
Western Division					
Raiders	6	3	1	4	6
Chiefs	5	5	0	4	6
Chargers	3	6	1	5	5
Broncos	3	7	0	4	6

NFC

	w	l	t	vs. spread w	l
Eastern Division					
Redskins	9	1	0	7	2
Cowboys	8	2	0	3	7
Giants	6	4	0	5	3*
Eagles	2	7	1	4	6
Cardinals	2	7	1	4	4*
Central Division					
Packers	7	3	0	6	4
Lions	6	4	0	7	3
Vikings	6	4	0	3	6*
Bears	3	6	1	4	6
Western Division					
Rams	5	4	1	4	5*
49ers	5	4	1	4	6
Falcons	5	5	0	4	6
Saints	1	8	1	5	5

* Tie

RESULTS

Colts 20, Bengals 19
Bills 27, Patriots 24
Cowboys 28, Eagles 7
Packers 23, Oilers 10
Vikings 45, Rams 41
Lions 27, Saints 14
Giants 13, Cardinals 7
Dolphins 28, Jets 24
Raiders 37, Broncos 20
Browns 26, Steelers 24
Chargers 27, Chiefs 17
49ers 34, Bears 21
Redskins 24, Falcons 13

BETTORS	w	l	pct.
Mr. Rich	26	10	.722
Lem Banker	43	29	.597
Merchant	29	20	.592
Fats–Mover	34	26	.566
Fast Eddie	24	21	.533

EXOTICA

Visitors 74, Home Teams 54
Favorites 72, Underdogs 53
Pros 50, Outlaw Line 33
Official Line 56, Public 40

Eleventh Week

TUESDAY

Vic Ziegel, friend and colleague, came back from Lake Tahoe with a story.

Frank Sinatra, part-owner of a hotel in the Nevada resort, substituted himself for a blackjack dealer at a small game one evening.

For a half dozen hands or so he proceeded to pay off each of the players—a dollar or two—no matter what the cards showed.

Catching on quickly to Sinatra's act, one player put $30 on the next hand.

"Don't," said Sinatra, pushing the money back at him, "be a pig."

Don't be a pig, or variations thereof, a number of which I have already expressed, is half of the most-important rule in gambling—the half that has to do with winning. The losing corollary is expressed in a rock song: "Only a fool gambles more than he can afford to lose."

The problem of course is that we all have the capacity to be pigs and fools. A genius may make a great fortune or a great work of art by shooting these extreme rapids. Gamblers can only make themselves poor, smashing themselves on the rocks of greed or panic and drowning in subconscious depths.

So, in reviewing last week, I conclude that I did a few

foolish things, perhaps even a few piggy things, but I did not play the pig or the fool. After winning for five weeks I resisted the temptation that must have been lurking somewhere to make grandiose betting gestures. But I allowed myself to get unhinged by the 49er thing and tried to compensate too heavily on the Falcons. Nobody's perfect.

So, back into the fray. To demonstrate my mastery of the situation I have bet only $2,000 on the Jets and 8 points over the Lions on Thanksgiving Day. I am a sprinter in the starting blocks anxious to go, but I am holding back. I like the Jets more than $2,000 worth. They have an offense that should do as it pleases against the Lions, and the Lions should do likewise to the Jets, and a good time should be had by all who take the points. The Jets are banged up after a rough game with the Dolphins, but I emerged unscathed and look ahead to the Lions fearlessly.

I made three $500 bets: the Bengals giving 2½ to the Bears, the Redskins giving 6½ to the Packers, the Eagles and 13½ against the Giants. The Bengals' offense, unspectacular as it is, should have an easier time with the Bears' defense than the Bears' offense, which is downright pitiful, should have with the Bengals' defense. Also I've won four straight weeks on the Bears, and this one is for Gail, who has begun to think that betting against the Bears is a vital part of the Medicare program. The Redskins' defense should contain the Packers in a game without many complicating factors. The Giants haven't been two-touchdown favorites since Y. A. Tittle, and the Eagles, bad as they are, played them honorably if losingly in their first game.

The lineup:

	My Line	Outlaw Line	Opening Line	
Lions	3	5	7	Jets
Cowboys	8	7	7½	49ers
Browns	10	9	11	Bills
Bengals	3	3	2	Bears
Falcons	10	9	10	Broncos
Redskins	10	6½	7	Packers
Chargers	10	11½	13	Oilers
Raiders	3	5	4	Chiefs
Rams	12	11	12	Saints
Vikings	3	P	2	Steelers
Colts	9	13	13	Patriots
Giants	10	13	13	Eagles
Dolphins	14	14½	14	Cardinals

WEDNESDAY

I interviewed the former cornerback implicated in a fix by my confessed dumper. He lives in an Eastern city. We met in a bar. I knew him vaguely as a player.

We talked for about an hour. He introduced me to an uncle and a cousin who are, he said, crazy bettors. "I don't understand point spreads," he said. "I don't know how they figure them out. Players know about them because it's in the papers all the time, but they don't look at a game like gamblers do. I bet a few dollars on some games after I retired, and lost. I don't touch it anymore."

I asked him if he touched while he was playing. Off the record, for this book I'm doing.

He said no.

I asked him if he had ever heard of players, teammates, who gambled.

He said no.

After a decent interval I turned the conversation to a famous story, perhaps apocryphal, of two members of a well-known backfield of the sixties who reputedly bet against each other in one game.

He took the bait.

"I never heard that one," he said, suddenly understanding the point spread, "but I damn sure know who had the best bet."

The one, of course, who, as my confessed dumper accused the cornerback, bet against himself.

Thursday

Blurted two more terrific expletives today.

One was "dog-ass Jets." That comes from Dan Jenkins' best-selling *Semi-Tough.* I read the novel standing on grocery lines, sitting in the dentist's chair, lying in the bathtub, and while semilistening to a Village girl recently returned from a yoga farm telling me to wear a hat in Las Vegas so I don't catch the bad vibes. Why would anyone go to Las Vegas if he didn't want to catch the bad vibes?

Anyway, the dog-ass Jets cost me $2,200 by losing to the Lions. They were tied going into the fourth quarter, which meant I was leading by 8 points. Then the rape and the pillaging.

And I heard myself cry out, from deep within and long ago, "Sheet fahr!"

That's Oklahoman for shit-fire.

Oklahoma was playing Nebraska on ABC. I'd look at it

during commercial breaks on NBC. My heart isn't in Oklahoma much anymore, except when they play Texas. I've got four years of me in Oklahoma, though, and today, when a bet was crashing all around me, an afternoon on the practice field twenty-three years ago erupted.

Like I said, I was a last-stringer, which is more accurate than fourth-stringer, which I was too, because that implies that there were lower stringers I beat out. There weren't. We had four and a half strings. I scrimmaged the first three strings a lot, got run over a lot, went after them as best I could. If you told me there was a place where I could have more fun I'd have thought you were addled beyond repair.

Now on this afternoon we were supposed to be scrimmaging lightly, at three-quarter speed, but a couple times I felt myself being hit, carrying the ball, with what seemed like five-fourths zeal. Finally I got the idea that some people weren't playing the same game as I was, and the next time, picking on someone nearly my own size, I butted him on his back.

An assistant coach gave me hell for that, and I exploded, "Sheet fahr! If they're gonna hit me I'm gonna hit them" (getting a smile out of him).

I wasn't Sooner born and Sooner bred and I didn't intend to become Sooner dead, as the school fight song goes, but I was a Sooner. I ate chicken-fried steak, got so I could tolerate country music, and knew how to say "Sheet fahr" like a native. Right there, I reckon, was 90 percent of my education.

The other 10 percent I got from Bud Wilkinson, whose cool teacher style appealed to me because I fancied myself a student of the game.

Which is why my behavior today while watching the

Lions–Jets in my studio astonished me. I sheet-fahred and picked up a tennis racket and forehanded a helpless sofa like a boarding school teacher caning a miscreant. Me.

Until now only my excitable kidney has given me away, to myself, measuring my emotional input and output in this season to the last drop. I have rationalized this as a middle-aged version of kickoff butterflies, although, come to think of it, those faint flutterings in my stomach recently weren't Lady Windermere's fans.

But then I've been able to settle back and look at the game as I always have—until midway into the third quarter at least—trying to plumb the chemistry of one team probing and reacting toward the other team, trying to catch the significant drifts, and so on. (I want to emphasize that my technical knowledge of contemporary football is limited, if that. A good thing too, because too much knowledge, like too much information, can be dangerous to the handicapper.)

But today I lost my grip. Me, student of the game. Me, sportswriter schooled in the decorum of press box etiquette. Me, observer by training and inclination. Good grief, what if I were losing money? I might be cowering in a catatonic lump in my fireplace.

That shakes me, and so does the call I made to Billy when the game ended, dialing urgently, to bet the 49ers and 7 points over the Cowboys for $500. I didn't like the game, but I needed a win. The winning has made me manic, hungry for more wins. I have arrogated the divine right of winning to me. True, I beat the sofa with a devastating service and well-placed ground strokes, six-love, six-love, but it still shakes me.

The 49ers won. I felt limp and redeemed, like having good sex right after bad.

And to think that Thanksgiving used to mean mushroom stuffing and candied yams.

Friday

Department of I'm Not-the-Only-Crazy-One.

Item: Lion's Head drinking buddy, Tony Hayes, a mad dog Englishman, was in traction for a slipped disc in a hospital ward. No phones, so he managed somehow to raise himself from bed at noon Sunday to get to an outside telephone to call a friend to make a bet for him. He bet a five-team round-robin—ten two-team parlays.

The five teams won, and a miracle of healing took place. He left the hospital weeks ahead of schedule.

Item: My agent went to a Sunday wedding. There were three television sets in the reception room, how else could you get your best friends to come? The men, according to my agent, were dancing around the sets like lunatics under a full moon. The women presumably danced with each other.

Item: I got a letter from the soccer-style quarterback I met in Copenhagen last summer. She writes, "What do you want out of life?" That's the end of that. I'm afraid that what I want out of life at this crossroad in the starry sky is a middle with $3,000 on one side and $2,000 on the other. She'd never understand.

I'm going to Las Vegas to calm down.

Saturday

If you look on the other side of Grant Wood's painting, *American Gothic*—stern-faced Puritan couple in front of farmhouse, pitchfork at parade rest—you'll find Las Vegas, where the pitchforks have fiery tips.

Take this big brute of a brute I met here last spring. Rug salesman. Family man. And a former pro lineman who got a $100,000 bonus to sign during the height of the AFL–NFL war in the mid-sixties. Married to a Miss America contestant, he was playing his last game in college while she was being wined, dined, and promised a modeling career by the NFL team that drafted him, in its city. He was scheduled to follow her out right after the game. Enter the AFL team, mustachios twirling, with $5,000 in $100 bills and a proposition: "How about a party in Vegas?" Varoom, an all-night ride. "And the most beautiful redhead I ever saw," he recalled. And the AFL won another.

Las Vegas is all glitter and gold, America's frontier Sodom, its Hangitalloutsville, its red satin fantasy of thou-shalts.

I put $6,000 in a safe-deposit envelope and charged into the night to see what kind of trouble I could get into. It's a thirty-six-hour town and I'm going to be here for three weeks. A feat of endurance that, if I survive, will undoubtedly be recorded in the *Guinness Book of Records.*

SUNDAY

Yakapoola, I am here.

You can make half-time bets in Vegas, with a brand new line on the second half. You can bet on total points in Vegas, in which you must choose whether a game will go over or under a given number. My head isn't ready to handicap that action yet, but I did get down on a "teaser."

A teaser is a teasing proposition reputedly invented by a professor at the University of Chicago in the 1920s. The basic idea is that the bettor gets points to play with but must pick two or more winners to collect at even money.

The Churchill Downs Race & Sports Book, one of several legal bookmaking emporiums in Vegas, offers 6-, 6½-, 7-, 10- and 14-point teasers. This means that you get the number of points specified in the bet to add to or subtract from the point spread. For example, the Falcons are favored over the Broncos by 10. If I decide to play a 6-point teaser I can take the Falcons giving only 4 (10 minus 6) or the Broncos with 16 (10 plus 6). The tease is that you must pick two games. If you pick three you get 8–5, four 5–2, five 4–1, six 6–1. If you want 6½ points you must lay 11–10 odds, 7 points 6–5 odds. If there is a tie the bet is off. With a 10-point teaser you must pick three winners and lay 6–5 odds, and a tie loses the bet. With a 14-point teaser you must pick four winners and lay 6–5 odds, and a tie loses.

I played the Falcons and the Redskins in a 7-point teaser laying $1,200 to $1,000. I preferred to lay the odds, risk an extra $200, and have the extra point, because it could be a crucial point with a 10-point spread. I took the Falcons giving 3 to the Broncos, and the Redskins, who were favored by 6½, with half a point over the Packers.

That $200 saved me $1,000. The Falcons beat the Broncos by a field goal for a tie on the teaser. The tie canceled the bet no matter what the Redskins did, but they won.

They didn't win by enough because the Packers, trailing by eight with two minutes left, elected to kick a field goal. They lost 24–19. That cost me one $500 bet. I got it back when the Bengals beat the Bears 13–3 for Gail and me. And I lost it back, ignominiously, on the Giants. The ignominy was threefold. They beat the Eagles 62–10. Sitting in Churchill Downs, watching the touchdowns march by on the electronic ticker tape board (identical to stock exchange tickers), I shook my head in self-ridicule. I mean you can't get mad when you lose 62–10. Not even at yourself.

But it meant that I lost my $5 bet to Archie Mulligan because it was the Giants' seventh win. And it meant that I need another win over them to pay for the sculpture. Are you sure that this is how the Mellons started their collection?

My misery again had company in Danny Lavezzo, whose travails top anything I can offer. Having bet the Giants all season, doing nicely although losing once because he got the worst of the line, he decided to show that he wasn't a sucker. The line was 14 and 14½ in New York and he was offered 15½. So he shrewdly took the Eagles.

Lem Banker won one (Steelers) and lost four (Redskins, Jets, Bills, Chiefs). Fats and The Mover won two (Lions, Steelers) and lost two (Cowboys, Bills). Mr. Rich won two (Lions, Steelers) and lost two (Chiefs, Bears). Fast Eddie won one (Lions) and lost two (Redskins, Vikings).

Frankie the Doorman became the first casualty of the wars. He said he wasn't going to bet for a while. "I got a $100 band job New Year's Eve," he said. "I'll have a few bucks to bet on the Super Bowl."

MONDAY

Take the gambling mentality one step further, from a gambler who looks for an edge to a hustler who wants the whole table, and you have Jack Molinas. Jack Molinas is here. Where else?

Jack Molinas was an All-American basketball player at Columbia and rookie of the year in the National Basketball Association and a two-time loser as a fixer. He was sent to jail, got out on parole, and while under surveillance by the police got nabbed again for fixing. The manipulation of people and money to beat the system, the game, whatever, were more exciting for him than making use of his considerable talents. He has graduated now to pornographic films (producing, not starring).

Molinas took time out between bouts at a crap table to tell me an amazing story of another football line—the one he made while booking games at Attica prison, a maximum-security institution in New York.

Because it was difficult to communicate with all parts of the prison, he said, his assistants would meet with him in the chapel during the football season. Molinas said he made up the line himself because no matter what it was he would be sure to win. (The currency was cigarettes, which have real purchasing power.)

"This is how I would give the line out," Molinas said. "We'd be praying, 'Our father who art in heaven'—*the Packers are 6*—'Hallowed be thy name'—*the Rams are 3½. . . .*"

I have it on excellent authority that the line originating out of Las Vegas is neither as haphazard nor as sanctified as that.

I have an appointment to talk to The Main Man, the man who sets the national line, tomorrow.

	My Line	Outlaw Line	Opening Line	Closing Line	
LIONS (17)	3	5	7	8	Jets*
COWBOYS	8	7	7½	7½	49ers* (21)
Bengals* (10)	3	3	2	2½	BEARS
FALCONS (3)	10	9	10	10	Broncos
REDSKINS* (5)	10	6½	7	7	Packers
CHARGERS (14)	10	11½	13	13½	Oilers
RAIDERS (23)	3	5	4	4½	Chiefs
Rams	12	11	12	13	SAINTS (3)
Vikings	3	P	2	1	STEELERS (13)
COLTS (31)	9	13	13	13	Patriots
GIANTS (52)	10	13	13	14	Eagles*
DOLPHINS (21)	14	14½	14	15	Cardinals

The public had seven winners and two losers, the pros three winners and eight losers. Favorites won eight and lost five, home teams won ten and lost four.

I lost $2,405, losing $2,000 on the Jets and $550 apiece on Eagles and Redskins, and $5 on my social bet, winning $500 on the 49ers and $400 on the Bengals ($500 minus $100). The bottom line sinks to $4,980.

It gives me a sinking feeling too, and reminds me of another conversation with my friend Vic Ziegel. When the bottom line was over $9,000 I wondered aloud whether I would bet all my winnings on the Super Bowl. "Who said you'll still be winning?" Ziegel zinged.

With friends like that, who needs bookies?

THE STANDINGS

AFC

				vs. spread	
	w	l	t	w	l
Eastern Division					
Dolphins	11	0	0	9	2
Jets	6	5	0	6	5
Colts	4	7	0	5	5
Bills	3	8	0	4	7
Patriots	2	9	0	3	7
Central Division					
Browns	8	3	0	8	3
Steelers	8	3	0	8	2
Bengals	6	5	0	7	4
Oilers	1	10	0	1	10
Western Division					
Raiders	7	3	1	5	6
Chiefs	5	6	0	4	7
Chargers	4	6	1	6	5
Broncos	3	8	0	4	7

NFC

	w	l	t	w	l
Eastern Division					
Redskins	10	1	0	7	3
Cowboys	8	3	0	3	8
Giants	7	4	0	6	3
Eagles	2	8	1	4	7
Cardinals	2	8	1	4	5
Central Division					
Lions	7	4	0	8	3
Packers	7	4	0	7	4
Vikings	6	5	0	3	7
Bears	3	7	1	4	7
Western Division					
49ers	6	4	1	5	6
Falcons	6	5	0	4	7
Rams	5	5	1	4	6
Saints	2	8	1	6	5

RESULTS

Lions 37, Jets 20
49ers 31, Cowboys 10
Browns 27, Bills 10
Bengals 13, Bears 3
Falcons 23, Broncos 20
Redskins 21, Packers 16
Chargers 34, Oilers 20
Raiders 26, Chiefs 3
Steelers 23, Vikings 10
Colts 31, Patriots 0
Giants 62, Eagles 10
Dolphins 31, Cardinals 10
Saints 19, Rams 16

BETTORS	w	l	pct.
Mr. Rich	28	12	.700
Merchant	31	23	.574
Lem Banker	44	33	.571
Fats–Mover	36	28	.562
Fast Eddie	25	23	.520

EXOTICA

Visitors 78, Home Teams 64
Favorites 80, Underdogs 58
Pros 53, Outlaw Line 41
Official Line 58, Public 47

Twelfth Week

TUESDAY

Bob Martin ran a bookmaking operation with three associates in a house next to the State Department in Washington, D.C. (laying odds, no doubt, on everything from the Berlin airlift to the Bay of Pigs). They were arrested, tried, convicted, and sentenced to five years in prison. The case went to the Supreme Court, stewarded by Edward Bennett Williams, the trial lawyer who is now president of the Redskins. Evidence had been gathered through presumably illegal wire-tapping.

Bob Martin was so certain that the verdict would be reversed that he took 10–1 odds from one of his associates, for $1,000 to $100, that the decision would be 9–0, unanimous, a forfeit. When the decision was handed down, he was sunning in Miami.

"I knew what the call was about as soon as I got it," Martin said today in his office at Churchill Downs. "I didn't ask for the verdict, I asked for the score. It was unanimous."

Bob Martin is fifty-three years old. He has a prominent forehead and Nixon-like jowls and blue X-ray vision eyes that give him the look of a wise old cherub. He grinned warmly as he spun the yarn, relishing it, I thought, because yarns like this are the chocolate soufflé of the eight-course banquet that the world of gamesmanship is to him.

"I middled a Supreme Court decision," he said, delighted to see the glee in my own baby blues.

This is a story that defines Bob Martin perfectly as a man of nerve and conviction, the qualities that make him The Main Man of bookmaking.

The Mover calls him "The Grandaddy."

Mr. Rhodes calls him "The Taj Mahal."

Lefty Rosenthal, perhaps the most important bettor in the country (whom I will interview during my stay in Vegas), calls him "An original."

Lem Banker says, "He's the leader. Everyone else is a follower."

Bob Martin is in effect the commissioner of games betting in America, the David Rockefeller of odds and spreads. He is an ordinary, pleasant, likable fellow whose word is taken as gospel by a multibillion-dollar industry.

He has achieved his status in the free marketplace of betting because he is better than anyone else at his job. He said one thing that describes his preeminence:

"I don't bet money—I bet faces."

What this means is that he couldn't care less if you or I walked off the street and wanted to bet him the mortgage on a football game. He would smile, write the bet down and stick the mortgage in a drawer. He would not move the line a half point.

But, he said, if a professional, a man whose opinion he respects, bet a couple or three thousand or more, then and only then might he make an adjustment.

That is profound. It is the essence of how the line is formed and what makes Bob Martin the last of the super bookies. Unlike lesser men who nervously shift the line around, Martin refuses to be intimidated by public money (except on the Super Bowl, where the volume is overpowering). He has absolute faith in his own judgment, refined by a consensus of betting pros and backed by the 11–10 odds. Just tell him what you want to bet and you're down. He is willing to take financial risks because he knows that you are likely, over a period of bets, to stay down.

Martin conjures a line every Monday from a witch's stew of records, power ratings, horned toads and intuition, which includes a feel for how the public backs certain popular teams—this season the Dolphins, Redskins, Steelers and Packers—called public teams. That's the only concession he makes to public taste. He has a United Press International sports wire in his office, keeping him abreast of developments (i.e., serious injuries). The final stage:

"I ask myself whether I would bet a game at a number," he said. "I keep moving the number until I feel I wouldn't bet either side. That's the number."

The numbers are exposed to "eight or ten" pros during the day. This is the line that is called the outlaw line, or the early line, or the service line. Martin has a limit (higher than his competitors) that can be bet into this line at half-point increments (as bookies universally do). If he makes a game 3 you can bet it to the limit, then bet it again at 2½ or 3½, as the case may be. This process shakes the line down to the hard numbers that will be posted for all comers Tuesday.

This is how Bob Martin sets the line that is the basis, with regional adjustments, for the line from Seattle to Miami, San Diego to Boston, Memphis to Saint Joe.

(Other bookies in Vegas follow a similar procedure, but they don't have Martin's acumen, nerve or capital. His steadfastness, like the steadfastness of a strong bank, gives his jumpy competitors courage to stand firm.)

"I wish I had 100 professionals," Martin said. "They all have good opinions, but half of them would like one side and half the other. And they're easy to do business with. They pay."

Martin conceded that the system is imperfect. But nobody has come up with a better one, and it works—which is all that counts. "I make mistakes," he said. "I might like a team and stay with my opinion too long. I think I've had about fifteen losers in a row on my opinion. Last year we lost quite a bit on football because there were an unusual number of middles. The numbers we had were too good, so they weren't good for us."

What he meant by that was that the biggest danger to the bookie is a game landing right on the spread, say 4, because he might have had bets on 3½ one way and 4½ the other. On the weekends, when the pros and betting groups make their big plays, Martin adjusts the spreads accordingly, in a large-scale repeat of the Monday shakedown. He takes no interstate calls for betting purposes, but it is apparent that bets are relayed to him by local representatives of groups and individuals from around the country (the same representatives who early in the week phone out reports of Martin's line and changes).

A paradox in Martin's perception of the pros is that he is more willing to pit himself against them than his respect should seem to warrant. His very lack of jitters—"My wife says I'm a robot," he said—in opposing their theoretically well-informed money suggests a certain contempt. He squares the paradox by reminding you of the 11–10.

"I'd like to go on a cruise with any of them," he said. "If I have the 11–10 they won't beat me."

I'd like to test him myself, providing the cruise stopped off at Saint-Tropez, Hong Kong, Honolulu and San Francisco.

"What about dry land, though, where the pros supposedly have access to so much terrific information?"

"Same thing," Bob Martin said.

"How do they make a living then?"

"They do other things. They have ways."

"What ways?"

"Ways. Ask them."

I assume he means scalping (which is a form of bookmaking), betting other pros to avoid the vigorish, touting and "bearding" (secretly betting for groups or for individuals who don't want to broadcast their selections). I will have to ask them.

"They've had good seasons," Martin said. "But I don't believe a player (professional) can beat me. Not year in and year out."

"What about a football player?" I asked him about fixes, suspicions, great dumps of yesteryear.

"If a player isn't greedy he can probably get away with it," he said. "But if he tries to make a lot of money it's easy to spot."

"How so?"

He explained why the Chiefs were not bettable for several games in 1966 (about which I will comment on further before I leave Vegas).

Martin said two or more players were involved in a

point-shaving conspiracy. He said they had an acquaintance bet $1,500 for each of them against themselves. The acquaintance, naturally, added something of his own. Suddenly a man who was betting a thousand or two was betting $5,000 or more.

"It pyramids," Martin said. "The bookie they were dealing with smelled something, so he bet another bookie $10,000, right down the line until someone in Texas tried to win the whole world. He bet $200,000."

An alarm, a red light, a siren, and sun spots went off, alerting the betting community to a probable coup. The Chiefs were taken off the board.

In the course of our discussion on dumps of the past, Martin mentioned a name that rang an alert bell in my head. A player is known among veteran bettors as "Offsides -----" because in a game in the fifties, according to Martin, he got himself penalized to avert a late touchdown that would have affected the result for bettors. The player is the one identified by my confessed dumper as having arranged a fix with eleven teammates.

Martin said he was not suspicious of hanky-panky this season, nor has he had strong suspicions since the Chiefs. He said there was an NFL official he was "curious about." If his curiosity was aroused again he would, first, check every game the official has worked and, second, collate that with his memory of where the important money came from on those games. If there is a significant trend, Martin said, he would make sure it got back to Pete Rozelle, somehow.

"The money always shows up here," Martin said, meaning that whenever and wherever big money is bet in America it will be reflected in Las Vegas, meaning with himself. I asked him why this was so. He cited two reasons that The Mover gave—few big offices, few of those remaining that will take big bets close to game time—and a third.

"We pay," he said. "Some people might not."

What did he mean by that?

He had a parable. "A few years back the mob declared themselves partners with a bookie in Baltimore," he said. "This was in the baseball season. The first week they lost. The second week they lost. The third week they lost. The fourth week they lost. The fifth week the mob declared itself out. They don't like to lose."

WEDNESDAY

Public team.

That phrase has been haunting me since yesterday. Public team. I've heard players and bookies use it any number of times in the few days I've been here, and today, studying the board at Churchill Downs, the significance of the term hit me.

Theory No. 11 is that you bet on the public team early in the week and against the public team late in the week. Every season has its public teams, teams that win convincingly and are backed by the public, usually glamour teams like the Dolphins or Packers. The public supports these teams and the sharp bettor can capitalize on it. If you like the public team to win, bet early because you'll get less or give more points as the game approaches. If you don't like the public team, wait until the last minute when chances are that you'll get more or give less points. I've been doing this instinctively all season, but the concept of the public team may make it easier to keep track of. This is another way to squeeze every half and full point to your advantage.

But do as I say, not as I always do. I immediately bet $1,000 on the Lions with 2½ over the Packers because I'm not sure, on this game, what funny bounce the line might take. If the money is on the Packers, as is likely, I may bet more on the Lions. These two teams were separated by a point the last time they played, and Charlie Sanders didn't play then, and the Packers, though winning, have been struggling on offense in their last three games.

	My Line	Outlaw Line	Opening Line	
Colts	10	11	10	Bills
Vikings	13	12	12½	Bears
Steelers	10	7	7½	Browns
Cowboys	13	10	11	Cardinals
Chiefs	4	6	6	Broncos
Packers	6	2	2½	Lions
Falcons	13	16	15	Oilers
Dolphins	20	17	16	Patriots
Jets	10	12	11	Saints
Bengals	P	2	1	Giants
Raiders	6	4	3½	Chargers
Redskins	20	17	17	Eagles
49ers	6	6	5½	Rams

Two more thoughts for the day occurred to me as I scanned the lines. One is that the collective wisdom of the pros is not that far removed from the collective innocence of the public. Two is that I am bucking the collective wisdom more than the collective innocence because the pros are more instrumental in establishing the line.

Three: great. The Walter Mitty in my romantic heart

is now engaged in direct mortal combat, dueling on castle steps, with the pro football betting establishment. *En garde.*

THURSDAY

For recreation, between duels, I've been exchanging my Errol Flynn saber for the Cincinnati Kid's poker face. I'm better with the saber.

I blew $1,900 in three marathon poker sessions of eight to ten hours. Had a wonderful time.

My last active experience in poker dates back to spring training with the Phillies, when I played for a dollar and two and laughs with Richie Ashburn and Solly Hemus and others on rainy days. I sat down here with a bunch of cutthroats and assassins in one of the hotels on The Strip. Table stakes stud poker. I was the mare.

First night I called the bluff of a guy named Slim and damned if he wasn't bluffing. Not every day a tourist beats a guy named Slim out of a $200 pot. I wound up $400 in the hole.

Thought that was it, but I won the $400 back at a crap table in ten minutes. Went back the next night for more, and felt cruel for driving a nice kid out of the game by outdrawing his jacks with queens. If it wasn't me it would have been someone else, but it was me. I wound up $500 in the hole.

Thought that was it, but I won the $500 back at a crap table in fifteen minutes. Went back the next night for more, and found out why I'm not a poker player. I raised a guy $200 and had him licked, my aces to his best-possible kings—which is like betting a football game when you know the score—and still my hand trembled when I pushed the chips in. I don't have the nerve or the skill or the vulturelike patience of the pros. I wound up $1,000 in the hole, busted, and was consoled by a wizened dealer who said it had cost him a quarter million dollars and he never did learn the game.

Here lies a man, to paraphrase an old tombstone epitaph, who tried to beat three fives with aces up.

FRIDAY

Had a blissful spat with Gail, long distance, today. She was unhappy that I was betting on the Lions for her. It had to come to this.

"We've won every time we bet against the Bears," she said. "Why don't we bet against the Bears?"

"The Vikings, love, are favored by 12," I said. "I don't bet games in which I have to give that many points."

"I don't care," she said. "I want to bet against the Bears."

"Then bet against them," I said. "I'm betting the Lions."

"Who am I going to bet with?"

"That's your problem."

"That's mean. Then bet $100 on the Lions and $100 on the Bears."

"Nope. I don't want you to get sane too fast. I'll never catch up."

"Pooh."

"Give my regards to Misha."

These conversations are so free of the usual undertone of tension that I wonder why I didn't think of sharing my betting experiences with her before. In five years we have metamorphosed from a bettor's noncommunication to a couple held together by telephone wire and betting palaver.

And now for a few choruses of "Adelaide's Lament."

SATURDAY

I had breakfast with Joe DiMaggio today. Mark it down as one of the highlights of the season.

Joe DiMaggio was the mythic centerpiece of my childhood. Like most budding baseball sophisticates of his time, I aped his mannerisms, lingered over his name in boxscores, treasured bubblegum cards with his likeness. I rooted for the Yankees because all my relatives did—it being instilled in me like religion: They never took me anywhere but Yankee Stadium until I had experienced communion—and I suppose they rooted for the Yankees because, as Yankee fan Paul Simon once explained, with all the other troubles in life who needed the Dodgers? And Babe Ruth was their Joe Namath.

So now, in answer to Simon's plaintive "Where have you gone, Joe DiMaggio?", we are in Las Vegas in the year 1972 having breakfast. He peeked into Churchill Downs this morning, looked around for anyone he might recognize, and it was me; I have interviewed him several times in recent years. Imperial and imperious as a player, he is a gracious, silver-haired old-timer, nearing sixty, looking much younger, maintaining his mythic presence.

We talked about banking and fishing. Banking because his face is a quality brand for a New York bank's recent advertising campaign, twenty years after he retired. Fishing because it was a major prop of the DiMaggio legend.

His father was a commercial fisherman in Italy and San Francisco; his early baseball riches were invested in a restaurant on Fisherman's Wharf; there were annual spring training stories about DiMaggio fishing; indeed, the old man in Ernest Hemingway's *The Old Man and the Sea* fished for his marlin with DiMaggio's legend as his mate. DiMaggio fishes no more. He has a boat, a thirty-footer, he said, but he hasn't been on it in two years. His brothers Vince and Dom fish off it, for Pacific salmon. Joe is the world's guest, traveling, playing golf, posing for bank ads. No Captain Ahab he.

For breakfast he had Cream of Wheat with skimmed milk. I was a Wheaties and oatmeal kid myself.

SUNDAY

When you're in a slump, hit the ball up the middle, don't swing from the heels. That's what they told us, and that's what I did today. I think I'm out of my slump.

The Packers wasted the Lions, forced six turnovers in their first nine possessions and ran all over them 33–7. I can't imagine what consequences this will have on my love life, but I played two safe teasers and they promise to compensate for any teasing from Gail that I may have to deal with.

Lem Banker said he plays teasers on rare occasions, but he offered me some sage advice about them: "It looks like an easy way out, but it's a sign that you're losing confidence in your handicapping. You have to keep battling it."

I wanted to battle it, but seven of the twelve games had spreads of more than a touchdown and I wasn't enchanted with the remaining five. So I played a 14-point teaser for $1,000, reducing the Dolphins (16-point favorites) to 2 over the Patriots, the Redskins (15-point favorites) to 1 over the Eagles, the Falcons (15-point favorites to 1 over the Oilers, the Raiders (4-point favorites) to 10 under the Chargers. I had four playoff contenders playing four bad teams, three of them had only to win and the fourth had to lose by about a touchdown at worst. The big favorites won easily, but the Raiders were on the brink of a disaster for me before rallying to win.

The second teaser, a 7-pointer, also for $1,000, is half won. I took the Steelers (a 9-point favorite) at 2 over the Browns and the Rams (a 6-point underdog) with 13 points over the 49ers tomorrow night. The Steelers mashed the Browns 30–0. Feeling better about things, guaranteed a winning week if the Rams don't fall off the edge of the earth, I also bet on them straight up, with 6 points. I didn't feel as positive about them as did Lem, who wrote in his column in the *Review-Journal,* "If you don't bet the Rams, you ought to quit betting," but they should dominate the 49ers at the line of scrimmage a nickel's worth.

I got my first taste of the total-points line and the half-time line too, but I didn't swallow either of them. The average number of points in an NFL game is 39 or 40. These were the numbers you had to go over or under today: Redskins–Eagles 39, Giants–Bengals 40, Jets–Saints 44, Dolphins–Patriots 38, Falcons–Oilers 39, Packers–Lions 42, Chiefs–Broncos 42, Vikings–Bears 36, Colts–Bills 38, Raiders–Chargers 44, Cowboys–Cardinals 39, Steelers–Browns 42. There were two overs and ten unders.

A half-time line is available only for television games (so the linemaker can check injuries). The Bengals led the Giants 6–3 and were 1-point favorites in the second half. The Steelers led the Browns 10–0 and were 4-point favorites in the second half. Lem showed what a sophisticated bettor can do with these propositions. He had the Bengals giving 1 point in the game, so he hedged a part of his bet by taking the Giants with 1 in the second half. Result: He caught a middle. The Bengals won 13–10; the second half was a 7–7 tie.

Lem had a big day, winning seven (Bengals, Patriots, Oilers, Steelers, Vikings, Chargers, Eagles) and losing three (Jets, Lions, Cards). Everyone else went into mourning. The Mover won two (Steelers, Bengals) and lost four (Lions, Bills, Chiefs, Falcons). Fats said he has already lost $8,000 this season betting with The Mover. "I think the bookies start all those rumors to get people to bet," he said. Mr. Rich lost both of his bets (Lions, Giants) and Fast Eddie lost his three bets (Giants, Jets, Raiders). Lem has the Rams tomorrow, the others have the 49ers.

Monday

Mrs. Cavanaugh would have a stroke if she saw what I saw tonight. I saw a parliament of "wise guys."

Mrs. Cavanaugh was my seventh-grade math teacher. Driven by raging carnal desires, I'd throw spitballs at Cherry the blonde, and Mrs. Cavanaugh would snarl nasally, like Eliza Doolittle in the first act, "Wise guy, eh? Stand up in the back where I can see you, wise guy."

Mrs. Cavanaugh, wherever you are, in Las Vegas "wise guy" is a term of approbation, of endearment even. It is, one gathers, just about the biggest compliment you can give a guy, calling him wise. It is a synonym for a player or a pro.

The Rams had won the TV game and now the wise guys were sitting around a green felt-topped card table, kibitzing, sounding each other out. From this klatch would emerge a proposition or two or a dozen. It is an informal ritual, outside the formal rituals that determine the consensus on next weekend's action, but a part of it in the way that nonpublic stock deals are part of the stock market dynamic.

"If you went into a room with them, you'd come out bleeding," Lem Banker said. "They are the sharpest guys around, triple-sharp. You have to play dumb with them, listen to twenty bad propositions until you get one you can step in on."

They are sports-wise, angle-wise, odds-wise guys who have gravitated to Vegas from all over the country. Sessions like these are their shootouts. They carry notebooks and pencils in their jacket pockets as though they are pistols and holsters. At the drop of a proposition they whip them out and it's every man for himself.

Propositions may vary from the odds on division races to individual yardage leaders in a game to guessing the number of freckles on Archie Manning's nose. But the main game is what Lem Banker called "turning numbers over." Two bettors pick a game or games to bet, at a predetermined figure. They write down the spread they think each game should be on a slip of paper, then turn them up. The bettors must then bet either way on their opponent's spread. For example, one bettor may have made the 49ers 7-point favorites, the other bettor may have made them 4-point favorites. One bettor had to decide whether to give or take 7 points, the other 4 points. If one bettor took the Rams and 7 and gave the 49ers and 4, he could win both bets—a middle—if the game landed on 5 or 6.

Mrs. Cavanaugh, I stood in the back of the room, but I didn't play. I'm not a real wise guy.

The week that was:

	My Line	Outlaw Line	Opening Line	Closing Line	
COLTS (28)	10	11	10	10½	Bills
VIKINGS (13)	13	12	12½	13	Bears
STEELERS (30)	10	7	7½	9	Browns
Cowboys (21)	13	10	11	11½	CARDINALS
CHIEFS (3)	4	6	6	6	Broncos
PACKERS (26)	6	2	2½	3	Lions*
FALCONS (10)	13	16	15	15	Oilers
DOLPHINS (16)	20	17	16	16	Patriots
JETS (1)	10	12	11	13	Saints
BENGALS (3)	P	2	1	P	Giants
Raiders (2)	6	4	3½	4½	CHARGERS
Redskins (16)	20	17	17	16	EAGLES
49ERS	6	6	5½	6	Rams* (10)

The pros won nine and lost two, the public won six and lost four. Home teams and visitors won five games apiece. Underdogs won five, favorites four.

I won $1,510 for the week, winning two $1,000 teasers and $500 on the Rams, losing $990 on the Lions ($1,100 minus $110 for Gail). The bottom line is $6,490, and God is in His heaven.

THE STANDINGS

AFC

				vs.	spread
	w	l	t	w	l
Eastern Division					
Dolphins	12	0	0	9	2*
Jets	7	5	0	6	6
Colts	5	7	0	5	5
Bills	3	9	0	4	8
Patriots	2	10	0	3	7*
Central Division					
Steelers	9	3	0	9	2
Browns	8	4	0	8	4
Bengals	7	5	0	8	4
Oilers	1	11	0	2	10
Western Division					
Raiders	8	3	1	5	7
Chiefs	6	6	0	4	8
Chargers	4	7	1	6	5
Broncos	3	9	0	5	7

NFC

	w	l	t	w	l
Eastern Division					
Redskins	11	1	0	7	3*
Cowboys	9	3	0	4	8
Giants	7	5	0	6	4
Eagles	2	9	1	4	7*
Cardinals	2	9	1	4	6
Central Division					
Packers	8	4	0	8	4
Lions	7	5	0	8	4
Vikings	7	5	0	3	7*
Bears	3	8	1	4	7*
Western Division					
Falcons	7	5	0	4	8
Rams	6	5	1	5	6
49ers	6	5	1	5	7
Saints	2	9	1	7	5

* Tie

RESULTS

Colts 35, Bills 7
Vikings 23, Bears 10
Steelers 30, Browns 0
Cowboys 27, Cardinals 6
Chiefs 24, Broncos 21
Packers 33, Lions 7
Falcons 20, Oilers 10
Dolphins 37, Patriots 21
Jets 18, Saints 17
Bengals 13, Giants 10
Raiders 21, Chargers 19
Redskins 23, Eagles 7
Rams 26, 49ers 16

BETTORS	w	l	pct.
Mr. Rich	28	15	.651
Lem Banker	52	36	.591
Merchant	34	24	.586
Fats–Mover	38	33	.535
Fast Eddie	25	27	.480

EXOTICA

Visitors 83, Home Teams 69
Favorites 84, Underdogs 63
Pros 62, Outlaw Line 43
Official Line 62, Public 63

Thirteenth Week

TUESDAY

The wise guys have a saying: "I swept the board." This means they won all their bets. Skeptic that I am, I always assume it means they won two out of three or three out of four.

The wise guys have another saying: "I held my own." This means they broke even. Skeptic that I am, I always assume it means they lost two out of three or three out of four.

What I really think is that there is something Freudian about this holding your own.

If you don't want to wind up holding your own, this is the time of season when a bettor has to be as cautious as the bookies are. All but three games this week are "circle games." A circle game is a betting-limit game because there is nothing at stake in it for one or both teams. The wise guys call them exhibitions because a team that has already clinched a playoff berth, like the Redskins, may not play regulars for the entire game (George Allen already has stated that he will rest Larry Brown); and a team that is out of the race may experiment or, according to the wise guys, play with less zeal than a team with a shot at the playoffs. The three uncircled games this week are the Packers–Vikings, Falcons–49ers, Browns–Bengals—all six teams are playoff contenders.

I bet one of those games, putting $500 on the Browns with 3 points over the Bengals. I like the Browns because they get into the end zone better than the Bengals when they have to. The strength of the Browns is their offense, the strength of the Bengals is their defense: I think the Browns' strength will prevail.

(This could be a game in which the line influences the public. But Bob Martin said, when I asked him whether the betting pattern would change if the Browns were favored, "No, they'd bet the Bengals until they were favored by 2 or 3.")

There were two circle games that appealed to me, for myriad reasons, not all of which had to do with Hegelian handicapping. I went for $500 on the Dolphins giving 6½ to the Giants. Need I say more? This is the best of all possible worlds, a bet combining logic and emotion. Logic says the Dolphins are more than a touchdown better than the Giants. The wise guys say the Dolphins won't be putting out 110 percent because they've clinched the division, but I think they want to be great men and go undefeated. Also I need the $500 to get back what the Giants owe me for the sculpture.

I put $500 on the Chiefs giving 1½ to the Colts. The Colts have won four games since Marty Domres replaced Johnny Unitas, but three of them have been over the Patriots and Bills. Hank Stram has been quoted that he will play all his first-string people, including several just recovered from injuries, and that's all I need to know. The Chiefs' people are better than the Colts' people.

The lineup looks so:

	My Line	Outlaw Line	Opening Line	
Bengals	3	3	4	Browns
Cowboys	4	3½	6½	Redskins
49ers	6	6	6	Falcons
Chiefs	4	3	2½	Colts
Bears	1	3	4	Eagles
Lions	12	12	12½	Bills
Vikings	6	3	4	Packers
Rams	6	7	11	Cardinals
Dolphins	10	5	6½	Giants
Saints	7	9	10	Patriots
Steelers	13	14	14	Oilers
Chargers	4	3½	3	Broncos
Raiders	8	3	4½	Jets

The pros made a strong move on the Cowboys not so much because Larry Brown is unlikely to play (which to me is the crucial factor), but because Billy Kilmer suffered a minor injury Sunday, for which he was briefly hospitalized. Their thinking is that George Allen won't risk him in a meaningless game for the Redskins. Conversely, the bookies, anticipating letdowns by the Dolphins and Raiders, made the spreads so low that the pros jumped on them.

WEDNESDAY

"Gambling," said an old-time gambler known as Cheesecake Ike, "is the worst, meanest business in the world. Everyone hates one another."

If this be true, Lem Banker is an orchid grown wild in a garbage dump. Everyone seems to like him. Gene Mauch, the baseball manager, said of the saintly Alvin

Dark, "He's the kind of guy we'd all like to be if we had the time," and that's how Lem Banker is regarded by his peers. They recite his virtues as though he were a Boy Scout: loyal, trustworthy, honest, friendly, industrious, nonimbibing. I'm sure he helps old ladies across the street.

I also marvel at his audacity in betting so many games —and winning.

The credit probably goes to clean living. Although he decks himself out in Las Vegas mod (suede Ike jackets, two-tone shoes), Lem Banker would be thrown off the set of *Guys and Dolls* as an impostor. Few athletes take care of themselves as well, are as dedicated, or construct an environment as harmonious to their profession. Animated by a wry feeling of tribal fellowship, he glides unobtrusively among the brasher hustlers and wise guys. He regards their schemes and dreams as colorful incense. He regards himself as a businessman in an exciting business.

"A gambler is like anyone else who uses his head in his work," Lem said. "You have to keep a sound body and sound mind. You need a good wife who won't be involved in keeping up with the Joneses. You have to avoid emotional involvements. Gamblers get screwed up when they lose their heads over beautiful women. There are millions of stories about that. You need stability to think clearly. Health, stability, credit. You have that, you have everything."

Lem lives with his wife Debbie and thirteen-year-old daughter and a menagerie of cats and dogs in a Spanish-style ranch house. There's a pool and a heavy punching bag and gym equipment out back. Lem said he works out nearly every day. He jogs. He rides a bicycle. He takes steam two or three times a week. He is, at 6′–3″, age forty-six, built like a tight end. He doesn't smoke, drinks only socially. But he isn't perfect. He has a sinful weakness for ice cream.

An adding machine on the kitchen table, a typewriter nearby. This is Lem's office. His tools are notebooks crammed with records and ratings, notebooks that are neatly inscribed ledgers, sports magazines and other publications, a telephone with three exchanges, sharpened pencils and colored pens. He is as meticulous as a tax accountant, as organized as the Dallas Cowboys.

Lem emigrated to Vegas from Union City, New Jersey, eighteen years ago. His father was a bookmaker. He was an outstanding high school basketball player, went to Long Island University and the University of Miami. "It's ridiculous: you cross the state line and you're legitimate. I came here because I wanted to be a first-class citizen," he said. "I tried to make it in every kind of business, but gambling is the only one I'm good at. It's my profession. If you know what you're doing it's like almost any other business. Sometimes I have losing streaks and I wish I had a normal job, but then I win a few and I'm okay."

Selling stationery or building skyscrapers it isn't. "Lem can't eat without a telephone," his wife Debbie said. Or a transistor radio. Lem tells the story of the gambler who inexplicably cracks up and cries at his uncle's funeral. Nobody understands it. Lem does. The gambler's transistor has just given him a terrible result. Lem has a calico cat that he cradles when he needs to pull a game out. And a lucky sweat shirt that Debbie readies for him on television game days. Magic can't hurt.

"Sure there's tension and nerves," Lem said. "But you take the greatest dramatists in the world—Shakespeare, Shaw—they couldn't improve on the scripts you get in ballgames."

Lem's philosophy of handicapping and betting can be summed up in three maxims:

"It's a game of values."

"You're only as good as your information."

"You don't go overboard on one game. You're dealing with human beings. Anything can happen. A kid athlete could jump out of the fourth story of a hotel the night before a game to impress a girl."

By a game of values, Lem means, "You're in a store. There's something for $125, you wouldn't look at it. But if the same thing cost $25, you'd look at it, maybe buy it. It has value. That's how I bet a game. Certain games, certain teams have values."

Lem is saying that there are known statistical quantities that you start with—the Browns shouldn't be 7-point underdogs at home, the Chiefs seldom cover a big spread, the Redskins are a bargain at 6 but no bet at 8 over some teams, etc.—and work from there. One thing I've noticed is that this formula betting encourages Lem to bet on more underdogs than I do and on many more than the public does.

From that basic start, he works with information, knowledge, opinion. Despite his businesslike approach, he often bets intuitively, picking a team and then looking for reasons why, as I probably do at times. But he knows the game well. We have discussed games, matchups, personnel and so on at length, and we've come to respect and handicap each other's views. This exchange of ideas is included in what Lem calls information, as it should be.

As the season wore on, he got increasingly disenchanted with injury reports, declaring that the chances of seizing an advantage on such information in pro football are small today.

Does he only bet on games, or does he have a side dodge? There are so many bettors in Vegas that he probably saves the vigorish by betting with them when he can, but that's hardly a dodge. He can play a money game similar to scalping, or what is known on the stock market as arbitrage, by "buying and selling points." He can bet early in the week, anticipating the movement of the line, and sell the bet at a more favorable price later in the week, giving him a free bet.

I told Lem that Bob Martin said no player beats the odds consistently. "Every housewife thinks she makes the best spaghetti sauce, and every gambler thinks he's the best," he said, tooling along The Strip in his new Mark IV.

THURSDAY–FRIDAY

What am I doing here?

I've said that to myself any number of times. Hitchhiking from New Orleans to Oklahoma one Easter recess, I took two hours of a record of Eddie Arnold singing "Any Time" on a loudspeaker outside a roadhouse and picked myself up and walked into the pitch black Louisiana night. What am I doing here? Got a ride from a drunk who careened through thick fog at eighty miles an hour, deposited me in the lobby of his father's motel, where I slept until father appeared. What am I doing here?

And the first time I bargained for hay with a farmer near my fifty acres (forty rented) and twelve boarded horses in New Jersey. Bought the hay for $25 a ton right out of the field, like I knew what I was doing. What am I doing here? I was going to take a course in hay at Rutgers when my marriage broke up. Took up betting instead.

So I asked myself what I was doing here Thursday morning flying to Chicago, Illinois, from Las Vegas, Nevada. Gail called very early. I was expecting flak over the Lions' bet, but this was going too far. Misha wants to see me—us. Her play's run has ended, and there are six weeks until she goes into rehearsal for her Broadway debut, and what do we do now? I'm a gambler. I went.

Cabbed to Misha's office from the airport. We talked about the book. He was, as were two other analysts I've met while researching, incredulous over my winning. Psychiatrists, like law enforcers, don't come across winners in their work. I liked Misha although I knew his function was to preside over a defeat. I like anyone who asks me to talk about myself.

We talked for two days, Misha and me, Misha and her, Misha, her and me. We played parlor games of psychodrama. (What am I doing here?) And at the end we were exactly where we were at the beginning, at an impasse. I wanted to try to patch up our blowout. She wanted to hobble along on a flat. I said good-bye to all that and we split again. All bets were off.

Thirty seconds before the plane was scheduled to leave the terminal, the finality of this split made me say to myself once more, what am I doing here? Blurs of all the times I responded too late with too little, or too much, to someone else's need flashed on and off like the fasten-your-seatbelt-sign. Photo slides of desperation passes on last down. Rust-colored carpeting retreated rapidly under my feet. Airlines people converged on the entrance. I was inside the terminal, calling her.

Coaching a championship high school game, I stood on the sidelines next to our line coach, muttering the plays I thought our quarterback should be calling. Every play I called he mind-read, guiding the team to a touchdown. The line coach asked me if I had given the quarterback a sequence of plays. I hadn't. The quarterback, who was my pupil, and I were tuned to the same frequency.

Our defenses down, remembering things past, luminous clock hands moving on, Gail and I found that pore-to-pore rapport on our last night.

Sometimes I also ask myself, why can't a woman be more like a man?

SATURDAY

I arrived back in Vegas for the fourth quarter of the Browns and Bengals. Chicago seemed as unreal, or real, as a clear dream. I slipped into my football mindset and watched the Browns cling to a lead and win $500 for me. There were some hairy moments, but I never wavered. Subdued, or numb, or sleepy, I watched dispassionately. I couldn't decide whether my love life was an anesthetic for my betting life or vice versa.

I had a dinner engagement with the Bankers. We were to meet at a bar in the Dunes. There was a roulette wheel in front of the bar. Three blacks came up in a row. I put a $5 chip on black. It multiplied into $500. That woke me up like a shaft of sunlight hitting me in the eye. I went to a blackjack table and quickly won $200. I grabbed the money and ran to a crap table and won $400. This seemed as good a time as any to try baccarat. Baccarat is a dull card game favored by gamblers because the cut of the house is the smallest of any game, 5 percent of winnings. I lost $800 and joined the Bankers for dinner.

"How was Chicago?" Lem asked.

"What I expected."

"Anything exciting happening?"

"Same old stuff."

I had a dream. Muhammad Ali lost a fight and toured the ring by himself, acknowledging wave upon wave of tumultuous applause.

Phil Esposito told me winning is losing. Muhammad Ali tells me losing is winning. Plainly, I need to go in for repairs. Meanwhile I can't wait to hear from Hank Aaron, Don Meredith and Billie Jean King.

SUNDAY

I swept the board.

With the win by the Browns tucked away, I bet another $500 on the Dolphins, giving 7 to the Giants. The Dolphins won 23–13. Thank you very much, Giants. The Chiefs did away with the Colts 24–10.

"You're back on the beam," my self said to myself.

"When you lose you want to win, and when you win you want to win more."

"I noticed that on Thanksgiving Day. You went slightly berserk, as I recall."

"I like winning. I like wanting to win. But I try my lousy best to win in tennis, and I'm a sensational loser: gracious, cheerful, good sport. Losing control of myself because I was losing a bet still astonishes me. Guess I don't really care about tennis."

"Maybe what astonishes you is that you're feeling. Not holding back."

"Maybe I was toilet-trained only to be a good winner; losing was left out. Undefeated in high school. Two out of three undefeated seasons as a coach. Oklahoma never lost. Yankee fan in my formative years; hell, my mother took me to see Babe Ruth when she was pregnant with me."

"Life's not that simple."

"Profound. Maybe I should have rooted for the Dodgers, gone to Columbia, and had my mother take me to the stock market crash."

"You did take a big loss well this week."

"Maybe I didn't care anymore. No, scratch that. I'd be celebrating, not cerebralizing, if I didn't care. It hasn't hit me yet."

"What was it Casey Stengel said? 'The trick is to grow up without growing old.' "

"I imagine it's a nifty balancing act if you get the hang of it, maturity and adolescence on a seesaw. Right now I've got to go with my strength, got to win."

"Might be hard on your sofa. And your tennis racket."

"If one of us has to come unstrung, I'd rather it was the racket."

"Maybe you'll get restrung in a pro shop together."

"Maybe I'll keep winning and live happily ever after."

Lem Banker had another good week, winning seven (Cowboys, Dolphins, Oilers, Cardinals, Chiefs, Bills, Broncos) and losing three (Bengals, Vikings, Saints).

Fats and The Mover finally had a big one, going four-for-four (Bills, Bears, Dolphins, Cardinals). Mr. Rich won one (Browns) and lost two (Redskins, Colts). Fast Eddie split, winning two (Chiefs, Dolphins) and losing two (Redskins, Steelers). Lem is betting the Jets tomorrow, everyone else is on the Raiders.

MONDAY

Flew to Oakland for the Jets–Raiders, leaving a $200 bet behind on the Raiders, giving 6½. This is what I call a contrary bet, contrary to conventional wisdom. There is a contrary streak in me that is connected to the bullshit-detector that most journalists are born with. What I'm contrary to is the cynical theology of Vegas.

With the second exhibition season upon us, there is much furious cogitating and inside-informationing going on as the wise guys grope for their coveted edges. There is a down-home logic to this that has some credence. As in preseason exhibitions, a coach may rest first-stringers (for the playoffs).

But I am skeptical of claims that gamblers are keen students of human nature and therefore can divine the (late-season) moods of athletes. All gamblers play this game occasionally, and when they win they think they are entitled to hang out a shingle at $50 an hour and when they lose they blame fumbles. Their insights into the motivational behavior of a highly motivated species are simplistic—the corollary to a "must" game being a who-cares game—and spiritually unacceptable to me. I don't know about you, but I'm not a sinner. A little loony is all.

Two examples of Las Vegas motivational research practically applied:

Saturday the money was on the Cowboys, who hadn't clinched a playoff spot, over the Redskins, who had. The word was "The Redskins aren't trying." In the sense that they aren't trying if they don't play Larry Brown, that's true. In the sense that therefore everyone else, being human, would roll over and die, that's galloping know-nothingism; despite the injury, Billy Kilmer started and finished. The Cowboys roared to a big lead and cries of "The Redskins aren't trying!" drowned out the squeals at the slot machines and banzai shouts at the crap tables. The Redskins then roared back and very nearly tied the game. The word of their rollover suffocated in many dry throats.

The Cowboys won, but on Sunday the Lions didn't. The Lions, still in the running for the playoffs, were tied by the Bills, who were out of it. Were the Bills trying? The word was that they were "loose" because they had nothing to lose.

The word then, whatever it is, is a two-headed coin. Heads ("they're not trying") the wise guys win. Heads ("they're loose") the wise guys win. There is an explanation for everything, except what the game is about.

I bet on the Raiders because they're the better team, because star runner John Riggins wasn't going to play for the Jets, and because word was that the playoff-bound Raiders wouldn't play their top players for the full game. Confirmation of Riggins's injury status turned around the late betting toward the Raiders, it being prized intelligence that transcended religious preferences for the Jets. What happened was that everybody was wrong, though the Raiders won 24–16. Everybody was wrong because the Raiders—all of them—played themselves to a state of exhaustion as Joe Namath put on a Joe Namath fireworks show, and everybody was wrong because the Jets had the ball on the Raiders' three-yard line with less than a minute to go. They didn't score, but you could have bought Raider bets for 10 cents on the dollar at that point. I would have swapped mine for a bound anthology of Wellington Mara's pep talks.

This week's week that was:

	My Line	Outlaw Line	Opening Line	Closing Line	
BENGALS	3	3	4	4	Browns* (3)
COWBOYS (10)	4	4	6½	7½	Redskins
49ERS (20)	6	6	6	6	Falcons
CHIEFS* (14)	4	3	2½	1	Colts
Bears (9)	1	3	4	4½	EAGLES
Lions	12	12	12½	12	BILLS (0)
VIKINGS	6	3	4	4	Packers (16)
Rams	6	7	11	10	CARDINALS (10)
Dolphins* (10)	10	5	6½	8	GIANTS
SAINTS	7	9	10	10	Patriots (7)
Steelers (6)	13	14	14	16	OILERS
Chargers	4	3½	3	4	BRONCOS (25)
RAIDERS* (8)	8	3	4½	7	Jets

The pros won five and lost six, the public won six and lost three. Underdogs won seven, favorites six. Home teams won eight, visitors five.

I won $2,200, $1,000 on the Dolphins, $500 each on the Browns and Chiefs, $200 on the Raiders. The bottom line now reads plus $8,690.

I'm not holding my own.

THE STANDINGS

AFC

	w	l	t	vs. spread w	l
Eastern Division					
Dolphins	13	0	0	10	2
Jets	7	6	0	6	7
Colts	5	8	0	6	6
Bills	3	9	1	5	8
Patriots	3	10	0	4	7
Central Division					
Steelers	10	3	0	9	3
Browns	9	4	0	9	4
Bengals	7	6	0	8	5
Oilers	1	12	0	3	10
Western Division					
Raiders	9	3	1	6	7
Chiefs	7	6	0	5	8
Chargers	4	8	1	7	6
Broncos	4	9	0	6	7

NFC

	w	l	t	vs. spread w	l
Eastern Division					
Redskins	11	2	0	7	4
Cowboys	10	3	0	5	8
Giants	7	6	0	6	5
Cardinals	3	9	1	5	6
Eagles	2	10	1	4	8
Central Division					
Packers	9	4	0	9	4
Lions	7	5	1	8	5
Vikings	7	6	0	3	8
Bears	4	8	1	5	7
Western Division					
49ers	7	5	1	6	7
Falcons	7	6	0	4	9
Rams	6	6	1	5	7
Saints	2	10	1	8	6

RESULTS

Browns 27, Bengals 24
Cowboys 34, Redskins 24
49ers 20, Falcons 0
Chiefs 24, Colts 10
Bears 21, Eagles 12
Bills 21, Lions 21
Packers 23, Vikings 7
Cardinals 24, Rams 14
Dolphins 23, Giants 13
Patriots 17, Saints 10
Steelers 9, Oilers 3
Broncos 28, Chargers 13
Raiders 24, Jets 16

BETTORS	w	l	pct.
Mr. Rich	30	17	.638
Merchant	38	24	.613
Lem Banker	59	40	.595
Fats–Mover	43	33	.565
Fast Eddie	28	29	.491

EXOTICA

Visitors 88, Home Teams 77
Favorites 90, Underdogs 70
Pros 67, Outlaw Line 49
Official Line 65, Public 59

Fourteenth Week

TUESDAY

Jimmy the Greek is the Minnesota Fats of pro football betting. In my book that's a terrific compliment.

Minnesota Fats (Rudolph Wanderone) is the greatest of all poolroom hustlers. Reason being that he is a raconteur-bullshitter extraordinaire. With practice, anyone can put the 8 ball in the side pocket with enough English on the cue ball to make it sing "God Save the Queen." Only Minnesota Fats had the wit, bombast and presence to turn himself into an institution. While better players denied his outrageous tales of conquest, issued winner-take-all challenges, etc., he waddled into a cushy job with a billiards table manufacturer, became a brand name, and helped elevate the game from subterranean social standing to pastel recreation halls. In the process those better players made more money from tournaments and appearances. Nobody suffered. Many laughs were racked up.

There probably were better generals than Patton and better hoofers than Astaire too, and they undoubtedly bleated and howled about life's injustice, with some justice; but some guys are theatrical and some guys aren't and what are you going to do? So Jimmy the Greek has many critics in Las Vegas, with some justice, because he is not the high roller or the big bookmaker or the national linemaker that his popular image makes him out to be. He is a performer.

Bob Martin is the eminence that Jimmy the Greek is thought to be. Martin apparently is satisfied to be himself, commenting dryly, "Jimmy knows pro football," leaving it at that. The wise guys, who would memorialize Bob Martin on Mount Rushmore, see Jimmy the Greek as an opportunist at best.

Jimmy the Greek is an invention of the sports betting phenomenon as well as of himself. As in time of war Patton came across as what a general is, and as in time of peace Astaire came across as what a hoofer is, in the time of pro football and point spreads Jimmy the Greek comes across as what a gambling man is. He looks like a swarthy Buddha. He combines the glib smarts of a morning disc jockey with a sorcerer's incantations. He knows more about pro football as a betting game than 99.99 percent of the people, and he dazzles them with his song and dance. Billy the bookie and Lem Banker sitting at kitchen tables and Bob Martin quietly setting and holding the line are not theatrical.

So it is Jimmy the Greek whose commentaries appear on the Mutual radio network, whose line is published in many newspapers (giving the mistaken impression that it is official, i.e., bettable), who is paid handsomely by Time, Inc. to appear at business luncheons, who is in demand as a speaker, who is writing a book, who has done a commercial for a shaving cream called Edge, who has a deal with columnist Jack Anderson to use his election odds, whatever they are. And God knows what else.

The Jimmy the Greek industry began innocently enough before the first Super Bowl in 1967, when *The New York*

Times did a story on how he computed the spread on the game between the Packers and the Chiefs. Inventively, he broke it down to its component parts. The Chiefs got so many points for linebacking, receiving, quarterbacking, et al., the Packers got so many more. Add a half point here for team speed and a half point there for intangibles and a point for coaching and, presto change-o, you have the spread. Which is like analyzing a Jackson Pollock painting stroke by stroke. It can't be done. But who's to stop you if you try? Who knows, the Museum of Modern Art might go show biz and make you curator. By shrewdly cultivating the press, showing up at important events, promoting himself, Jimmy the Greek went on to become the star he is today.

In private life Jimmy the Greek is Jimmy Snyder, who is in fact a promoter. He does promotional work for the Tropicana Hotel in Las Vegas. He has a half-dozen employees, including a writer and researchers.

He computes his line from his own power ratings and from what he hears around town and from tips he gathers from informants. This is not a bookmaking line, it is one man's opinion. Oddly however, it varies from the official line by a point or two at most. Jimmy the Greek wisely rejects the role of a common tout. A sorcerer could lose his license if he doesn't pick winners.

I've had lunch twice with Jimmy since I've been here and found him to be as entertaining as ever. He is the hero of his stories, like all of us, but unlike most gamblers he is the hero victim as often as hero victor. A former bookie, his stories have oodles of zeroes in them and, come to think of it, he seems to enjoy the ones where he gets ripped off more than the ones where he does the ripping. Maybe that's why he has risen above the Vegas crowd: He understands that losing big is as glamorous as winning big.

A gambler could get blackballed from the fraternity for the sin of modesty, which probably is why Jimmy the Greek doesn't strain to correct the misconception that he is the commissioner of games betting. His acceptance nationally by people who once considered gamblers reptilian is an important symbol of the change in attitudes toward betting, and they mustn't be disillusioned.

WEDNESDAY

I made one bet today and I have my eye on two more games. I bet the Chiefs at pick over the Falcons for $500. This is a tough game, but the Falcons have made a habit of losing tough games, and the Chiefs should be able to handle the Falcons' offense, and I'd like to bet against the Falcons once this season anyway to get over my hangup.

I like the 49ers over the Vikings, but the spread is 4½ 49ers, and I'll wait it out until it comes down to 4. The 49ers need the win to get into the playoffs, they have beaten the Vikings in the playoffs the last two years, and the Vikings of this year aren't the Vikings of those years. The 49ers should be able to pass on them.

I like the Steelers over the Chargers, but I'm going to wait for the result of the Browns–Jets before I get involved. If the Browns win the Steelers must win to take their division. If the Browns lose I'll stay away from the game because this close to the playoffs the Steelers are likely to hold people out if they don't need the win.

The lineup:

	My Line	Outlaw Line	Opening Line	
Dolphins	8	10	10½	Colts
49ers	6	4	4½	Vikings
Redskins	10	12	13½	Bills
Raiders	7	10	10	Bears
Bengals	10	8	8	Oilers
Browns	4	3	3	Jets
Rams	P	2	1	Lions
Packers	7	9	10	Saints
Chiefs	3	P	P	Falcons
Broncos	9	10	11	Patriots
Cowboys	7	8	9	Giants
Cardinals	7	8	9	Eagles
Steelers	4	3	4	Chargers

I made the Jets favorites over the Browns, unaware that the Browns could still win their division and that Joe Namath was a questionable starter for the Jets. Namath finished Monday's game on wobbly ankles and it is assumed that, with nothing at stake, the Jets won't jeopardize him. I spoke to him after the game. Ice bags were toweled around his ankles, which didn't look that bad to me. He could play if there were a reason to.

Money on the Browns has materialized in Las Vegas from Birmingham, which is Joe Namath country. They hold a wet finger to the wind on Namath in Birmingham, betting with and against the Jets. They aren't, according to my sources, unusually successful.

THURSDAY

They say Lefty is deep. We had a long talk tonight. He's deep.

Lefty Rosenthal is a split end to Lem Banker's tight end. Lem hauls in a ton of short passes and breaks a big one now and again. Lefty bets few games, goes for the big ones.

Lefty is built for the role. He is tall and lanky. He wears dark pin-striped suits, white shirts and ties on his public relations-floor job in the casino of the Stardust Hotel. He is in semiretirement as a gambler, he said, concentrating on football and his family. He comes from Chicago, made his reputation in Miami. He is forty-seven. His appearance and attitude forge an exclamation point of thin steel.

"When I bet, it's on the national wire in five minutes," Lefty said.

"I can create an avalanche," he added, ever so lightly dotting the exclamation point.

Lefty has respect, capital, followers—power. I have no idea what his relationship is with his followers, little men who buzz around him like commas and apostrophes. But when Lefty bets, the betting establishment salutes, and I suspect that these little men have something to do with it.

The power to cause an avalanche, to stimulate betting on one side of a game, speaks of the reputation Lefty has, and of opportunity. It suggests the power and opportunity of a Rothschild influencing the stock market to go one way, so he can buy cheap the other way. You must pick your spots. It is said Lefty went with the Vikings early and the Chiefs late in the 1970 Super Bowl.

"A live underdog is the best bet," Lefty said, meaning an underdog that could or should win the game. "The Chiefs were live."

Sayings from Chairman Lefty:

"The difference between an amateur and a professional gambler is the difference between a general practitioner and a heart specialist. The only similarity is that they're both called doctors."

"An amateur who wins is just borrowing the bookmaker's money."

"You can't be a successful gambler when you're young. You have to go busted a few times."

"There are no geniuses in gambling. It takes a lot of hard work, dedication and discipline."

"You can't beat the [blackjack, crap] tables, because of the PC [percentage] and the limit. The only gambling game you can beat is a game of opinion."

"I don't want good luck. I just don't want bad luck."

"I've been a bookmaker and a player. I respect a good bookmaker. But I admire a player. We're on the outside. We're warriors."

Lefty said his only aim as a handicapper is to pick winners; he isn't concerned with middles and other point games. I had to agree it was a distraction. The way to pick winners, he said, is to remember that football is still decided "in the trenches" and by staying two or three weeks ahead of the linemaker by anticipating a team's changing fortunes. Injuries, he thought, are overrated. Of course I loved him for all of that, since it confirmed my own findings. His insights into the specifics of teams and individuals were so dead-on that I got the feeling of comparing political notes with a stranger who had made the same clear-headed, enlightened discoveries. In some cases he went farther than I had, startling and exciting me at once.

We discussed the Vikings–49ers game. He said, "Alan Page is the greatest lineman in the history of football." I've thought that but never felt compelled to put it that boldly. A bettor knows Page's worth because he creates such havoc, forcing fumbles and interceptions, that he is indirectly responsible for many scores. (Fran Tarkenton once said that if he were starting a franchise Alan Page would be his first choice, over any quarterback.) I said I liked the 49ers because they run just well enough to throw effectively. He said that without Ken Willard in top form the 49ers don't run that well. I said Vic Washington was a pretty good football player. He cut me dead with, "He's a fumbler." (Some pros, wise guys, players I've met have impressed me with their knowledge of the turnover tendencies of teams and individuals. I haven't concentrated on that as much as I should. *Pro Football Weekly* runs a turnover chart that can be a valuable aid.) I said I liked Steve Spurrier. Lefty said he did too, "But this is his first big game. Experience is a factor in a big game." I pointed out that Spurrier passed for 300 yards against the Vikings in his only start against them. Lefty repeated firmly, "Experience is a factor."

I was chastened by this exchange. It is perfectly plain why people all over the country are waiting for Lefty to bet. He does his homework. He knows the game.

I asked him about Bob Martin's comment that nobody can beat the 11–10.

He said, "Ask him what happened last year."

I asked Lefty what happened this year.

He said, "Nobody's winning this season. It's a hard, tough season."

I was glad he didn't say he was holding his own.

FRIDAY

The theory of cheesecake, art and sex in relation to gambling came to me in the steamroom as Lem Banker was getting basketball scores on the phone. I had just weighed myself in at 167 pounds of solid cheesecake.

There aren't many things as good as good cheesecake, and Las Vegas may be the good cheesecake capital of the world. The reason so much of it is eaten here, I think, is that, one, our vision of heaven is a place where you can play games endlessly and chomp on a cheesecake cloud as it drifts by; and two, it's the second-best form of mother's milk yet invented. Losers, my survey indicates, eat twice as much as winners.

I met a fellow who lost $400 at the crap tables and redeemed himself by buying a $200 Leroy Neiman serigraph of Bobby Hull. See, he hadn't been a total fool with his money. There's an art gallery near every hotel casino. Losers, my survey indicates, buy twice as many *objets d'art* as winners.

Las Vegas also leads the world in hookers. Losers, my survey indicates, restore their virility twice as often as winners. "Sometimes," one gambler said, "I feel like getting laid out of pure meanness."

Which reminds me. I've been losing at the tables. There are people who think Vegas is hell on earth; I think that after thirty-six hours it's simply boring as hell. So a couple times a day I peel off a bill and get some chips and play some games. The bill usually is a hundred because that's the common denomination here. Ben Franklin, whose picture is on the bill, is revered in Vegas because he caught lightning, not because he penny-saved and penny-earned.

I'm losing $3,500. This is about $200 a day, which my agent tells me is a triumph of willpower beyond compare. I played a number (2) for him at roulette, and it hit and he had a long-distance orgasm. I've won at roulette, lost at blackjack and dice (and poker). I played blackjack one night with Sid Luckman. He lost and bitched, bitched and lost. I'll bet he kicked a lot of ass in huddles. I shot dice with Ernie Banks. He played for silver dollars, I played for basic units of $10 to $20, and we both won, and we never stopped laughing and slapping hands and telling each other how great we were. "This is the land of opportunity," said the eternally cheerful Banks, "and nobody deserves that opportunity more than you and me."

I credited, or debited, the losing to The Las Vegas Experience. I've won $3,600 on football. It isn't money, it's pieces of paper and chips. If Dostoevski could self-destruct, who am I to stay aloof from the battle?

Which brings me to Monique and the horny dwarf. Monique is a striking French girl. She's fun and I'm fun and we funned around at a bar one night. Then she announced that she had to go to work, and she didn't work with fun guys like me. She was a hooker, a funny hooker if not a happy hooker. Why didn't I call her sometime and we'll eat and dance and have fun? It was an offer I couldn't refuse. Tonight we did it all. And I, out of goodness and gratitude, will voluntarily leave her a Ben Franklin in the morning. Clever, these French.

But I've sworn off cheesecake, and I'll not collect guilt-edged art. Certainly not Leroy Neiman's. It was Leroy who borrowed the limousine that got us to Hialeah just in time for me to miss that $1,100 daily double four years ago.

SATURDAY

Now let me tell you about the ten more Ben Franklins last night cost me. I was going to put $1,000 on a teaser today, the Dolphins and the Vikings, but I didn't wake up until the fourth quarter of the Dolphins–Colts. You win some, you lose some, and you sleep through some. Some things you can't put a price on.

I did put $1,000 on the 49ers, giving 4, which was 1 too many. It was a bizarre day.

Around noon there was an authoritative report that Carl Eller wasn't going to play for the Vikings. The way he's played this season that didn't seem crucial. But he played, and he played like he's supposed to play, like one of the premier defensive ends. How did the rumor start and spread?

It was first published in the Los Angeles *Examiner*. In Vegas, where rumors of conspiracy thrive like mosquitoes in a swamp, it was theorized that a gambler fed the item to the paper to stimulate action on the 49ers to send the spread still higher. (It didn't work in Vegas, possibly because the paper arrived too late to start a panic.)

I spoke to Bud Furillo, sports editor of the *Examiner*, and this is the anatomy of a rumor he outlined:

Don Klosterman, the general manager of the Rams, called Jim Finks, the general manager of the Vikings, to discuss the game. A victory for the Vikings would give the Rams a chance to win their division tomorrow. Finks saw an opening to agitate him. He told Klosterman that, alas, Eller was doubtful. Klosterman reported the bad news to Furillo. Furillo put it in the paper.

That was the conspiracy.

Alas, there was no conspiracy in the game either, because the crazy thing that happened on the last play didn't fall on the point spread. If it had, the conspiracy meter would have exploded.

As Lefty was saying, Steve Spurrier wasn't up to the assignment. Which is putting it charitably. The Vikings led 17–3 in the third quarter. Enter John Brodie after eight weeks of inactivity. Herosville. The 49ers vault ahead 20–17 in the last minute.

Now it is the last play, the Vikings just inside 49er territory. But, yoiks, instead of going for the one-chance-in-a-thousand touchdown—the ethical thing to do because the Rams and Falcons still can beat out the 49ers—the Vikings try a long field goal. The 49ers begin cheering themselves as soon as the ball is kicked, because good or bad (it was bad) they have made the playoffs. Bud Grant, coach of the Vikings, explains that a tie would have given them a winning season and let the other guys take care of themselves.

Can you imagine the uproar if the point spread were involved? Could you convince conspiracy-minded bettors, and fans, that coaches do crazy things sometimes? You would have an easier time convincing cynics in Vegas that the Chiefs are a solid bet tomorrow. What they say about the Chiefs is: "I wouldn't bet Kansas City if the game was over."

SUNDAY

And then there's Joe Namath, of whom I heard it said that he was seen Thursday in the company of his former movie co-star, Ann-Margret, right here in Las Vegas, 2,700 miles, as the conspiracy flies, from the whirlpool and diathermy machines where he was taking treatment.

I still haven't found out how The Mover learned about Namath's missing knee brace on the first weekend of the season—although I do remember that he lost the bet on the game—but I know for a fact that neither The Mover nor the Las Vegas underground had information on Namath's pregame illness last week. Four hours before the game in Oakland everyone in the motel where the Jets were staying knew that Namath was retching and feverish in his room. Two hours before the game I saw him in the lobby bundled in a heavy jacket looking like a survivor of a death march. I called people in New York and Las Vegas to ask if they had any information on the game. Nothing.

This morning I was awakened by a call from a pro I met casually in Vegas. He asked me if Namath would play against the Browns. I said I'd check with friends in New York. Fast Eddie was my only bettor betting the game, on the Browns. He said it was so cold and windy that it wouldn't make any difference if Namath did play but he doubted that he would. It was a perfect reading. The weather kept 17,000 ticket-holders away from the ballpark. Namath warmed up but didn't play. Apparently other bettors reached the same conclusion Fast Eddie did because, according to Billy, money was pouring in on the Browns. The line went as high as 5.

Yet there were rumors that the gamblers or bookies or both knew something, suggesting that they must have been tipped off that Namath wouldn't play. With the history of Namath's legs, that was like attributing an epileptic seizure to a betting coup.

Because he is a super athlete and celebrity, it is always open season on Joe Namath. In Vegas they have an affinity for owners too. Everyone seems to know someone who knows someone who has a pipeline into an owner. Bets actually were made on the Bills against the Colts two weeks ago because the owner of the Colts allegedly told this ubiquitous someone that it would be a tough game. (The Colts romped.) What qualifies an owner as an expert is beyond me. They are emotional fans who have the added disadvantage of being close to coaches and players. I'd rather use a gypsy on speed as a tout. I'd bet that betting owners have lost more often than they won.

Why is professional football such fair and unfair game for rumor-mongering and conspiracy-mongering?

Well, for openers, few bettors beat it. Until this season, they claimed to do better with college football. Adding one and one they got eleven. Since they did better with college football, there must be something wrong with professional football.

There's the point spread. If nirvana for a bettor-player is hitting a middle, why not the same for an athlete-player who can win the game but lose by the points?

There's the difficulty of comprehending the nuances of football. (Even coaches often don't know what they saw until they study films.) At Churchill Downs during the baseball season the bettors interpret the electronic tape reports like historical novelists. If there's a change of pitchers in Chicago, they can tell you who's hitting, who will pinch-hit next, whether the infield is drawn in, and how many bags of peanuts have been sold in the bleachers; and they will debate whether Leo Durocher should order a bunt, giving cogent arguments, with asides on his private life and wardrobe. In football the bettors are lost. Bad breaks and conspiracies are easy to understand.

Conversely, when a bettor is right he may concoct or embellish conspiracies because that's more interesting and has greater machismo prestige in his circle than picking a winner, which would be regarded as mere luck. Never underestimate the value of malicious gossip as a negotiable social currency. It is the tribal cant of gamblers, like the griping of infantrymen.

And so to the Kansas City Chiefs. And the Pittsburgh Steelers. Both won for me today. After the Browns beat the Jets, I went with the Steelers for $1,000, giving 3½ to the Chargers. The Steelers led the league in forcing turnovers and the Chargers led the league in committing turnovers, and guess what? The Chargers had seven turnovers to the Steelers' one. The Steelers won 24–2.

The 17–14 victory of the Chiefs over the Falcons pleased me because it was another contrary bet. I've made seven bets involving the Chiefs this season and won six of them. I've always had success betting on and against the Chiefs, which is why I have always retained a scintilla of doubt about the exact nature of their alleged misdeeds.

I believe, absolutely, Bob Martin's revelation about the betting pyramid that resulted in the Chiefs being taken down from the line in 1966. What I'm not so sure about is how the pyramid started. It is conceivable to me that a gambler had as much success as I have handicapping them, and boasted that he had a sure thing. It is conceivable to me that innocent remarks by players were translated into winning bets. According to the NFL, Len Dawson has twice passed lie detector tests. In 1963, after Paul Hornung and Alex Karras were suspended for betting on themselves, while a couple of players were cleared of suspicion after taking lie detector tests, I took one in a Philadelphia police station. Every lie I told shook the machine like an earthquake. A guilty man, law enforcement agents say, can fool the machine only if he's a congenital liar or a psychologically trained liar (spies). I believe them. If Dawson passed the tests, I believe him. (Opponents of such tests claim five percent error.) If the Chiefs were guilty, the butler must have done it. Or other players.

I've dwelled on conspiracies because they remind me of the boos of summer. A thousand fans booing persistently can dominate a ballpark in which 30,000 fans are cheering or sitting on their hands.

Top professional gamblers have a saying that "Money is strong." They acknowledge the possibility of larceny. But if a deep-sea diver worried about sharks all the time he'd never go into the water. The pros are too busy figuring out their next move to worry about it.

I have not met a single respected player in Las Vegas who thinks that the National Football Lottery is dishonest.

The way he is going, Lem Banker, for one, wishes the NFL would play on indefinitely. He won seven again this week (Dolphins, Chiefs, Browns, Bills, Giants, Saints, Bears) and lost three (Rams, Chargers, 49ers). Fats and The Mover won two (Bengals, Steelers) and lost one (Saints). Mr. Rich won his two bets (Vikings, Steelers). Fast Eddie won two (Browns, Dolphins) and lost two (49ers, Cowboys).

The last full week that was:

	My Line	Outlaw Line	Opening Line	Closing Line	
DOLPHINS (16)	8	10	10½	10½	Colts
49ERS* (3)	6	4	4½	4	Vikings
REDSKINS	10	12	13½	12½	Bills (7)
RAIDERS (7)	7	10	10	9½	Bears
Bengals (44)	10	8	8	10½	OILERS
Browns (16)	4	3	3	4	JETS
RAMS	P	2	1	1	Lions (17)
Packers (10)	7	9	10	11	SAINTS
Chiefs* (3)	3	P	P	3	FALCONS
BRONCOS (24)	9	10	11	11	Patriots
COWBOYS	7	8	9	7½	GIANTS (20)
CARDINALS (1)	7	8	9	8	Eagles
Steelers* (22)	4	3	4	3½	CHARGERS

The pros won five and lost four, the public (represented by pros in Las Vegas only, because the line changes there are caused by pro money) won six and lost three. Visitors won nine, home teams two. Underdogs won six, favorites five.

A few observations about betting statistics at the close of the regular season:

The opening, or official, line was closer to the final score ten more times than my line during the season. That's consistency. I picked the exact spread on eleven games, the official line had four. That is an example of what an opinion can do.

An unusually high number of favorites won this season (ninety-five to seventy-seven underdogs). Figures I've seen in the past always were within a few percentage points of .500. The preponderance of winning favorites should have made it a relatively successful season for the public, but of course there is the tendency after "borrowing the bookie's money," in Lefty Rosenthal's magnificent phrase, to impale oneself trying to leap high fences to riches.

Because so many favorites won, the public did respectably betting into the line, winning sixty-four times, losing sixty-nine. Although the professionals got stung, in part because they go to underdogs more than the public does, they won seventy-two and lost fifty-three betting into the outlaw line.

The performance of my bettors is interesting, but, again, wins vs. losses is not necessarily a reflection of how the money game went. Also, bettors don't distinguish between the colleges and the pros when they count their money, and there was a national plague betting on college games. I'm a pro freak. I don't even want to try to keep up with sixty or seventy college teams. I didn't bet a single college game.

If I wore a hat I'd tip it to Mr. Rich. He had 65 percent winners, betting a disciplined three or four games weekly. He bets the way I did in the second half of the season, laying off high-priced (over 7-point) favorites and long shots. Lem Banker did extraordinarily well considering the fact that he bet so many underdogs. He hit 60 percent and had twenty-three more winners than losers. Greenwich Village Fats and The Mover had a respectable 56 percent, yet they insist it was a disaster. Fast Eddie's near-50 percent was reasonable for an amateur. If he bet his basic $200 bet on every game he would have lost $820.

I'm not ecstatic with my 61 percent, but I won $400 this week, winning $1,000 on the Steelers and $500 on the Chiefs, losing $1,100 on the 49ers, making the bottom line plus $9,090. I had ten winning weeks and four losing weeks, and that's good enough to get a player into the playoffs.

MONDAY

Men have been walking on the moon lately, picking up rocks. Three weeks in Las Vegas, with no electronic umbilical cord to whisk you back to earth, isn't bad either. It took a lifetime of living to survive this ordeal. I may not be as young as I think I am.

"We've come a long way from Monte Carlo."

"Seven thousand miles."

"Nine thousand dollars."

"Beating them three weeks in a row in Las Vegas is like going into the lion's den and coming out with meat under both arms. Maybe there's nobody as smart as a dumb New Yorker."

"Lem had it the other way around."

"It was a good warning; kept me on my guard. I dig Lem. And Lefty. I respect the real pros. They are players —warriors. They may be the last of the rugged individualists, making it on their own, bucking the system alone."

"You could be a Lem or a Lefty."

"No question about it. If I devoted that much time to it, better. We all think we're the best, don't we? I may not be able to do much else, but I can pick winners."

"Sounds like you're ready to go West, old man."

"Live in Vegas? No way. I'd look like a cheesecake in six months. I couldn't work at it as hard as those guys do anyway. It's too much like work."

"You going to send it all in on the playoffs?"

"Don't know. But if I win $30,000 I could middle the book. Give the publisher his money back and forget it."

"Who do you like to win it?"

"Me."

FINAL STANDINGS

AFC

	w	l	t	vs. spread w	l
Eastern Division					
Dolphins	14	0	0	11	2
Jets	7	7	0	6	8
Colts	5	9	0	6	7
Bills	4	9	1	6	8
Patriots	3	11	0	4	8
Central Division					
Steelers	11	3	0	10	3
Browns	10	4	0	10	4
Bengals	8	6	0	9	5
Oilers	1	13	0	3	11
Western Division					
Raiders	10	3	1	6	8
Chiefs	8	6	0	5	8*
Broncos	5	9	0	7	7
Chargers	4	9	1	7	7

NFC

	w	l	t	vs. spread w	l
Eastern Division					
Redskins	11	3	0	7	5
Cowboys	10	4	0	5	9
Giants	8	6	0	7	5
Cardinals	4	9	1	5	7
Eagles	2	11	1	5	8
Central Division					
Packers	10	4	0	9	5
Lions	8	5	1	9	5
Vikings	7	7	0	4	8
Bears	4	9	1	6	7
Western Division					
49ers	8	5	1	6	8
Falcons	7	7	0	4	9*
Rams	6	7	1	5	8
Saints	2	11	1	8	6

* Tie

RESULTS

Dolphins 16, Colts 0
49ers 20, Vikings 17
Bills 24, Redskins 17
Raiders 28, Bears 21
Bengals 61, Oilers 17
Browns 26, Jets 10
Lions 34, Rams 17
Packers 30, Saints 20
Chiefs 17, Falcons 14
Broncos 45, Patriots 21
Giants 23, Cowboys 3
Cardinals 24, Eagles 23
Steelers 24, Chargers 2

BETTORS	w	l	pct.
Mr. Rich	32	17	.653
Merchant	40	25	.615
Lem Banker	66	43	.605
Fats–Mover	45	34	.567
Fast Eddie	30	31	.491

EXOTICA

Visitors 97, Home Teams 80
Favorites 95, Underdogs 77
Pros 72, Outlaw Line 53
Official Line 69, Public 64

Part III
Superbet

I hope he follows his heart, his frightened heart.

—TENNESSEE WILLIAMS

The Playoffs

TUESDAY

During a hot roll at a crap table a Southerner leaned over and shook a fist of encouragement at me. "Cut ya sef a new piece a bait," he said, "and fish a little deeper."

That's what the postseason games are about for the betting man.

The season is reduced to the eight best teams and, more important, the eight best-known teams. There are no secrets. Even the inside-information crowd has to go on outside information. On opinion.

The games are so tough, the line so tight, that a wise man, as opposed to a wise guy, probably would pass most of them up as betting propositions. But if you've been involved with the season there's no holding back. This is where you put yourself on the line—with new bait—and fish deep inside the game for the big ones.

I left two unusual bets behind in Las Vegas, where I'll be stopping en route to Los Angeles for the Super Bowl. Stopping to pick up my money.

I bet on the Raiders at 7–1, for $1,000, to win the whole thing. I don't expect them to win the whole thing, although I give them the best shot among the long shots. But there's a method to my madness.

(Other odds were: Dolphins 2–1, Redskins 3–1, Cowboys 6–1, Steelers 6–1, 49ers 8–1, Packers 10–1, Browns 25–1.)

The Steelers figured to be favored by about a field goal. To me that means they have to win the game to win a bet on them; few games are decided under 3 points. The same goes for the Raiders. So, in effect, my 7–1 bet is an opinion that they will win this game, and this game alone, because if they do, I'm in the driver's seat with the odds. If they win, I can insure the bet by hedging next week. Assuming they would play the Dolphins, I can bet $2,000 or $3,000 on the Dolphins, and if the Raiders should win again I would still have 7–1 going into the Super Bowl, and could again take out insurance. Since I like, but don't love, the Raiders to beat the Steelers, the 7–1 appealed to me over a straight bet. I am returning to that grand old Polynesian pastime—yakapoola.

The second bet is serious stuff. I bet $3,000 at even money that the Redskins beat the Packers and the Dolphins beat the Browns—with no points. I would never bet a points parlay. This is a different breed of yakapoola.

In the old, old days, before point spreads, betting propositions were based on pure odds. Your friendly neighborhood bookie might get skunked on pure odds betting today—because so much money would be bet on favorites—but in Vegas you can still get down with odds. The Redskins, as 6-point favorites, were 8–5. The Dolphins, as 12-point favorites, were 3½–1. Together they were 6–5 or even money. The bookie who gave me the proposition said there was a bettor in town who would take the 8–5 on the Packers, so the bookie was getting a free shot at a fat middle if the Browns pulled an upset: If the Redskins win he'll beat the Packer-backer, and if the Browns win he'll beat me. Where a middle normally is a 20–1 shot, the bookie reduced it to 3½–1 for himself. Longer long shots than that have come in.

(The odds on other point spreads are approximately: 1 point, 6–5; 3 points, 7–5; 4 points, 8–5; 6 points, 9–5; 7 points, 2–1; 10 points, 3–1; 13 points, 4–1.)

This is how I fished deeper into the playoffs:

Raiders vs. Steelers I made the Raiders 3, the Steelers are favored by 2 or 2½. The Steelers beat the Raiders convincingly in the opening game of the season. I see it as an even rematch because (*a*) the Steelers' powerhouse running game (Fuqua, Harris) can't dominate the Raiders without a supplementary passing attack; (*b*) Terry Bradshaw, who completed just 48 percent of his passes, will be throwing into one of the better secondaries, in his first playoff game; (*c*) the offensive line of the Raiders, one of the best, should neutralize the Steelers' front seven, which is their strength; but (*d*) the Raiders don't have a breakaway back to pop one; and (*e*) Daryl Lamonica is a risk in a big game. I'm going with the Raiders on their experience in playoffs.

Cowboys vs. 49ers I made this a pick game, the Cowboys opened at 1. The 49ers thrashed the Cowboys four weeks ago when they turned two early turnovers into touchdowns. Both teams are erratic and have pronounced weaknesses. The quarterbacking of the Cowboys leaves much to be desired, their secondary is vulnerable. The 49ers aren't much of a running threat, their defensive line has been whipped. The Cowboys should run on the 49ers, the 49ers should throw on the Cowboys. These teams covered the spread eleven out of twenty-six times between them this season. I lean to the 49ers, but not so you'd notice.

Packers vs. Redskins I made the Redskins 7, the line has dipped to 5 from 6. The Redskins beat the Packers soundly last month, though the score was close because Chester Marcol kicked four field goals. The Packers are another team with half an offense, running, and you can't get away with that in the playoffs, not against a tough, experienced team like the Redskins. Scott Hunter, a second-year quarterback with no outstanding receiver to throw to, is over his head. The Redskins should get enough points on a pretty good Packer defense to win handily. If the spread dips to 4, where field goals are unlikely to overcome me, I may go another $1,000 or $2,000 further on the Redskins.

Dolphins vs. Browns I made the Dolphins 10, they are up to 13 already. I don't see how the Dolphins can lose, but I don't trust Earl Morrall with all those points. The Dolphins have to play conservatively with him at quarterback. The Browns, with Mike Phipps and Leroy Kelly and many playoff veterans, could hang in there until the Dolphins cave in their defensive line.

Of course one of the things about fishing deep is that you could end up hooking yourself.

WEDNESDAY

A story broke while I was in Las Vegas that a player reported a bribe attempt to his team and the league last year. The story originated in Washington, where a House committee on crime had learned of the abortive caper. The FBI was investigating it. I found out today what the story was about.

A marginal player, a center, on one of the poorer teams in the NFL was approached toward the end of the 1971 season by a former teammate. The former teammate, whose business was collapsing under him, offered the player $10,000 per game to fix the last three games.

Three observations:

The player, a veteran who probably never earned more than $25,000 in a season, turned down $30,000 in hard, untaxable cash near the end of his career.

His team usually was a decided underdog. So was the team that my confessed dumper dumped most of his games for. Where conspiratorial gossip usually involves top teams in close games, who would suspect a 10-point underdog that lost by two or three touchdowns?

There's no way they could have pulled off a coup for three straight weeks. The probable scenario would be this: To make it worthwhile, a minimum of $25,000 would have to be bet. To bet that much you must deal with bookies who have dealt with you before. If you haven't bet in the high four or five figures, they are going to be suspicious, or they are going to try to cash in themselves. That would, by the second week, trigger the chain pyramid reaction that Bob Martin described. The second week would be the thirteenth week of the season, when games are circled for limited betting. If the warning system hadn't already sounded, it would go off from coast to coast by then, provided you could even bet that much. The game would be unbettable by the third week at the latest. As an isolated one-shot, it would be awfully difficult to pinpoint. Three in a row violates a cardinal rule. It's piggish.

THURSDAY

Decisions, decisions.

Bob Lilly has a back spasm. He's been in a hospital. If

he plays against the 49ers, his impact on the game will be reduced to normal human scale. That is a blow to the Cowboys. Without a superhuman Lilly to overoccupy the offense, who is going to rush the passer? If no one does, won't their vulnerable secondary disintegrate?

The 49ers are listed as slight favorites now, up to a point or a point-and-a-half.

But what about John Brodie? There's an interview with Brodie in the magazine *Intellectual Digest.* I've always wondered why Brodie was so flighty. Now I know. He has too much imagination for an athlete. He muses about experiencing "energy flows" and "a kind of clarity" and "sudden glimmers" and "beingness" during games. He speculated that a key pass he completed in the playoffs last year was lifted over a defender's reach by psychic forces. The gist of the article was that he marches to his own spiritual drummer. The implication is that when he trips up, it's because his beat is off, not because the other guys trip him up.

At the risk of being accused of unimaginative rationality, my cause-and-effect interpretation of these two events in relation to Saturday's game is this: If Lilly doesn't play, or doesn't play up to his standard, Brodie will experience wonderful things. If Lilly plays like Lilly, the drummer will influence Brodie to run for his life.

FRIDAY

Think I met a witch tonight.

The talk at the party turned to gambling, as talk usually does around me these days. I got into a rap about Las Vegas and dice. When a dozen people from all walks of life and all parts of the country, betting all kinds of money, find themselves at a hot table, they are transported across boundaries into a closely knit team. People who never saw each other fifteen minutes before, and will never see each other again after fifteen minutes more, are caught up in a frenzy of laughter and enthusiasm, of life.

The witch, a beauty animated by a rubber mouth and enormous green eyes, said she liked to play dice.

I said that I felt a visceral hostility toward the Judases who bet with the house, against the roller, against the team. They are, I said, collaborating with the enemy, siding with the devil, opting for death. When one of them is driven from a table, losing, I feel as though I have conquered Mr. Dirt.

She said that she bets on the house because it is easier to win and winning was opting for life.

Later I was told that she always dresses in black when she plays. And that she sleeps in a bedroom done in black, with dolls hanging from the ceiling—by nooses.

SATURDAY

"God," said Albert Einstein, "does not play dice with the universe."

Bet?

Somebody up there rolled deuces and boxcars, crazy bounces and fumbles today. For me. Sevens and elevens for some.

I handicapped expertly. I fished patiently. I brushed my teeth and cleaned behind my ears and drank my orange juice. And I lost 1,880 unbelievable dollars.

I put another $200 on the Raiders, taking 2 points from Mr. Rhodes, because I'm still trying to get even with him. I bet $600 on the 49ers. Between Lilly's back and Brodie's head, I had a feeling in my neck that, since nothing has happened to alter my preseason judgment that the Cowboys couldn't repeat as champions without Duane Thomas and Roger Staubach, I should go against them. If they win I'll go against them again next week. If they win then I'll go against them in the Super Bowl. If they win again I'll become a hermit in the Sierras.

Watched the game with Jonathan Schwartz and Vic Ziegel. Jonathan had $50 on the Raiders. Vic made the Raiders his annual bet, for $200. Lem Banker had the Raiders and Cowboys (and Redskins and Dolphins). Mr. Rich had the Steelers and 49ers (and Packers and Browns). Fats and The Mover had the Steelers and 49ers (and Browns). Fast Eddie had the Raiders and 49ers (and Packers and Browns). Danny Lavezzo was in Florida betting on horses.

The Steelers and Raiders played a scoreless first half, putting Vic to sleep. I grimaced in disgust, with myself, when Lamonica hurried a pass despite good protection. The Steelers went ahead 6–0 on two field goals. Ken Stabler replaced Lamonica in the fourth quarter. I like Stabler. He's not a classic thrower, but he has a winning temperament. Vic and Jonathan didn't think so. They gave up.

I had my concentration face on, my antennae trying to pick up the vibes that Stabler might be radiating on the field. With less than four minutes to go he marched the Raiders fifty yards to the Steelers' thirty, their deepest penetration. Then he scrambled outside a blitz and ran unmolested for a touchdown.

Whoops and hollers. I leaped up and punched the air with both fists, a double uppercut the likes of which hasn't been seen since Hurricane Jackson. I congratulated myself on my unwavering professionalism, my faith, in the company of panicky amateurs. Vic said he knew it all the time. Jonathan ran to the telephone.

"Watching the game?"

"Oh, I glance at it now and then."

"Just wanted to know. Talk to you later."

There was a little more than a minute to go. I didn't give the Steelers a chance with Bradshaw. He got the Steelers to their own forty and threw three incompletions. With twenty-two seconds left he heaved down the middle. There was a violent collision. My immediate flash was: I'm going to Miami to see the Dolphins play the Raiders next week.

The action switched to Franco Harris chugging down the sideline. Alone. Scoring. I knew what had happened —it could only have been a deflection—instantly. I fell to my knees and buried my head in my hands.

Sonofabitch.

Vic: "What happened?"

There was an instant replay.

The telephone rang.

"Hamburger Heaven," Jonathan answered.

"Watching the game?" his friend asked.

Vic cried, "I'm going to write my bookie a check that bounces too."

"You have to pay on acts of God," I said.

I have the writer's affliction of unconsciously clicking into and out of focuses. There's a click, a lens adjustment, and suddenly I'm behind the camera instead of in front of it, or both, observing myself.

Jesus, I thought, can you imagine what's going on in America right now? The exulting and despairing? How many trays of peanuts flung at the screen? How many cocktail tables kicked? How many wives hugged? How many trips planned for the holiday—mine to Miami was canceled before the first replay—with money that fell from the sky? It's wild.

So was the second game.

Lilly played two series and sat down. The 49ers led 28–13 going into the fourth quarter, capitalizing on turnovers, Brodie throwing two psychic touchdown passes. Roger Staubach replaced Craig Morton in the third quarter. Staubach and Jim Plunkett are the two best college quarterbacks I ever saw. Staubach is a winner, but this would be his longest appearance since he was injured last summer. It was asking too much.

No, it wasn't. When the Cowboys got a field goal with six minutes left to move within two touchdowns of the 49ers, I slumped in my chair, fearful that the lightning would strike again. The Cowboys scored with a minute and a half left to make it 28–23. There would have to be an onside kick. I leaned forward, mouth pursed, mind agape. The ball bounced off a 49er and the Cowboys recovered. I slumped back. The game was over. Staubach made it official forty seconds later.

In strawberry fields of fantasy I jog alongside Roger Staubach, flipping a football. He can play for me. I don't ever want to bet so much that I lose sight of that.

I felt strangely buoyant at the Lion's Head tonight. I could afford the luxury of being the good loser because it accrued to my credit that I had been victimized by a parlay of miracles. It was the biggest thing since Mike Reardon, the bartender, got hauled into court as a $4,000 scofflaw on the same day that his sailboat was torn from its mooring and wrecked in a storm. I did not feel reduced by the twin disaster at all. If anything, I reveled in the role of expert shot down by fate, whim, magic. It elevated me above the crowd of resident experts at the Head. It took some mighty powerful stuff to defeat me.

I met a fellow who bet on the Raiders and said he was going to church tomorrow for the first time in ten years. I don't give up that easily. But I wondered what I could be hit with next.

SUNDAY

I Einsteined the game today.

And I Lem Bankered it.

And I Mel Sokolowed it.

Einsteining it, my equations were mathematically perfect. I had the right teams for the right reasons.

Lem Bankering it, I made betting moves that I learned from the master himself.

Mel Sokolow is my agent the gambler. He goes nutty during games. His children keep a respectful distance. His wife feeds the squirrels in Central Park. I didn't go that nutty, but if higher powers were going to interfere with my lofty deliberations on the playoffs I wasn't going to just sit there. I wasn't going to let my kidney do all the work. Fighting fire with water wasn't enough yesterday, so I summoned deeper reserves. With every muscle, gland and capillary in me, I leaned opposing field goals off course, stretched yard markers, guided footballs. (I did not dictate strategy. I leave that to coaches, quarterbacks and fans.)

I won $6,500.

The bottom line is plus $13,710.

As Danny Murtaugh said after the Pirates beat the Yankees in the 1960 World Series, I feel handsome.

At the very last minute I bet $2,000 on the Redskins, giving 4 to the Packers. The Packers were the public team. The line came down, predictably.

They were no match for the Redskins. George Allen showed contempt for their passing game by substituting a middle guard for his middle linebacker. It was a masterstroke. The Packers banged away and banged away with their two big backs, John Brockington and MacArthur Lane, and they were banged back and banged down. They were challenged to throw, and couldn't. The Redskins won 16–3.

I was $2,000 ahead and had won the key half of the $3,000 odds parlay. I decided to insure the second bet by going with the Browns. Here I did something that would never have occurred to me before Las Vegas. I negotiated with a bookie, as I had seen Lem Banker do. It is, after all, business you're conducting.

Doctor reported that the Dolphins were 13½ over the Browns. Obviously there was a flood of Dolphins' money.

I said, guessing that he might welcome Browns' money, "Do you have any 14?"

He said, "Why not?"

I took $1,500 worth of the Browns at 14.

This violated my rule about betting underdogs unless you think they can win. But, having bet the Dolphins without any points in the parlay, I had a 13-point middle going for me, and that takes precedence over any nine rules I can think of.

As things stood, I would come out $500 ahead for the day if the Browns won (losing the $3,000 bet, winning $2,000 and $1,500).

I would come out $3,350 ahead if the Dolphins covered the spread (winning $3,000 and $2,000, losing $1,650).

And I would win it all if the Dolphins won by less than 14.

I won it all.

They won 20–14, nearly blowing it. The Dolphins scored a touchdown on a blocked kick in the first quarter, sat on a lead and didn't score a touchdown on their own offensive initiative until they fell behind midway through the fourth quarter. Earl Morrall played poorly, as the Browns ganged up on the run and dared him to throw, but he completed a clutch pass to Paul Warfield on the winning drive. The Dolphins blasted the length of the field in seven plays. For pure football—as opposed to the drama of celestial crapshooting—it was the most impressive single thing I saw all weekend.

I saw it in a momentary state of calm. The football person in me wanted to see how the Dolphins would respond to the test. The betting person in me, who could do no worse than win $500 on the day, was subdued in appreciation for the bookie's side of the odds bet I thought I had all the best of. Damon Runyon put it best when he said, "Where human beings are concerned, nobody is more than 3–1." That is why the pros take the big points. That is why the bookie took a stab at a middle based on the Browns winning the game.

After the Dolphins scored, I squatted on the counter in

my kitchen, legs crossed under me, arms folded, grinning like a balmy guru getting hot flashes of truth. When the game ended my calm ended. It was the calm before a shrill storm. I started phoning people and reciting the details of my conquest in high C. Relatives, friends, long-lost friends, seldom-seen friends, the rookie quarterback. She got so excited that I caught her hysteria and got a stitch in my side.

I saw a man win $15,000 at a crap table in the Bahamas, pocket the cash, and walk around the casino like a horse being hot-walked after a workout, walking the excitement out. I went for a walk in the cold Christmas Eve night. I aimed myself at a friend's restaurant a good walk away. It was closed. I felt a pang of need. Gail, usually a continent away, is an ocean away, in London. And I can't swim more than 200 yards.

At the Lion's Head there was much celebrating. The star of the game, I rhapsodized endlessly about my home run, my half-court basket, my touchdown. Friends basked in my moonglow.

The shrill high carried into the early morning like a radio signal. I thought of my daughter, Jamie, who lives in Florida with her mother. Summer before last I took her to the game preserves of East Africa. At a lake outlined in pink flamingos, hippopotami yawning offshore, she sighed, "Daddy, this is my day of days."

Sweetheart, I just had a day almost as good as that one.

The Championships

MONDAY

Genius confirmed, skeptics converted, cynics quieted, critics awed, I sense that the timing is right to summarize the rules and guidelines of playing The National Football Lottery.

I've been told that if the book were entitled *How to Bet Pro Football and Win Money* I'd make a fortune. I'll settle for a fraction of a fortune by saying that it's possible, but highly improbable, for an amateur to beat pro football.

There's no way I can impart my knowledge and instinct for the game as a betting proposition to the casual fan and bettor.

There's no way to do what Lem Banker does with the points unless you devote your life to it.

And even then it's a battle.

If Lem Banker can admit after a long season of betting —the pros and colleges—that it was a battle, that ought to sober any amateur hotshot.

If Bob Martin says that even a pro can't beat the 11–10 and if Lefty Rosenthal says that an amateur who wins is only borrowing the bookie's money, that ought to be an additional forewarning about what you're up against.

So I recommend, first, that amateurs limit themselves to parlay cards, which provide action, and social bets, which provide fun.

And, second, since you can't keep a good bettor down,

and because I'm all for the guy who pits himself against the odds, I'll set down some do's and don't's that might save someone a nickel or a dime along the way.

A few all-purpose generalizations:

Winning isn't going to change your life. So don't bet so much that you can get hurt. If that's what betting is all about for you, wear dog tags so they know where to ship the body. This stuff can't help you.

Don't be a pig. Step up your bets a little when you win, but don't try to capture the deed to Fort Knox.

Don't be a fool. When you have the inevitable losing streak, cut down on your bets a little and try to win your losings back one game at a time. There's no reason why a bettor who loses five in a row can't lose six, seven, or eight in a row. If you panic, you won't have anything left to bet with when it turns around.

Putting these generalizations together in one handy football package: Try to win one weekend at a time. That should keep you from blowing your winnings and doubling your losings.

All right, but how do you win? A few pro football generalizations:

Don't try to make money by betting on a bad team.

Don't give more than 7 points.

Don't bet an underdog unless you think it can win the game.

Bet a clearly superior team any time it is favored by less than a touchdown.

Bet the team you like regardless of injuries, home field, etc. Those factors have already been included in the line.

Don't bet games in which the weather is likely to be a factor. You're guessing.

Bet convictions, not hunches. When in doubt, pass the game up.

Bet with your emotions, but don't be carried away.

A few generalizations about bookies, betting, and the points:

Russian proverb: "Believe not your own brother, believe instead your own crooked eye."

Don't be intimidated by the line. If you think a favorite isn't favored by enough or an underdog is underdogged by too much, bet it. The line is fallible.

Bet on the public (popular) teams early in the week, bet against them as late as possible.

Try to get the best of the line by using two or more bookies. If a game is 3½, 4½, 6½, etc., and you're not interested in it unless you can get another half-point or give a half-point less, tell the bookmaker. He may give it to you immediately, or get back to you when and if it becomes available.

Ask for a rundown of the line, not for a specific game. A bookie will take advantage of a bettor if he can figure out on whom he wants to bet.

Don't bet parlays.

Two generalizations for the bettor who can't pick a winner to save his life:

Bet against the movement of the money. If the points go up, bet on the underdog. If the points go down, bet on the favorite.

Raise titwillows.

TUESDAY

I made a couple of nervous bets. The Dolphins should handle the Steelers and the Redskins should handle the Cowboys, but I bet $2,000 on the Dolphins, expecting to hedge some of it, and I bet $2,000 on the Cowboys, expecting to hedge all of it and then some.

I'm nervous about Earl Morrall and Roger Staubach. I'm nervous about Morrall because he made the game with the Browns too close for comfort. I'm nervous about Staubach because he changes the known factors in the equation between the Redskins and Cowboys.

The Dolphins opened at 2½ over the Steelers. I made them 4. They should win the game. The Steelers' offense is inconsistent, frequently triggered by the turnovers forced by their defense, much as a basketball team whose offense is triggered by defense and rebounding, and the Dolphins rarely turn the ball over. The Steelers will have to earn their points and I don't think they can beat the Dolphins at that. But the Steelers terrorized Daryl Lamonica, so they could do the same to Morrall.

I also have reservations about Don Shula. Shula is a terrific coach. But he has lost the four championship games his teams have played in, and in three of them they performed below their best. His Colts panicked in the Super Bowl against the Jets. His Dolphins froze against the Cowboys last year, when he didn't use Mercury Morris for one offensive play; Morris gained 1,000 yards as a starter this season. Now Shula seems indecisive about using Bob Griese, who has recovered from his broken ankle. In a tough game the coaching and quarterbacking will make the difference, and the background on these factors makes me nervous about the Dolphins, as much as I like them.

If Roger Staubach hadn't entered the picture, I would make a good bet on the Redskins and forget it. They beat the Cowboys coming from two touchdowns behind in their first game and they threw a scare into them coming from farther behind in their second game. Which tells me the Redskins can handle this team when they have to. Plus they have the game-breakers and the Cowboys don't. And George Allen seems to know how to defense scramblers, and this will be Staubach's first start of the season. But I am constitutionally unable to send it in against Staubach and that's that.

The $2,000 I put on the Cowboys is to take advantage of a spread that figures to drop. I took 4, having made the Redskins favorites by 3. I think there will be heavy action on the Cowboys at 4, knocking the number down to 2 or 3, in which event I'll come back with $3,000 or $4,000 on the Redskins, giving me a good shot at a middle or side.

Playoff games are so tough that by yakapoolaing I can make more than I can lose, safeguarding my winnings in the process. I don't want to be so cocksure that I give back my hard-earned easy money, and I don't want to be so careful that there is no risk. Playing between those extremes you can win and have fun. If you can pick winners.

WEDNESDAY

Stick your head above the crowd, Leo Durocher said, and somebody will take a shot at it. I got shot at tonight. It hurt. It hurt so much that I trembled, fighting to control rage welling into violence.

A casual friend came into the Head. He was smiling. I thought he had heard about my coup and that, as a bettor himself, he would dig my temporary insanity. I threw my arms around him.

He backed off and said I fantasized the whole thing. Those weren't the bets I said I would make when I saw him a few days before.

I thought he was kidding. He repeated it, still smiling. I could feel myself tensing. I said that, well, he had just heard wrong. He repeated it again, adamantly. I said, in that case, he had my permission to check with the lawyer to whom I mailed my intended bets (although he wouldn't have the late, late bets). I felt futile offering such an ineffectually civilized rejoinder. The occasion demanded rapier wit, or a challenge to a duel. He was calling me a liar about something that was very important to me, an experience that has insinuated itself into every molecule in me.

The more patiently, and vehemently, I explained my brilliant manipulations, the more insistent he was that I was fantasizing. His patronizing smile enraged me. At a point where I felt myself physically resisting the urge to lash out at him, I said, "If you could do anything half-well you wouldn't be so hostile." It was cruel, and I meant it.

And I was sorry for it immediately. I had been provoked, it was a well-deserved kick in the groin, but I was reduced by it. I am still embarrassed for beating up my sofa, which never said a word to me, much less impugn my integrity.

The remark stung him. He offered to buy me a drink and forget it.

I said no. And no eight times, returning his insult with a violent breach of pub etiquette. I will not drink with you, I said. Each time I said it he reacted as though I slapped him in the face. I had.

On the night Bobby Kennedy was assassinated I pub-crawled through the Village with Norman Mailer. The air was charged with tension that sobbed, "Not again, the bastards." A friend of his got into a fight and suffered a deep gash over one eye. Norman, challenged at another bar, puffed up his chest and was ready to go, but it cooled out. I asked him what all this macho was about. He said, "You're the kind of guy who's saving it all up for one big fight."

Though I am a devout coward and a determined Mr. Nice Guy, I sensed that he was right. Tonight, in my own fashion, I hit someone. Superficially it was over an argument whether I picked winners or not, over being called a liar. Actually it was about betrayal and rejection. Twice this season I've been shot down from a high I wanted to share, with a lover and with a friend. We weren't both in love and we weren't that friendly.

Thursday

Jack Danahy, a former FBI man, is the director of security for the NFL. Howard Samuels, a former big businessman, runs the offtrack betting operation in New York City and wants to expand it to sports betting. I spoke to both of them today (not about each other). Samuels disappointed me.

Danahy has one part-time assistant and correspondents in every NFL city and a $200,000 budget to ward off scandal. It isn't much, but there isn't much more they can do.

The correspondents, Danahy said, are former FBI men and lawyers who are in constant touch with bookies. They report line fluctuations on a weekly and sometimes daily basis. Danahy showed me charts listing the changes on every game. We compared notes on a few games and they jibed. In some cities, notably Saint Louis and Houston, where the bookies are conservative, Danahy said, the fluctuations were most extreme.

These charts are the NFL's early warning system. When a game jumps by a point or point and a half or more, Danahy said, they try to trace the cause. Usually it is an injury report, a rumor, or what Danahy called "heart money," local sentiment. "Gamblers may start a rumor of an injury to make the public bet one way so they can bet the other way," he said. "If they win they tell people they had inside information. They're the biggest braggarts in the world. Before you know it people are saying that players are spilling information."

Injury rumors are checked and denials are issued when they are false. But the real problem is that the overwhelming majority of rumors are initiated by the traditional deceit of coaches who hide injuries. Pete Rozelle tries to discourage the practice with fines, to no avail. This season there were dozens of pregame "injuries"—players pulling muscles and suffering all sorts of hideous ailments while jogging in place—most of which happened during the week. If Rozelle is serious about his contention that it is the rumor of scandal and not scandal itself that is the enemy, he would either make coaches declare injured players in or out of the starting lineup no later than Friday afternoon, or he would appeal strongly to owners to protect their interests by insisting that their coaches issue accurate injury reports.

Danahy makes the rounds of teams during the exhibition season to lecture players on gambling and gamblers. He reminds players not to frequent "hazardous" places where unsavory characters hang out.

One of those places he mentioned to me was the one (before NFL security was established in 1964) in which my dumper said he made his first betting contact.

Bumped into Howard Samuels at a Christmas party. I asked him about his plans to institute games betting if the state legislature approves it and the public votes for it in a referendum. There was a rock band blaring at noise pollution decibels, but, unfortunately, I heard him.

He said he was thinking of using a tote board system: giving both points and odds, with the city taking a percentage out of the betting pool. This would mean that you could bet the Dolphins this week, giving the points, but you wouldn't know the payoff until all bets were in, when you might collect at 8–5 or 1–3, depending on the distribution of the money. Theoretically the odds would balance out to near-even money because the Steelers could be attractive with the points and possible odds.

This is an intriguing concept, but I doubt that it can effectively compete with the 10–11 you lay with a bookie. Nothing is going to make me think the Steelers will win, and if I'm right about the Dolphins I don't want to take the chance that I'm going to collect less than 10–11. If I like the Steelers, though, I might bet on them legally, if I thought the odds would be favorable; and provided that I can wake up early enough Sunday to get to a betting office, or that the telephones aren't jammed five minutes before game time.

Samuels prefers the tote board system because it eliminates the possibility of the city losing money, either by a short-term turn of fortune or on a giant coup. But if the possibility of a coup is intrinsic—because with over a hundred betting offices it would be impossible to trace the origin of the money—what protection does football have?

The sensitive apparatus of the illegal system is far better equipped to detect a betting conspiracy. The answer is to absorb the apparatus into legal betting.

Bob Martin said in Las Vegas that he has a syndicate prepared to put up $50 million to run the operation for New York. If run properly, he said, there would be no greater danger of a conspiracy than now exists.

When I relayed this to Samuels he said he was afraid underworld money would be involved. Which would be politically hazardous.

I don't know who Martin's backers are, but I do know his reputation for running an honest bookmaking business. It is impeccable. Would the government hire bureaucrats to cut meat if it went into the butcher business? Without experts to operate a system that can compete with illegal bookies, the government won't compete successfully; or it might be an amateur bookie only borrowing the bettor's money.

I've come around to the belief that government should involve itself only to the extent that it licenses and taxes legal bookies, as they do in England. A tidy profit could also be made by offering fairer odds on parlay cards than illegal distributors do. Millions would be saved, too, by reducing the role that the police and the courts play in gambling.

But all of this is academic until the tax loopholes are filled, until we get an equitable betting depletion allowance. Gamblers of the world, unite.

Friday

What magnetic field pulled Heshye Seidenberg back into my orbit today? I met him on a movie line (*The Heartbreak Kid*). I hadn't seen him in twenty-five years, since he went on to stardom at Cornell and I went on to obscurity at Oklahoma, and he has been darting in and out of my head all week.

I've been making laundry lists of my greatest days, trying to find the proper niche for my $6,500 score. It fits somewhere between my sixty-two-yard run at Ebbets Field and the time I had to perjure myself in court, in order to establish legal grounds for divorce, by admitting that I punched my mother-in-law.

I was the fullback to Heshye's tailback at Lafayette High. He was a great high school player and I was a glorified blocking back who ran with the ball when he got tired. In the last game of our unbeaten season he got tired and called on me to run his weakside play. I went all the way, untouched. (It occurs to me now that I ran into the end zone at first base, where Jackie Robinson broke into baseball that year.)

Heshye is a lawyer in exurbia, gray flecks his only visible concession to time. We had dinner, his woman, his daughter, and us, and he brought up the run.

"This is the guy who ran seventy-two yards at Ebbets Field," he said.

"No, Hesh," I said, "sixty-two." (Back then we heroes were modest.)

"I never asked you, Hesh, what you were thinking as I scooted down the field."

"First I thought, look at the little sonofabitch run," he said. "And second, why didn't I call the play for myself?"

SATURDAY

Unbeknownst, unwittingly, innocently, I've become a tout and a conspiracy-monger. I'm flabbergasted.

Sunday mornings I talk to Mel my agent, among all the others. I tell him whom I'm betting on, why, etc. Sometimes he follows me, sometimes he follows his own star. It develops that he also gets calls from half a dozen business associates who ask for my picks. Because he doesn't want to identify me, as a columnist, he told them he has a line into a big betting syndicate.

If these people have been following me, the consequences are staggering. Six people call four people who call three people who call seven people—a geometric progression that, like a telephonic chain letter, can embrace thousands of bettors in an hour. All convinced they have inside information. Some, no doubt, who embellish their connection with conspiratorial fantasies that give them importance in their offices and country clubs.

One of the people is the athletic director of a major college in the East. Last week he skied down half a mountain in Vermont during a snowstorm to call Mel for my picks.

SUNDAY

I haven't been drunk on New Year's Eve since, at age sixteen, I took a date to see the immortal musical *Terplitsky of Notre Dame* and afterward drank two beers and a glass of wine and threw up. Never saw the girl again, which grieved me because her mother was a fabulous beauty who excited me by using a brassiere as a fly swatter.

I got drunk tonight, drunk on me.

I hedged my bet on the Dolphins by putting $1,200 on the Steelers, taking 4. The Dolphins won 21–17, giving me a side, giving me $2,000 even though I was risking just $1,000.

I bet $3,000 on the Redskins when the line dipped to 2½. They won 23–3. I won $800.

The bottom line is now plus $16,510. Cha-cha-cha.

Don Shula was magnificent. The score was 7–7 at the half, the Dolphins' touchdown coming as a result of a run on a fake punt. Morrall couldn't generate anything. Shula brought in Griese in the second half and he generated two scoring drives, on a team that hadn't given up a touchdown in half their games this season. And both touchdowns came after Shula ordered the Dolphins to go for a first down on fourth and short yardage; he did it a third time, adding up to a bruising statement of his determination to win everything this time around.

The Redskins never gave Roger Staubach a chance. Their pass coverages confused him and their defensive line smothered him. The Cowboys got eight first downs.

"Are you going to bet it all on the big one?"

"Don't know yet. Let me calm down."

"You must know. Out with it. Don't be coy."

"All I know is that I'm getting the feeling that I don't pick the team that wins the game—the team that wins the game is the team I pick."

"Heavy."

"So is $16,510."

The magnetic field I live in these days must be irresistible. I'm not the kind of guy who walks off with the stunner at the party. My style is to grow on them, like a tumor. To-night I walked off with her.

Happy New Year.

The Super Bowl

Monday

"I think the Dolphins will win, but I also think the Redskins will win," Jonathan Schwartz said. "I feel very strongly about that."

Precisely.

This is a game for fans, and I am a fan of the game. It shapes up as the most attractive matchup of the seven Super Bowls: two outstanding teams, finely balanced, stocked with offensive stars, coached by the dominant coaches in the NFL.

The fan in me wants to see it. The newspaperman in me wants to write it. The bettor in me wants to win it. Right now that's all there is to me.

It is too early to examine it in detail. I want to creep up on it, surround it, pounce on it, suck out its marrow. That may be the killer instinct in me. I dream of lions and leopards, being among them as though I am them.

There are two questions to be resolved by the game. Are the Dolphins, with Bob Griese, a great football team? Is George Allen, with these Redskins, going to emerge as the reigning ogre of the NFL? The Dolphins will have to be a great football team to beat the Redskins. Allen has all the qualities of ogrehood, much as Vince Lombardi, Paul Brown and George Halas had when they reigned over professional football. Pro football seems to demand one, and Don Shula is too straight for the role.

Allen is a disturbing factor. He is a brilliant fellow. He has to be to overcome himself. His brilliance is manifest in pioneering the no-draft draft, by trading all his prime draft picks for proven talent, and in motivating old ballplayers to play like young ones, by paying them handsomely, and in coaching very sound and yet at times bold football. Himself is manifest in his compulsion to create demons to overcome—oddsmakers, reporters, fans, all the "theys" out there who are plotting to do him and his team in—and in his proudly proclaimed philosophy that winning-isn't-just-the-only-thing-but-there-is-nothing-else-in-life. Supporting that philosophy, he twice has been caught cheating (once when an assistant was caught spying on the opposition's practice, once when he traded a draft pick he didn't own). Cheating is the only aspect of the game that Allen doesn't excel in.

I am probably more annoyed than I should be about Allen's calculated emotionalism. I rather like him for being open about his own feelings, but, really, I got a game ball and danced victory dances in high school, how can the Washington Redskins go for that stuff? It seems so staged, so unspontaneous, so George Alleny. What annoys me, I guess, is that it works. The players seem to dig it. Perhaps I would too if he paid me more money than I had ever earned before and made a hero of me by winning. George wants dancing, give him dancing.

There was a television first after the Redskins beat the Cowboys: a public prayer session. The Redskins broke the freestyle record for postgame thankfulness. If I had a conspiratorial turn of mind I'd wonder whether Allen was trying to win public support and influence the point spread. I'm cynical about it because George Allen would make a deal with the devil to win a football game, and claim he didn't remember it when he had to pay his dues. He's a sweetheart.

The disturbing factor, then, is that, while I have the highest respect for Allen as a coach and have won more money betting on the Redskins than any other team, how am I going to ignore him as himself for two weeks? His philosophy is abhorrent to me. The Super Bowl is a showcase for that philosophy.

There is, however, no room in a handicapping equation for moral judgments. Does a horseplayer inquire into the guiding principles of the Phippses and Vanderbilts? There is no room for ideology either. Unlike some of my friends, I couldn't care less about President Nixon's rooting interest in the Redskins. I applauded Larry Csonka's statement that he was making football seem much more important than it is (although I feel safe when the President is involved in football, because how much trouble can he be making then?). But still, as a bettor how can I overlook his 1971 "bet" that the Redskins would win a championship in a year or two? He went to Whittier College, and George Allen coached there. Maybe the Prez had inside information.

Regardless, Allen disturbs me. The intense experience of the season has put me in touch with some things about myself, and I'm not sure I can—or want to—prune my feelings from the sturdy trunk of coachly logic I lean on. I am only sure that I want to win the Super Bowl, want to be right and pick up the money.

TUESDAY

To further discombobulate my head, the lines came out today. It was 2 Redskins at noon and 2½ a few hours later, after opening in Vegas with outlaw bookies at 1 Dolphins. I made it a pick game. The pros are betting as though they have advance copies of Super Monday's newspapers.

That offends my deepest sensibilities about football. To bet that confidently against a team that is undefeated sends a shiver of contempt through me, like a phonograph needle scratching a record. Maybe the pros are right, but I'm contemptuous of their disrespect for a fundamental truth, a truth that also has been missed in stories that question the severity of the schedule the Dolphins had to overcome. The truth is that all you can do is beat everyone in front of you. How many teams have done that? (None in the NFL.) The Dolphins have. It must be respected.

Last week, looking ahead, I thought that if it came down to the Redskins vs. the Dolphins I would have to go with the Redskins if the Dolphins had to go with Earl Morrall. Considering what happened to Roger Staubach in his first start after a long layoff, I must still reserve some doubt about Bob Griese. But the Dolphins scored the touchdown they needed in the fourth quarter on the Browns, and they dominated a powerhouse Steeler defense in the second half, and that's what the game is about. And that's why you have to fish deeper than matchups and data in the playoffs.

That makes it look like a wrap on the Dolphins, but the Redskins have an imposing truth to contend with: In two seasons they have lost exactly one game in which all their superstuds played. They will all play in the Super Bowl.

WEDNESDAY

Mr. Rhodes called and said he'd take any bet I had on the game, any amount. I asked how come no Christmas presents this year, hadn't I lost enough to him? He said he was getting hard-luck Christmas stories from the customers who owe him money, and, incidentally, my bill is $650 and he needs the money. I visualized his shoulders stooping with a hod-carrier's burden. I expected a litany that began with holes in his shoes. I said I hadn't made up my mind on the game, I'd leave the money in an envelope at his hangout. The bum beat me, and that's it. I'm not going to try to get even with one bet. I'll give my Super Bowl business to Billy or Doctor or both; they owe me more than $2,000 apiece. Not that I'm superstitious. It's just that, where bookies are concerned, I believe in the biblical injunction that it is better to receive than to give.

My other doctor had good news today. I'm alive and well. I took my year-end physical last week, and laboratory tests showed one inconsequential change from the preseason tests. My thyroid has acted up a bit. That could reflect tension, the doctor said, but it's inconclusive.

To be on the safe side, I'll go somewhere and lie down for a while. How much do I have to bet on the Super Bowl to buy an island in the Caribbean?

THURSDAY

Like most young athletes whose fathers worked long, hard hours, my first serious relationship with a man was with my high school coach. He recognized me, led me through the fire. I sometimes wonder whether I have made it all the way through that rite of passage, but that is my problem. Harry Ostro was a good teacher and an enormously successful coach. He still is.

We communicate once or twice a year. I check the high school results during the football season to see how he's doing, and it always comes as a surprise when he loses. Before I left for Las Vegas today I talked to him about the Super Bowl. It was something I felt I had to do, going back to a source.

He said, "If I was a bettor I'd bet coaches. I have to go with Shula. Somehow I think Allen is getting on his knees and praying too much."

FRIDAY

I looked under every roulette wheel in Vegas and couldn't find a soul who loves the Dolphins. The best I could do was a neutral observer, Bob Martin. "It's a good game to watch, not bet," he said.

Fat chance. All America will be betting. Hundreds of millions of dollars, a billion maybe. The gross national product of Uruguay or someplace. That's why Martin bets money, not faces, on this game. When the Colts were favored by 17 over the Jets, he was asked what influence Vince Lombardi would have on the spread if he endorsed the Jets. "It depends," said Martin, "on how much he bets."

Lem Banker and I kicked the game around. He's the only pro I encountered who has any feeling for the Dolphins. He took them at 2–1 to win it all, when I took the Raiders at 7–1. But he got burned on the bowl games, so he may hedge. By betting the Redskins he would in effect have a free bet on the Dolphins: If the Redskins win, he breaks even; if the Dolphins win, he wins the odds.

When I argue for the Dolphins I am playing devil's advocate. It's not a conviction, it's a contrary response to the overwhelming surge to the Redskins. It's not that easy, I keep saying, the game can't be that easy. The Redskins' defense is good, but it's not as massively impregnable as the Colts and Vikings were. Teams have moved the ball on them, the Vikings and Giants, neither great. They haven't been tested by an offense that can do as many things as well as the Dolphins.

I threw this at Lefty Rosenthal: What if the Dolphins expose the old side of the Redskins' defense (Jack Pardee, Ron McDole, Pat Fischer) the way the Jets did to the old side of the Colts' defense (Ordell Braase, Don Shinnick, Len Lyle)? He said, "Allen won't let that happen." I said, "You're right. But Csonka will tear them up inside then. You can't stop everything." I didn't persuade him. I'm not sure I persuaded myself. I simply was trying to determine if there were sound reasons for the surge to the Redskins. For me, there has to be more to the game than the scores of the playoffs.

I solved the dilemma, temporarily, by betting on both teams. I bet $1,000 on an over-under proposition. The number is 33. I bet it will go over. I'll take a 20–14 final.

My thinking is that both teams can score from anywhere on the field, and neither team is capable of dominating the other's line in a close game. As long as he has the threat of Larry Brown to freeze the defense, Billy Kilmer functions beautifully throwing to Charley Taylor and Roy Jefferson. Bob Griese is bolder than Morrall and should put more points on the board. If the game breaks open, the ball will fly around and someone usually scores when that happens.

In my present state of indecision—and until I back my opinion with money, it is indecision—the prospect of rooting, "Come on, somebody," is very appealing. It may be the best way to bet a game like this.

There's another proposition floating around: three field goals. You have to bet whether there will be more or less than three field goals in the game. Curt Knight has kicked seven in two playoffs for the Redskins. Garo Yepremian has kicked two for the Dolphins. Bets like these are great between friends, for about 50 cents. There is a limit to my craziness.

I'd like to bet Shelly Rich on Knight vs. Yepremian. Shelly Rich is a waiter in the Village who bets the colleges but won't touch the pros "because I don't want to lose to a 5-foot soccer player from Armenia."

SATURDAY

Social notes from all over:

Jimmy the Greek lost a bundle on the Raiders. "I'll never bet more than a dollar again," he said. It seems to me I've heard that song before. Successful gamblers usually calcify into stonefaces from playing percentages. Jimmy is too good a showman, too ebullient, to be a good gambler.

I learned that Mr. Rich once lost a big bundle here. He had a system in baccarat.

Rodney Fertel says he's running for Congress. Rodney is my favorite character at the Churchill Downs Sports Book. He is a wealthy realtor from New Orleans with an I-don't-care-Howard-Hughes-look about him: an old Tulane tee shirt that is part of his skin and four or five days of beard. Democracy, it's wonderful. When Rodney paces between television sets on Sundays, turning the joint into a maternity waiting room, the cigars in the back bellow, "Sit down, shithead," or "Back to the jungle, gorilla man."

Rodney is known as gorilla man because he travels around the globe collecting gorillas and the like for the New Orleans Zoo and for research at Tulane. He tolerates the insults with the good-natured air of a rich man who can afford to live poor. Give him a football game to bet on and he hears nothing but the squawking of his nervous system.

Today Rodney gave me a preview of his political platform. He had two typewritten pages of curatives for the ills of Louisiana, not a few of which concerned the Communist menace. Rodney convinced me there are more Reds than boll weevils in the South. And I convinced him that he could use a provocative local issue.

"Here you are, Rodney, thousands of miles from home because the law harasses you when you want to bet," I said. "Why don't you stump for legalized gambling?"

"I think you've got something there," he said, scribbling it down.

Pick a few winners and the world beats a path to your door. Today Congress. Tomorrow it could be the Prez himself.

"Let me make this perfectly clear, Larry, I don't bet, much, but who do you like in the Super Bowl?"

"The way I see it, Dick. . . ."

SUNDAY

The bad news was horrid.

"I'm quitting," Bob Martin said. "I'm tired of sneaking around." To survive, a bookie has to operate illegally in this haven of legal gambling. The state gambling commission has been putting pressure on Martin. Why don't commissions put pressure on auto mechanics who replace crankshafts because of a squeak in the trunk? Why don't commissions put pressure on businessmen who try to overthrow foreign governments? The only consumer complaint Bob Martin ever received was that the consumer picked the wrong team.

Martin said he would try to organize opposition to the federal gambling tax, redress the tax grievances of gamblers. This is a lobby I can support, a Common Cause for the betting man.

If Martin isn't bookmaking for the 1973 season, a handful of professionals may prosper. Without anyone to hold that line, they will be able to shop among bookies who change the numbers willy-nilly. But without a central bank to monitor national betting patterns, opportunities for and suspicions of conspiracy may escalate.

I thanked Bob Martin for his cooperation. He said, "From what I've seen, you have control. Not many guys have control." I felt the tap of the sword on my shoulder, knighted.

I had felt the tap once before. Bud Wilkinson called me into his office to tell me I was going to play a lot of football for Oklahoma. He was never wronger.

MONDAY

The first day of Super Bowl week is a circus within a circus. The players are trotted out like trained bears to submit to interviews in an arena.

At the Long Beach practice field of the Rams, I observed the three Dolphins whom I consider the heart of the team, Nick Buoniconti, Paul Warfield and Larry Csonka. They are gifted athletes and solid people, articulate, eager to share their enthusiasm and experience with the public. Buoniconti is a small boy telling you about a game he has just played or is going to play. Warfield is a community leader who leads with dignity and reason. Csonka is the underneath man in an acrobat act. He holds the team up. He exudes the strength of purpose of the great winners, of Bill Russell and Frank Robinson.

Don Shula, ringmaster, said all the right things. I like Shula because he seems committed without being obsessed, tough and yet not so hung up on toughness that he is threatened by nobler faculties, like laughter and intelligence. A privately religious man, he said, grinning, that he wasn't worried about the Redskins' postgame prayers because the Dolphins lead the league in pregame prayers. Asked how he sustained the players' high level of performance through a long season, he said he appealed to their intelligence by telling them it was foolish to need a defeat to be roused. As for their understated emotional approach to the game, he said, "Can you see me leading Larry Csonka in a chorus of 'Hail to the Dolphins'?"

The Redskins were trotted out at Anaheim Stadium. With George Allen around, it is difficult to get to know them that well. He draws them into a tight circle to fight the enemy without, which includes just about everybody. They parrot him.

A few strong personalities have emerged. Billy Kilmer is Bobby Layne reincarnated. There are Texas-sized legends about Diron Talbert and his football-playing brothers. Larry Brown runs every run as though he is trying to escape the ghetto he escaped from.

The Redskins' half of the circus was curtailed when thousands of kids invaded center ring. George Allen held court in a dressing room. He was disappointed that the

Redskins were favored, the oddsmakers having wrested a psychological weapon from him. But he was gracious and cooperative. It was the charm hour.

So it's out now: I want the Dolphins to win almost as much as I want me to win. This is so arbitrary that it makes me uncomfortable as a bettor. The irony of abandoning my detachment for the big game is sweetly perverse though. In sum, I'm confused. My head and my heart are so rarely synchronized on vital issues that I suspect myself of duplicity. I'm too close to the game; it's probably clearer from 3,000 miles away, like the lunacy of people who live on the San Andreas Fault.

I wish they'd play it tomorrow. In six days I could talk myself out of it.

TUESDAY

I decided to put some distance between me and the game today. I went to Hollywood. That's about as far as you can get away from the real world. It helped. I think.

Fast Eddie's boss arranged for me to get on a movie set through his friend Seymour Cassell, the Moskowitz of *Minnie and Moskowitz,* who introduced me to Peter Falk, the Colombo of "Colombo," and John Cassavetes, the director. Their perspectives on the game clarified my confusion by amplifying it.

Peter Falk is rooting for the Redskins. "I like Allen because he's obsessed," he said. "A man with an obsession is more interesting than a man without one. He's good at what he does. He works hard at it. I'd like to see him win."

I thought: Maybe I'm being unfair to Allen because I

recognize in him that part of me that is obsessive, and cunning. He is more willing to live in the extreme than I. Is he more willing to gamble in his profession than I am in mine?

Seymour Cassell is rooting for the Dolphins. "It's too important to Allen," he said. "I think he'll blow it because he wants it so badly."

I thought: Is this me too?

John Cassavetes had no opinion. He said he was excited about the prospect of a classic game.

I thought: Wouldn't it be nice if I didn't bet at all, just sat in the stands and watched, or even better, rooted madly?

I asked seven-year-old Michael Cassell what the movie he was rehearsing for is about. He said, "My mother goes in the nuthouse and gets out on page 102."

I thought: I get out of the nuthouse of this season Sunday. What page is it?

I made the obligatory appearance at the Polo Lounge of the Beverly Hills Hotel. Rudolph Valentino and Dolores Del Rio sat in a booth there, I assume, and tourists have been looking for them ever since. I didn't find them.

Fellow I know from Fire Island found me. He is associated with Dustin Hoffman somehow. Couple months ago he called to tell me that the actor was interested in a property with a sports theme, did I have any ideas? No, I said, I'm working on a book about pro football and gambling.

Now I thought: Hmm, Dustin Hoffman. The little man of *Little Big Man*. Ratso in *Midnight Cowboy*. He'd be perfect as a horny dwarf who bets.

I took the fellow's card and said I'd get back to him in New York.

I feel like I've been blowing up giant balloons of Popeye and Charlie Brown all day.

WEDNESDAY

They may take me away in a straitjacket soon. Now I'm a lightning rod for psychological and emotional signals on the game.

I try to pay no mind to psychological and emotional factors for many reasons, some of them personal. I wasn't good enough to be overconfident. As a coach I devoted my energy to detail, remorselessly, win or lose. I never felt that I was manipulated or that I manipulated players emotionally. The teams I was connected with won because they had good organization, good coaching, good players. The juices flowed from within ourselves, from the community we were, from the purity of our goals.

Coaches can't measure the psychological mood of their teams in advance, how can handicappers? As a reporter I've found that players babble about the abstract forces in a game as alibis, as crutches, as smokescreens. In Las Vegas there was babble that the Redskins are more emotional than the Dolphins, presumably because they pray and dance. The Dolphins won three more games than the Redskins this season. Whatever they did it with, I'll buy it. In the large economy size.

Which is why I've been listening with interest, and alarm, to the psychomotional angles on the Super Bowl. I don't think I believe them, but since they confirm my views of the game I don't exactly disbelieve them.

The big angle is that the Dolphins can cope with the goldfish bowl pressure of the extravaganza better than the Redskins because they've been in it before. The theory is that the distractions are more likely to distract players who are in love with themselves simply for getting here: They may forget what they got here for. The historical support for the theory is that the last three winners were appearing for the second time.

That's pretty flimsy support. It reminds me of the betting trend that developed on the first Monday night games, when teams in those games invariably lost by the points in their next game. The trend was noticed in the third or fourth week. The theory held that there was insufficient time to prepare for Sunday games. Coaches and players eagerly testified to the disruption in their lives. By the sixth week the trend, the testimony and the bettors received a quiet mass burial.

Still, I hear the things I want to hear. The Dolphins sound a common theme: They've been working for six months to win, not appear, here. There's no doubt they believe that. Nor is there any doubt that I would turn a deaf ear to the jabberwocky if Bob Griese wasn't ready to start.

George Allen, who loves an angle more than Euclid did, is playing this one to the hilt. And I suspect he may not be kidding. He's bitching so much about the distractions that the bitching itself distracts him. Is he alibiing for himself in advance? Pete Gent, a former Dallas Cowboy turned writer, said the Redskins were still gloating over their demolition of the Cowboys ten days ago. Was that their season?

Tom Catlin, an assistant coach with the Rams, dropped an innocuous line that hit me where I breathe. He was in my class at Oklahoma (educationally, not athletically; he was an All-American linebacker) and, like the Dolphins, he was a quiet, undemonstrative killer. He said, "I wouldn't have believed you could go undefeated in the NFL." I had been thinking of going back to another source, Bud Wilkinson. I didn't have to.

THURSDAY

Doctor called. The Redskins are still 2½. I bet $1,000 on the Redskins, chickening out. I should have bet more.

I'm speculating, playing yakapoola, trying to nudge the line up to 3. That's why I should have bet more. If it goes to 3, I decided, I will double back on the Dolphins, heavy. That would be, as Lem Banker said, good value.

I still don't trust myself completely. If the wise guys are so sure about the Redskins, how can I be so glib in the opposite direction? I can make a helluva case for the Redskins too: Allen, Brown, Taylor, Jefferson, defense, great kicking in the playoffs.

With the exception of The Mover, who likes the Redskins because "all the smart money is on them," my bettors are going for the Dolphins. Frankie the Doorman said he's betting the $200 he made playing the saxophone over the holidays on the Dolphins. Mr. Rich said, "They're worth a good bet." Fast Eddie said, "I liked the Redskins, but suddenly I like the Dolphins." Lem Banker said, "I'm going to stick with the Dolphins. What you said makes sense."

Wish I could say the same.

FRIDAY

Lem Banker's remark must have purified the circuits in my head. When I opened my eyes this morning I heard a voice, mine, say, "It's the Dolphins. The game is over."

It boiled down to three reasons, none of them George Allen. He has been purged from the equation, I think. After a week's inspection, he strikes me as a fanatic pipsqueak. Unlike George Halas, Paul Brown and Vince Lombardi, he is smaller than the game. I may be revolted by, but I refuse to be stampeded by pipsqueaks from Whittier College.

The football reason is this: The primary strength of the Dolphins is their offense, of the Redskins their defense, ergo the game probably will be decided when the Dolphins have the ball. If they move on the Redskins—and I think they can move on anyone—they should win. The Redskins scored only three touchdowns in the playoffs even though their defense controlled the games from start to finish, so how much will it do when the defense isn't in control? The unknown factor is how the Dolphins' defense will stand up; it has had lapses in the playoffs.

The second reason is this: If the Redskins win after I bet the Dolphins I would be unhappy; but if the Dolphins win after I bet the Redskins I would be miserable. I have an emotional commitment to the Dolphins because I relate to them more personally than I do to the Redskins—Larry Csonka, I romanticize, won't let them lose—and because a victory for them would confirm, for me, my thesis that most professional gamblers don't understand the science or soul of the game.

Third: The Dolphins have a chance to achieve greatness, to be perfect. They would be identified with their time in the way great athletes and teams have been in the past. And I will be a footnote to that time, or, in my head, they will be a footnote to my great season.

So in this, the big game, my emotions seem more tangible than my judgment. My judgment can be wrong. My emotions can't be. It's a beautiful middle. I can only lose money.

The question remains: How much will I gamble on my emotions? The answer is: I will bet judiciously. If the line goes up to 3 or 4, I might bet $5,000 on the Dolphins. If the line goes down, I probably will bet less. I will bet enough to win the game, to win the Super Bowl. I have worked too long and too well—winning on twelve of the sixteen weeks of the season—to throw it away on one grandstand play of a bet. You can't become a good gambler until you've been busted, as Lefty Rosenthal said, and I've been there. I'm a romantic, but I haven't abandoned all reason.

This is an important decision for me, more important than the decision on whom I should bet. It was not made, I should add, on the basis of the horoscope in the *Los Angeles Times* advising Aquariuses to "engage in the practical affairs that will increase your income in the future." Nick the Greek, the legendary high roller (no relation to Jimmy), said gambling was only a way to keep score, and this decision goes up on my personal scoreboard. I'm highly motivated to win, to control my destiny, even if it means damming up fantasies inside me. Betting with my emotions is a welcome if slight crack in the dam.

A psychiatrist told me a story that encourages me to frisk my past. An air force pilot completed his required combat missions and volunteered for another tour. He completed the tour and volunteered again. He completed that tour and volunteered a third time, but was rejected. When he returned to the states he gambled away $10,000 in savings. The psychiatrist shook loose symptoms of this daredevil mentality in the pilot's youth. As a five-year-old he blindfolded himself and raced back and forth across a street with heavy traffic.

I was a wild child but there was one activity I wouldn't join my friends in. Hitching rides on the back of trolley cars. There was, I could see, no percentage in that. Perhaps they thought I was a coward. Perhaps I was afraid. In retrospect I had common sense.

But consider: I married a woman with four children after I knew her for six weeks (thinking myself five times blessed). I went AWOL from an overseas assignment base for three months (and wasn't caught) so I could coach a high school team. I'm not your basic Mr. Milquetoast.

There are two things that are no fun for me in gambling then. One is gambling so recklessly that you must lose. The other is gambling so carefully that you aren't gambling. I travel the middle ground of using common sense and occasionally giving in to romantic impulse. That's who I am.

Who I am not is someone who bets thousands every week. That's a character I invented for a season, like a weekend horseback rider who spends a summer on a ranch. For an amateur, gambling regularly on this or any equivalent personal level is a substitute for gambling in life, using artificial courage. I will never do it again. I'd rather gamble at my work. I'd rather have affection with my emotion.

Saturday

Jimmy the Greek is holding open house in his suite. Jimmy likes the Redskins of course. So does Leroy Nieman, the artist. Leroy is a reverse tout. You find out which side he likes and you bet the other side. I am triply confident.

That is beside the point. The point is that a historic meeting almost took place, another Stanley and Livingstone. Jimmy the Greek, as a symbol of sports betting, is persona non grata around the sports establishment, but tonight he came within a whisker of a major triumph. Pete Rozelle, squiring the NFL executive's daughter I struck out with, actually went to the hotel floor that Jimmy's suite is on, knocked on the wrong door looking for him, and then, apparently reconsidering, departed.

SUNDAY

Faithful kidney, like the mighty Dolphins, rose to the occasion. It signaled to me on the kickoff, the first time this season that the siren call of nerves sounded that early. I took it as a vote of confidence, message being that the amount I bet didn't matter as much as winning and being right. But I'll take the money.

The line was Redskins 2 when Doctor reached me. The public was betting the Dolphins. I bet $3,000 on the Dolphins. And another dollar in the writers' pool, picking them to win 31–17. (Bob Marcus of the Chicago *Tribune* won the pool for the second straight year, indicating he is in the wrong business.)

The game was a spine-tingling anticlimax. The Dolphins proved they are a great team. Larry Csonka didn't let them lose. Bob Griese made them win. The defense was heroic. We won the Super Bowl 14–7.

George Allen, in his bid for ogrehood, had one George Alleny moment in the sun. On the first series of downs the Redskins deliberately interfered with the snap from center on a punt. Allen tried it despite a previous warning from the league that it was illegal. In the heat of battle he might have gotten away with it. He didn't. Everyone is against him.

When a coach pulls a stunt like that I interpret it to mean that he thinks he needs stunts like that to win. If that's what was behind Allen's brainstorm, he was right. The Dolphins were too good for the Redskins. They scored two touchdowns in the first half and had a third nullified by a penalty. Each of them came as a result of a pass on second or third down and short yardage, Griese specialties. The defense contained Larry Brown and zoned the patterns favored by Charley Taylor and Roy Jefferson. Trailing 14–0 in the second half, Billy Kilmer was forced to play from his weakness, pocket passing, because the threat of Brown's run was no longer credible. I gave up on my point-proposition bet after a long drive at the start of the third quarter stalled. When their defense broke down, the Redskins' offense was futile against a defense that took away the big play.

Proud as polished chrome, I drifted to the floor of the Los Angeles Coliseum (en route to the dressing rooms) for the last few minutes of the game. As I got to the field, Garo Yepremian authored a bizarre, hilarious anecdote to the spectacle. The carom of his low field goal attempt wound up in his arms and he flung the ball like Shelly the waiter's dread five-foot Armenian into the arms of a Redskin who returned it for a touchdown. The Redskins now could tie and send the game into overtime. I could still win or lose all of my bets.

I watched the last two minutes from behind the Dolphins' end zone. Down there you can't play God with the game. You can smell the grass and feel the hitting. In their crouches, from thirty yards away, the Dolphins and Redskins looked like all the players I had ever seen across the line of scrimmage. I remembered my brother, as captain of the first Lafayette team I helped coach, predicting they would complete an unbeaten season with a 40–0 victory. The score was 40–0 with two minutes left, when the other team completed a pass to the one-yard line. My brother made four straight tackles in the backfield, the game ending on the twenty-five. The Redskins weren't going to score on me.

Calculating my winnings—$799 for the day ($3,000 minus $1,100 on the Redskins, $1,100 on the point proposition and $1 on the pool)—I second-guessed myself for an instant. Why didn't I bet more? I was too pleased with myself for my first guess to let it linger. I wrote my column. Then I called Gail to tell her that the bottom line on the season was plus $17,309.

MONDAY

Sunday mornings on the way to the park to play ball I would pass a ruddy-faced, middle-aged shoe-shine man. He had signs on the side of his shoe-shine box and on a high metal chair that said he would recite the names of the forty-eight states in twenty or twenty-five seconds, I forget which, for a 10- or 15-cent tip. Sometimes, hoping to hear him, I'd spend minutes scanning the window of an electrical appliance store. Once I heard him. He was a machine gun. Brrrp. And I was sure every state was there. When he finished he was transfigured by a beatific smile.

I am on a 747, coming down from a four-month trip, with a beatific smile. Like that shoe-shine man, I can do a small thing well. Brrrp. I can pick winners in pro football. I said I could, and I did, and I feel good about that. I feel, as if in the afterglow of a moving sexual experience, sweetly spent.

Back on the ground, I will remind myself that I've done it before, that with my background and what I put into it, I should win. It is a game I am adept at. It is nice to be adept at games, as long as they are additions to, and not substitutes for, things that matter. Next season I will go back to betting $5 with Archie Mulligan that the Giants are lousy and $100 with Doctor, if at all, because, after this season, that can't be anything but an addition.

"You mean you're not going to be tempted to pick up a few thousand easy dollars?"

"Yup."

"That's like the woman who gives birth and says never again."

"I mean it. Winning is a full-time job. And I don't want to keep score that way anymore. It's time to move on."

"To what?"

"I'm not sure. I'm going to start by buying a pound of cherries, at any outrageous price."

About the Author

Larry Merchant is a sports columnist for the New York *Post.* His interest in football goes back to his days as a player and backfield coach at Lafayette High School in Brooklyn and as a member of the University of Oklahoma football team.

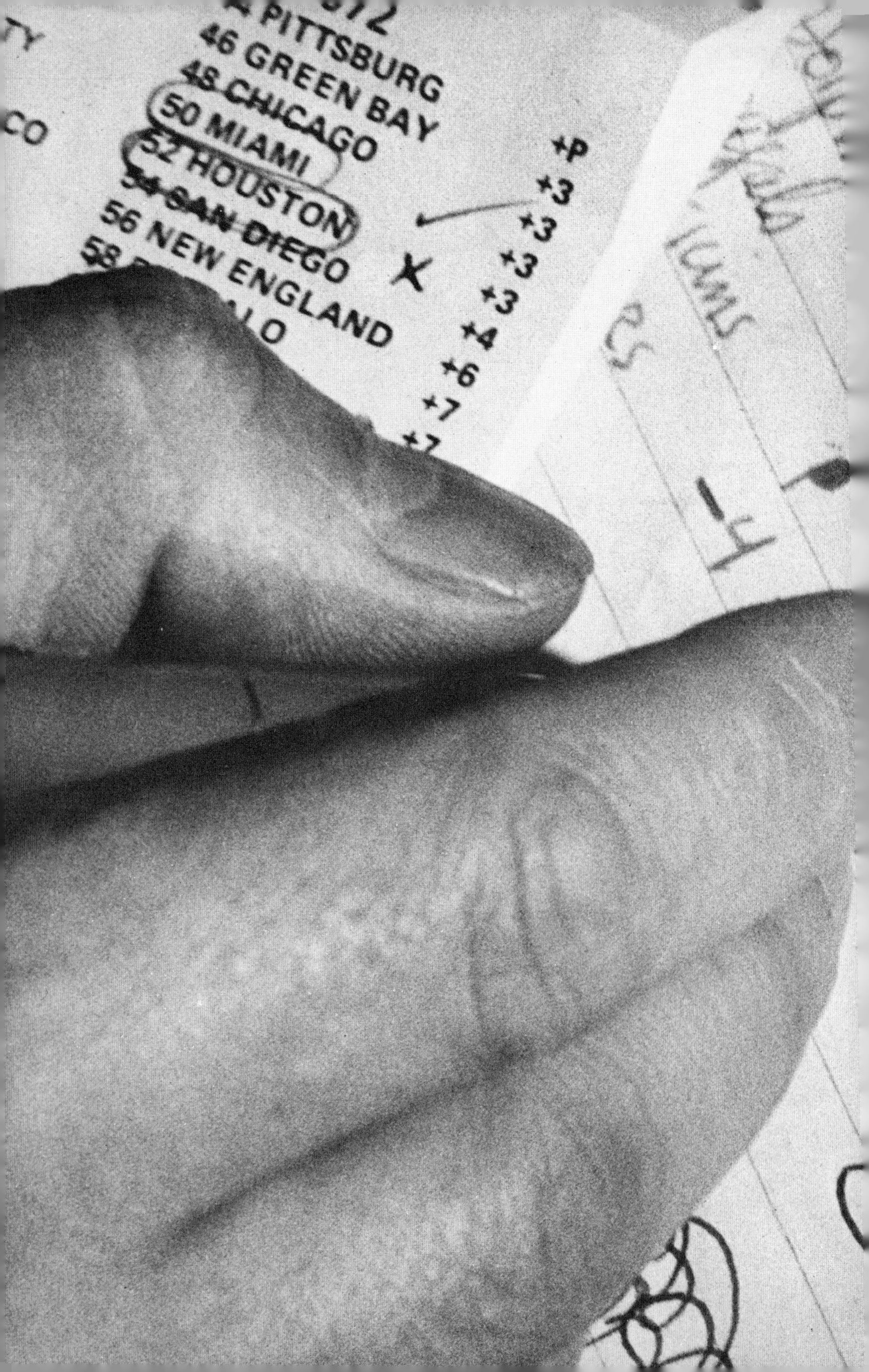

PITTSBURG
46 GREEN BAY
48 CHICAGO
50 MIAMI
52 HOUSTON
54 SAN DIEGO
56 NEW ENGLAND
+P
+3
+3
+3
+3
+4
+6
+7